The Girl from
No. 6

Based on a True Story

Vanessa Voth

 FriesenPress

Suite 300 - 990 Fort St
Victoria, BC, V8V 3K2
Canada

www.friesenpress.com

ISBN
978-1-5255-1900-0 (Hardcover)
978-1-5255-1901-7 (Paperback)
978-1-5255-1902-4 (eBook)

1. BIOGRAPHY & AUTOBIOGRAPHY, CULTURAL HERITAGE

Distributed to the trade by The Ingram Book Company

Dedicated to my Oma –
Thank you for sharing your story with me.

Maria Loewen
June 8, 1928 – January 21, 2017

WARKENTIN FAMILY

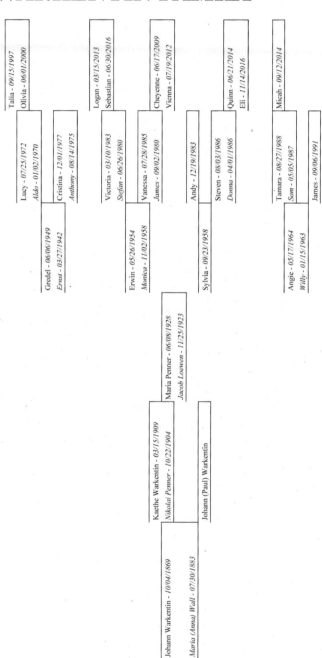

LOEWEN FAMILY

Abram Loewen - 04/12/1898
Helena Loewen - 09/04/1902

- Marieche - 12/25/1922 — Gerhard
- Jacob - 11/25/1923 — Maria - 06/08/1928
  - Gredel
  - Erwin
  - Sylvia
  - Angie
- Abram - 10/13/1925 — Tina
- David - 09/08/1927 — Aganethe
- Gerd - 06/07/1930 — Sara
- Heinrich - 01/24/1933 — Agnes
- Hans - 12/04/1934 — Gerlinda
- Lotte - 01/01/1937 — Heinrich
- Helga - 01/15/1939 — Peter
- Herta - 01/15/1939 — David
- Wilmar - 06/06/1942 — Elsie

ACKNOWLEDGMENTS

WORDS ESCAPE ME AS I REFLECT BACK ON THE LAST TWO YEARS. SO MANY people have supported me through this journey and made this book possible. I feel truly blessed.

Firstly, I'd like to thank my dad. He was the one who suggested I listen to Oma's stories and write them down. I had entertained the idea of one day writing a book, but never seriously considered it. Had he not mentioned it, the thought would never have crossed my mind, and I would have missed out on some of my most cherished moments with Oma. Thank you, Papi, for believing in me and for trusting me with your family's story, and for your support throughout the entire process.

Secondly, I'd like to thank my husband, James, for his continuous support and encouragement. He knew how much this book meant to me, and helped me in so many ways, from watching our daughters for a few hours – or days, when I went away on writing retreats – to cooking meals, and even reading various drafts of my book. James, I can't even express how much your support means to me – with this book and with all my dreams. I love you.

I'd also like to thank my mom for being my cheerleader, not just throughout this process but throughout my entire life. Mami, thank you for always being my biggest fan, for helping take care of the girls so I could write, and for sharing in my excitement over every little accomplishment.

Next, I have to give credit to my dad and his sisters for many of the details in this book. Papi, Tante Gredel, Tante Sylvia, and Tante Angie, it means so much to me that you were all willing to share your memories of your mother and your childhoods with me.

I couldn't have finished this book without the constant encouragement from my friends. If I could write down every name of every single person who gave me a word of encouragement or support, the list would be endless. But I do want to highlight a few of them.

Lesley, thank you for celebrating the milestones with me, for the memories we made on our writing retreats, and for helping me get through moments of writer's block.

Heidi, thank you for always being there for me despite the ocean between us. I appreciate how you listened to both my cries of excitement and my vents of frustration, and cheered me on along the way.

Frances, thank you for your support, your feedback, and for designing the cover of my book. You always know exactly what I'm envisioning in my head and make it become reality. Thank you!

To all my First Readers – Frances, Shannon, Hayley, Tamara, Scarlett, Papi, Tante Angie and Cristina - thank you from the bottom of my heart for taking time to read my book and send me your questions, feedback and constructive criticism. Having other people read my book was one of the most terrifying experiences, but your responses motivated me to refine my plot and make the story even better.

Thank you to my team at Friesen Press for making the publishing process feel effortless and easy. Special thanks to Code, my Publishing Consultant, and Zoe, my Publishing Specialist. Your guidance and help are very much appreciated.

Lastly, but far from least, I want to thank the one person who made this book possible. Oma, your presence in my life was so significant, and it wasn't until your absence from it that I realized just how much I needed and loved you. My heart aches and yearns to see you again. How I long to sit beside you at your kitchen table, picking fruit flies out of my coffee, listening to your sweet voice and looking into your shining eyes as you talk about your past. I miss that. I miss *you*. Thank you for everything you taught me about life, our heritage, and faith. I am forever changed because of you, and I hope others who read your story will be inspired by you, too.

And thank you to every single person reading my book. You're making my dream come true, and helping Oma's legacy live on.

With love,
Vanessa

INTRODUCTION

November 3, 2015

I'VE ALWAYS ENJOYED LISTENING TO OMA RECOUNT EARLY MEMORIES OF HER *life: what it was like for her growing up as a child; when she met Opa; how different it was to raise children sixty-plus years ago; and her favourite memories with her grandchildren. Her strong German accent, along with some broken English, make her stories all that much more interesting (and gives her grandchildren something to tease her about). She is a captivating and entertaining woman, to say the least. What she lacks in height, she makes up for with personality and passion.* Little but fierce, *is how she is often referred to by those who know her.*

Oma is a woman who has lived a long life, with many joys and struggles along the way. She has many stories to share, and willingly does so to anyone who will listen. Many of her stories have been repeated time and time again, that they are so ingrained in my mind, making them feel as much a part of my life as hers.

Today, while cutting my dad's hair, I told him about a recent conversation I had had with Oma, his mother, on the phone, and how much I loved visiting with her. She may be old, but she relates to me in ways no one else can. He then asked if I would be interested in listening to her stories and put them together in a book of some sort. I froze, scissors in hand, and smiled.

That was the lightbulb moment. I had always dreamed of writing a book, but had yet to determine a topic to write about – until now. I'm going to write the biography of my grandmother, one of my favourite people. The thought of sitting with Oma, and listening to all her stories – many of which are still unknown to me – makes me giddy with anticipation and delight. To say I'm excited about the task ahead would be a grand understatement.

The story you're about to read is based on a true story, that of my grandmother, Maria Loewen. It has been written as historical fiction, and some details have been altered to help the storyline flow more cohesively. Most of the characters in this book are based on real people, though some names have been changed.

I wanted to note a couple of key name changes. Maria's grandmother in the book is named Anna, but her real name is Maria Warkentin, whom she was named after. And her Uncle Paul's real name is Johann Warkentin, named after his father, Maria's grandfather. Their real names are used in the captions of any photos of them throughout the book.

Oma was very open with me about her life during our interviews, and I value her honesty and wisdom. Her one desire for this book was that it would glorify God, and be a testimony of His faithfulness throughout her life.

I hope that Oma's story will inspire and impact you the way it has impacted my life.

xoxo
Vanessa

PART ONE

1

April 1930

KAETHE WRAPPED HER FINGERS AROUND THE COOL METAL BAR AS HER BODY swayed with the rise and fall of each swell of the sea. Her stomach tightened as a wave of nausea washed over her and she closed her eyes, inhaling the cool, salty air. The wind moved weightlessly around her and she brushed a few strands of loose chestnut hair away from her eyes. Deep waters billowed as the propellers moved the ship forward, further away from home. Kaethe steadied herself and shivered from both the cool air, and the uncertainty and fear of the unknown future. She tried to shift her attention to her grip on the railing, a barrier between her and the endless miles of ocean surrounding her.

Kaethe pulled her shawl tighter around her chest, holding it tight with one hand while she tucked a few wayward strands of hair behind her ear. The last of the sun's warmth dipped beneath the horizon, casting a luminous glow across the sky. The beauty of the shimmering sea brought a momentary lapse to her memory, and for a minute she forgot where she was, until she sensed the unnerving presence of someone watching her. Before she could turn to see who it was, two arms closed around her waist. She started at the unexpected touch.

"Nikolai! *Du vefierst mie,* you startled me," she smacked his hand, feigning disapproval, though the upturn of her lips indicated otherwise.

Nikolai kissed her neck. The long hairs on his mustache tickled her skin and she rubbed the spot where his lips had touched her. "I'm sorry, my love. You looked so peaceful, I didn't want to disrupt you."

Kaethe relaxed her body into Nikolai's, grateful she was not on this journey alone. She felt the defined edges of his muscles pressing against her back, and the prickles of the stubble growing on his chin as he leaned his head on hers.

"Is Maria with my parents?"

"Yes," Nikolai answered, his lips still close to her neck, warming her skin with each exhale. "Maria's asleep."

Maria. The mere mention of her name reminded Kaethe of all the questions and worries that absorbed her thoughts, constantly. Her stomach turned, the nausea she was experiencing since their departure returned. Kaethe pulled herself away from Nikolai's grip and bent her body over the railing. With a sudden heave, she expelled her last meal. The wind whirled behind the boat, sending the vomit back toward her, instead of out to sea, and some of the bile fell on her shoes.

Nikolai offered his handkerchief to her, and she dabbed at the corners of her mouth without turning to face him. She was embarrassed, though Nikolai showed no signs of disgust.

"There's a bit on your shoes," Nikolai mentioned cautiously.

Kaethe looked down at her feet. She wiggled her toes and felt the warm liquid soak through her nylons, and run down to her toes. Mortified, she bent down and rubbed the cotton shoes furiously with the handkerchief. *As if things weren't bad enough*, she thought. *As if vomiting in front of your husband wasn't enough torture for one day, you had to vomit on the only pair of shoes you own.*

With bile-soaked shoes, she stood up, defeated. She looked at the soft, flickering lights from torches in the distance, and thought of her closet, where three perfectly clean, dry shoes sat unused, never to be seen or worn again. A tear slid down her cheek as resentment rose to the surface, yet again. She shook her head, willing God to see her disapproval. Nikolai placed his hands on her shoulders and she lowered her head as tears fell freely, one drop and then another, into the vastness of the ocean beneath them.

"Is everything all right?" Nikolai whispered.

It was the question she would expect him to ask, having just excreted her supper overboard, but the weight of it, and her answer, overwhelmed her. Kaethe wrapped her arms around Nikolai, and pressed her face into his shoulder. She cried unabashedly as Nikolai stroked her back.

No, everything is not all right.

2

August 1925

KAETHE FOLDED A LONG-SLEEVED SHIRT AND PLACED IT ON THE PILE OF neatly stacked shirts. The radio on the counter beside her hummed with deep male voices speaking through the static – another Russian Orthodox bishop had been killed. She reached for another shirt, her heart aching for the grieving families of the bishops. Surely all of the animosity and hostility in the nation would end soon. She longed to hear positive news coming through the wireless again. Though most of the tragedies were happening in other Russian villages, further away from Crimea, there was a cloud of fear and doubt looming over Ebenfeld.

The bell above the door rang. Kaethe's breath caught in her throat as she turned her eyes expectantly to see who was entering the shop. It was their neighbour, Sara Wieler. She was a stout woman, with her white hair pinned perfectly into place atop her head. She walked with a bounce in her step toward the counter where Kaethe sat perched on a wooden stool.

"*Goot Morje, Früling Warkentin*, good morning, Miss Warkentin," the lady greeted Kaethe in *Plautdietsch*, Low German. She smiled, making her face line with creases.

Kaethe looked past the woman toward the door, which had closed behind her. There was no sign of her father yet. She forced her lips into a smile and turned her attention to the women in front of her.

"How can I help you, *Frü* Wieler?"

Frü Wieler explained in elaborate detail the dress she was planning to sew for her daughter. Kaethe listened to the woman speak, her voice high as a mouse, and ushered Frü Wieler to the fabrics, pointing out a cotton material with bright yellow flowers. The woman's pale grey eyes widened and she clapped her hands together, oohing and aahing over the fabric.

The bell rang again and Kaethe was grateful for the opportunity to leave Frü Wieler's side. She turned toward the front of the store to greet the customer. A tall man stood just inside the shop, his arms full of burlap sacks and canvas bags bursting at the seams. The brown felt pork pie hat he wore shaded his eyes, but the thick grey hairs of his walrus mustache instantly gave away his identity.

"Papa!" Kaethe yelled and ran to her father.

Johann Warkentin lowered his bags and opened his arms. Kaethe fell into him, and wrapped her arms around his neck. His mustache tickled her cheek as she kissed him, and she embraced the familiarity of it. He smelled musty, a combination of sweat and horse hair, but Kaethe didn't mind.

"Papa!"

A cracked voice came from the back of the store. Her younger brother, Paul, ran toward them and joined their embrace. His voice cracked again as he welcomed his father home, affirmation that he was nearing adulthood. The boy's smooth face was scattered with short, bristly hairs, though more scarce than their father's. His hair was lighter than Kaethe's, though thicker, and curled at the ends. His body mirrored that of their mother's, wider in the frame and thick boned, with dark eyes and round cheeks.

"Oh, how good it is to see you! I missed you both," Johann took a deep breath, savouring the familiar scents of his children and his store. When he stood up, he noticed Paul now stood at eye level with him. He had only been away from home for a month, yet the boy in front of him hardly resembled the son he had left behind. Johann smiled and patted Paul firmly on the shoulder, and then gently placed his hand on Kaethe's cheek. She was looking more and more like a woman, and less like a sixteen-year-old, every day.

"What did you bring home?" Kaethe peered into the burlap sacks on the floor, eager to see the goods Johann acquired from his trip to Moscow.

Every few months, Johann visited Moscow to scour the markets lined with vendors selling their merchandise, and selected items to sell at his store. His taste was impeccable, especially when it came to coffee beans. Johann had a gift for choosing only the finest beans. With one swift inhale, he knew if they would result in good quality coffee or not. And good coffee was of utmost importance to the Warkentins.

Kaethe found the bag of beans and drew the opening close to her face, closing her eyes as she breathed in the sweet, nutty richness.

"Mama! *Papa es hüss*, Papa is home! Come see the beans he brought with him this time!" Kaethe called out, directing her voice toward the back of the store.

Anna instantly appeared from the back room. She wiped her hands on her grey apron, dodging tables displaying various goods as she hustled toward Johann. He stepped over the bags and reached his weathered hands outward, closing them around his wife's familiar body. He felt the pointed bones of her shoulders, and the soft curves of her bosom against his front. Her head rested on his chest, beneath his chin, cheeks sticky with sweat. He kissed the top of her head, where dark hair spilled out from the pins meant to keep them in place, and held her for a long time. She became more beautiful to him as the years went by, like a favourite book – the edges were slightly worn and weathered, but the story written inside never ceased to captivate him.

Johann thought of Anna incessantly whenever he was away. He knew she was more than capable of running the shop on her own, and with the children old enough to help, as well, there was no reason to fret. But he still worried about her and the children, praying there would be no major incidents to burden them with in his absence.

Anna pulled away from him, "You picked some good coffee beans, did you?" She smiled coquettishly, grateful to have him home. Johann searched his bags and handed Anna the beans. She held them in both hands and brought them to the back room. That evening, Anna would roast them in the same meticulous way she always did. Each step was done artfully with care and precision, while Kaethe and Paul looked on from a distance. Anna moved fluidly, and silently, through each step. First she spread all the beans on trays and roasted them very slowly. Then she added a touch of butter and a pinch of sugar when they were nearly finished roasting.

Every morning, their nanny, Olga, poured the rich, velvety liquid into their ceramic mugs. Steam journeyed toward the ceiling in whorls as the sweet fragrance filled their home and lungs. Kaethe and Anna enjoyed the silky taste of cream in their coffee, whereas Johann preferred his black, and thick enough to walk on.

Anna appeared from the back room again, this time with a handful of shirts draped over her arm. She placed them on the counter in front of her daughter and smiled affectionately, caressing Kaethe's shoulder before she turned back to where she came from.

Kaethe watched her mother walk back to her little room, and caught the wink her father gave to her mother as she passed him. Kaethe smiled at the gesture. If she could have a marriage as strong as her parents', she would be more than content. Kaethe went back to work, folding and stacking the shirts.

The store was quiet, save for the intermittent static coming from the radio, and the soft whir of the sewing machine. Kaethe's mood turned from awe to worry as she listened to the men on the radio speak of Stalin and his plan for 'Socialism in One Country'. Her heart clenched. They had witnessed so much horror since Stalin was elected into office only four years prior.

It had been over three years since The Great Famine ended, and though their store survived those trying years, Kaethe and her family were not blind to those that suffered from it. Kaethe looked out the front window, and slowly lowered her arms to the counter as she reminisced, the ghost of a little girl haunting her thoughts. The memory of that day was still vivid in her mind, despite having only been thirteen at the time. The young girl's hair was long and tangled in knots, the roots greased and unwashed, matted with dirt and grime. Her body was thin, though her stomach ballooned from starvation. Her skin, pale and translucent, showed every bone in her body as she stood naked in the snow, on the other side of the window. Steam outlined her hand where it gently touched the window. She peered at the table of freshly baked bread on the other side of the glass, and her eyes grew wide with wonder and desire.

Moved, Kaethe brought a loaf of bread outside and handed it to the girl. The child's eyes shone as she held the morsel in her hands, the smell intoxicating her. She thanked Kaethe and ran off, her feet leaving imprints in the white snow. Kaethe watched the girl run until she was out of sight. She never saw her again, but rarely a day went by that Kaethe didn't think of her. She wished she could have done more for the little girl – for all the children and families, for that matter, starving and in want of shelter and clothes.

Another memory from those awful years jarred her as the radio crackled beside her. Gooseflesh rose on her skin as she recalled the scene she witnessed on her walk to the pharmacy. A young boy hunched over a small piece of bread, devouring it as if it might disappear if he didn't act fast. His mother, feeble and weak, with a screaming newborn cradled in her arms, begged him to slow down. His stomach was not accustomed to eating, and she urged him to stop. With a raspy voice, muffled from a mouthful of bread, he told his mother he could not stop. He yearned to feel full, and the taste was too divine to pry himself away. Moments later, the boy vomited on the ground in front of him.

Another young boy, scrawny and naked, peered around a nearby fence. He instinctively ran toward them, falling to the ground beside the pool of bile and undigested bread pieces. With cupped hands, he scooped up the vomit and brought it to his mouth. Tears marked Kaethe's cheek as she regarded the hungry, desperate boy. If the boy, and the others struggling to survive, did not take desperate measures such as that, they would all die on the streets alongside the other adults and children who hadn't been as fortunate.

It was then Kaethe realized that, if the government continued down this path, it would be the end of Russia as they knew it. And then what? What would become of Russia? Of their home? A chill ran down Kaethe's spine and she turned away from the window. She switched the radio off, drowning out the sounds of the men's dejected remarks. She sighed again and forced herself to think of something more pleasant. Inevitably, her mind went to Nikolai.

—

The sun slowly lowered itself until completely hidden beneath the horizon, the orange and red streaks painted across the sky the only proof of it having been there. Nikolai unhooked the plow from the oxen and led them to the stable. Behind him, the fields were evenly lined with tilled soil. He wiped the perspiration from his brow as he ran toward the house.

Nikolai opened the door with much force, followed immediately by a loud gasp from the kitchen.

"Nikolai!" Aganetha, Nikolai's mother, exclaimed, her hand over her heart.

Nikolai smiled with a gleam in his eye. He put his arm around his mother's narrow shoulders and kissed her salty temple. Even though he was nearly twenty-one, he still had that boyish charm his mother was dearly fond of.

"I'm sorry, Mama, I didn't mean to scare you. What's for supper?"

He surveyed the ingredients sprawled across the counter. Aganetha reached for the headless chicken, her calloused hands covered with feathers.

"The usual," she winked at him before turning her eyes back to the half-naked hen. "Wash up and help me with the noodles."

Nikolai willingly did as he was told. He found his place at the counter beside his mother. Towering over her, he looked down at the top of her head, silver hairs glinting in the dim light coming through the window in front of them. He reached for the bin of wheat and ground the grains into a coarse powder. Squeals of delight echoed through their home as his younger siblings chased each other. Nikolai looked out the small window overlooking the fields. He saw the silhouette of his brothers, seeds falling from their fingers into the earth as they walked down the even rows of soil. Just outside the window, his father, Peter, sat in a wooden chair, a stack of lesson plans on his lap. With the new school year approaching, Peter spent most evenings preparing his lessons in advance, and adjusting the previous year's lessons as needed.

Nikolai worked hard in the fields so he could finish in time to help his mother with supper. Preparing meals for a family of fourteen was no easy feat. He took three eggs from the basket beside the window and cracked them swiftly over the flour, stirring the contents with a wooden spoon. He soon fell into rhythm as he mixed, and softly began crooning his favourite hymn, *It Is Well With My Soul*. His mother joined him, her soprano voice harmonizing his tenor notes perfectly.

They stood together for some time, singing familiar hymns until Nikolai's voice no longer carried the melody. Aganetha looked at her son. He had a familiar, far-off look in his eyes – dreamy, enchanted, in love. It was obvious, he was thinking of *her* again. Aganetha smiled fervently as she continued humming. That girl had changed him. Though Aganetha was thrilled for her son, she struggled with the jealousy she felt. She was no longer the love of his life. That title now belonged to the charming, confident girl from the other side of town – Kaethe Warkentin.

Kaethe and Nikolai had been courting for a few months. They had grown up together in their small Crimean village, but it was only recently that Kaethe returned Nikolai's affections. Nikolai was nearly five years her senior, and up until a few years ago, he viewed Kaethe merely as his sister's friend, not someone he thought of pursuing romantically. He always appreciated and respected her – her bright spirit and confidence, even at a young age, were admirable. But as Kaethe blossomed into a woman, Nikolai's attraction to her intensified. She was no longer a little girl, but rather a strong, passionate, driven woman, whom he regarded with much zeal.

The attraction was not mutual though, at least not for the first few years. Kaethe's lack of interest didn't deter him from pursuing her, and he continued to seek her out at their Sunday evening youth gatherings behind the church.

As often as possible, he sat beside her on the wooden bench, his body close to hers. When he felt the brush of her soft skin on his arm, a rush of electricity shot through him. Every time he succeeded in sitting close to her, however, she moved away from him. Her actions were subtle, though their meaning resounded in his heart – she was not interested in him as more than a friend. He respected her honesty, but refused to give up.

Nikolai pursued Kaethe relentlessly, until one fateful night, while sitting on the same wooden bench behind the church, when her arm brushed against his and she didn't move away. He knew in that moment that her feelings mirrored his own. Her slight smile, and flushed cheeks, affirmed his suspicion.

Nikolai startled as cold drops of water splattered across his face, bringing him back to the present, out of his daydream. His wide, shocked eyes met his mother's. She laughed and he turned away, bashful.

"*Waut denkjest du?* What are you thinking about, Nikolai? I've asked you to pass the salt ten times already," she winked, her eyes sparkling. He knew she was perfectly aware of what, or who, occupied his thoughts.

With red cheeks, he handed the salt to his mother, refusing to meet her gaze. He knew she was still smiling; he could tell by the way she hummed. He transferred the dough onto the counter and dusted it with more flour before kneading it with both fists. When his cheeks resumed their natural colour, and his heart beat at a regular pace, he sung the lyrics to the familiar hymns once again.

3

October 1929

KAETHE ROCKED BACK AND FORTH IN THE WOODEN ROCKING CHAIR. THE whitewashed boards beneath her creaked with each roll of the curved runners. A small, handmade doll lay in her lap, but her gaze was focused intently on the house across the fields. She was too far away to hear anything, but she didn't need sound to know exactly what was happening. It was an occurrence that was becoming far too common in their village.

Frü Wieler's arms reached desperately out toward her husband, who was being led by two members of the Soviet militia to their vehicle. Five children stood in a cluster beside the house, grasping on to each other's smocks and shirts, with balled fists pressed against their mouths, or covering their eyes to make the horror disappear. The man knew better than to fight with the soldiers as they arrested him and shoved him into the vehicle.

The whole ordeal lasted only moments, leaving Frü Wieler and her children standing in a cloud of dust as the truck drove off with her husband and the children's father. Kaethe's heart pounded inside her chest, and she tightened her grip on the armrests as she watched her neighbour fall to the ground, her face contorted with agony.

Footsteps thumped up the stairs to the porch. She turned to see Nikolai, his face streaked with dirt and sweat.

"They took him," Kaethe said breathlessly, her voice barely above a whisper. She turned toward her neighbour again. "Herr Wieler. They took him. One minute he was driving the tractor to the field, the next minute, he's gone." Nikolai knelt beside his wife and stroked her cheek. Kaethe turned to face him. Her lips quivered. "Oh, Nikolai, what if they come for you? Or Papa?" Knowing that either of them being taken away was not an unlikely reality sent a wave of nausea through Kaethe.

She gave in to her fears and bowed her head as she cried. Nikolai wrapped his arms around her, desperately searching for words that would encourage her, give her hope. But no words came to mind. His own fear gripped him as he watched their neighbour being ripped out of his wife's arms.

Nikolai and Kaethe had been married just over two years, and the thought of being taken from her, with no assurance of ever seeing her again, was too much to bear. He saw the doll in her lap and picked it up. A button hung loosely by a thread, leaving the doll with only one eye.

"I take it *Poppshe*, dolly, went on another wild adventure today," Nikolai's mouth turned up on one side. Kaethe sniffled and looked up. He moved the doll animatedly in his hand, making it look like she was walking. Kaethe smiled and reached for the doll.

"Yes, Maria thought *Poppshe* looked a little bored this morning. I'm not sure what exactly she did to her that would result in a lost eye." Kaethe smiled. The doll had been a gift for Maria's first birthday in June, and it had rarely left her side since. "When you're one, the world is filled with magic and wonder, and ample opportunities for adventure."

Kaethe had come outside to stitch the button back in place, but when tragedy befell their neighbours, mending a doll seemed like the least of her worries.

Kaethe felt a heaviness about her. The national strife had remained constant over the last few years, and there was still no end in sight. Stalin was determined to turn Russia into a "Soviet Paradise", as he liked to call it. His "famous land of freedom," though freedom was exactly what they were taking away from the thousands of Mennonites that had called Russia home for a hundred and fifty years. With his Five Year Plan in place, Stalin implemented his first step of collectivization, which was a hopeless cause for Mennonite farmers. The plan required farmers to pay incredibly high taxes they couldn't afford, which inevitably led to their arrest. If a family decided not to plant their seeds, to forego the tax, they were labeled as enemies of the state, and robbed of all their political and legal rights as citizens, and often arrested. Slowly the Mennonites were being deprived of their properties, farms and rights.

On top of that, religion was not to be spoken of at home, or taught in schools. Sunday was no longer a day of rest. Schools and shops were required to be open on Sundays, and closed on Wednesdays, instead. Nikolai's father had wrestled with the new law, feeling it was against his beliefs to teach on Sundays. But there was no other option, unless he, too, wanted to be arrested. With their youngest child only eight days younger than Maria, and ten other children still living at home, he couldn't take the risk. Nor could parents keep their children home on Sundays. If they did, the teacher was required to report their absence, along with their excuse, to the authorities.

There was so much unknown, and so much fear among Kaethe and her family, and the thousands of Mennonites in Russia. Hundreds had already left their homes and headed for Moscow in hopes of leaving the country, but many of their attempts had been for naught. Families were forced to leave Moscow and were sent to villages that weren't even their own homes, in an attempt to keep Russian citizens within the country. Husbands were constantly arrested and shipped either to the north to work as slave labourers, or sent to prison, charged with being an enemy of the state. In most cases, the men never returned home.

Kaethe woke often with nightmares, paralyzed with fear. What would happen to her and Maria if Nikolai were arrested?

She wrapped her fingers around Nikolai's calloused hands and he sensed her worries.

"Kaethe," Nikolai placed his other hand on top of hers, "we'll get through this. By God's grace, we'll get through this. One way or another."

"But what if we don't?"

"Despite what happens, we have each other, and God will always be with us, no matter where we are."

"How much longer will we stay here? What if we don't get to Moscow in time?"

Nikolai sighed. "I don't know, my love."

"You said we would stay to see if things got better. But they haven't, Nikolai. Things are not better. They're only getting worse. Every day more and more homes are being abandoned, and men arrested."

"I know," Nikolai looked at the cracked beams beneath his feet. Ebenfeld had been his home for his whole life. He met Kaethe there, and started a family in that very house. The thought of leaving it all behind felt like an anchor pressing against his chest, making it hard to breathe. The thought that they might be too late turned his stomach, and he swallowed hard, but the taste of bile lingered in his mouth for some time.

Nikolai stood up and put both thumbs around his suspenders. "It's not an easy decision to make," he said with a quiver in his voice. He bit his lip and cleared his throat as he walked into the house, not wanting Kaethe to see his emotion.

She was being strong for him, he could tell. She knew more details about the reality of the situation than she let on, and he knew that. Yet, he hoped. He hoped goodness would prevail, that God would right the wrongs of the Soviet government in due time. But time was running out. From the news they received from those forced to return from Moscow, the chances of being granted permission to leave the country were getting slimmer and slimmer. At this point, they may never leave the grasp of the Red Terror.

—

Johann and Anna arrived at the store promptly at six in the morning. They went about their usual tasks throughout the day, stopping only to eat for a few minutes before resuming their duties. Johann mostly dealt with customers while Maria sewed or baked in the back room. The bell above the door rang constantly. Customers flowed through their store, one after another, until Johann finally turned the wooden sign in the window from 'Op,' Open to 'Too,' Closed.

Johann sat behind the counter, a candle hissing as it burned. He counted rubles fluidly, noting their value on yellowed paper with black ink. He leaned in close to the paper, and focused intently on the numbers in the dull glow of the candlelight. The familiar clang of the bell sounded from the front of the store.

"I'm sorry, but we're clo—" he looked up. "Ivan!" Johann set his pen down and moved around the counter to greet his friend. Ivan adjusted the belt on his uniform, resting one hand on his rifle, and with the other he removed the green cap from his head.

It wasn't unlike Ivan to visit Johann at his store. The two often drank coffee after hours, conversing about travels, or weather, or politics. Ivan had extensive knowledge on the latter, being both communist and a soldier for Stalin. His presence in Johann's store that night was not out of the ordinary, but Ivan's standoffish demeanor was.

"Something wrong, my friend?" Johann asked him.

Ivan placed a hand on Johann's shoulder. "You're not safe, Johann," he spoke with a hushed voice, and looked over his shoulder, into the darkness on the other side of the glass door. "I don't have time to explain everything, but they're coming for you."

Johann looked at Ivan quizzically. "What do you mean I'm 'not safe?'"

Ivan moved closer, his mouth right beside Johann's ear, speaking even quieter.

"Listen to me," he spoke with authority, with an undertone of friendly affection. "Stalin is on the move. He's on a mission to kill all who claim to be Christian, or any other religion. He's bringing his plan of a Russian Paradise to fruition, which means anyone who has, or is, more than the average citizen is at the top of his list. That includes you, Johann. They're going to arrest you and take you to a prison camp if they find you. You must disappear, now. There is not a moment to spare. Soldiers are out right now with their lists of men to arrest. Please, my friend, leave now. I beg you."

"But, Ivan, I can't just leave right now. What about my family? And all our possessions? We'll need to have an auction to sell our things."

"Johann," Ivan's voice was stern, but his eyes showed his genuine concern. "Your friend, Herr Wieler – he's dead. As are many others you know. This is not something to take lightly, my friend. I know it's not easy, but if you want to stay alive, you need to leave – *now*."

With that, Johann shook Ivan's hand, thanking him immensely, and he turned and walked out of the store. The bell rang again, though it lacked the hope it usually brought with it. Johann heard a faint noise and turned to see Anna standing in the dark, the whites of her eyes reflecting the candlelight. The room was silent, save for Anna's quick breaths. The air was thick and dense. The needlework Anna held fell from her hands. The wooden casing made no sound as it touched the floor. The only sounds to be heard were the deep wails coming from Anna.

Johann moved quickly toward her and gathered Anna into his arms. Her cheeks glistened where tears descended. Johann looked into Anna's eyes, which mirrored the gut-wrenching pain he felt. He held her as close to his body as he could, feeling every familiar curve of her against him. Tears flowed from his eyes and fell off his jaw onto her, dampening her shoulder.

"We must go," he spoke softly, trying to make sense of what just transpired. "Quickly, grab a few cans of food and whatever else you can fit in the bag. I'll take whatever money we have in the store. We need to move fast."

"What do you mean you're leaving?" Kaethe sobbed. Nikolai stood beside her, holding Maria.

Anna hurriedly put her arms into her coat sleeves and wrapped a shawl around her neck. Her cheeks were glassy and the orange candlelight shone bright against them. When she was done, she went to Kaethe and hugged her. Unable to speak, she tightened her arms around her daughter.

"The authorities are coming for me," Johann interjected, composing himself with much effort. "We'll catch the next train to Moscow and wait for you there. I promise, Kaethe." He moved closer to her and firmly gripped her shoulder. Kaethe leaned her head to the side, resting her cheek on his leathery, familiar hand.

"But, how will we find you there? Where do we look? How will we know if you've arrived safely?" Her breaths became short and her eyes widened as panic set in. Nikolai placed Maria in Johann's arms and put his hands on Kaethe's cheeks, forcing her to look at him.

"Kaethe, we'll find them. I promise." Turning to Johann he said, "We'll leave as soon as we can. We'll sell what we can at the store, and around here, and then make our way to Moscow."

Johann nodded his head and patted Nikolai on the back. He lowered Maria to the ground and picked up the suitcase that held the only belongings that would go with them on their journey. Before stepping onto the porch, Johann, Anna and Paul looked around the house, savouring the last glimpse of their beloved home.

It wasn't until that moment that they realized how much of their identity was in that house, and in that land. Decades of memories seeped into every corner and crevice of the house. The crack in the wall from when Paul was a little boy and fell and hit his head; the large silver serving spoon, a gift for Johann and Anna on their wedding day. The notched carvings in the moulding around the kitchen doorway, marking how tall Kaethe and Paul had grown every year on their birthdays; the corner of the living room where the Christmas tree stood every year; the wooden rocking chair on the porch Johann had made for Kaethe when she told them she was expecting a baby; the armchair in the living room where Anna first held her granddaughter. The ashtray where Johann emptied his pipe after work; the hook on the wall beside the door where he hung his hat; the sewing machine in Anna's room, which had made all of their clothes, including Kaethe's wedding dress.

It was all too much. Anna clutched her chest and reached her arms out to Kaethe. Maria cried, unsettled by all the emotion.

"It's time to go," Johann said reluctantly. Nikolai nodded and slowly pulled Kaethe away from her mother.

"Until we meet again," Johann said. "Stay safe."

Kaethe, Nikolai and Maria stood motionless on the porch as they watched Johann, Anna and Paul ride off in the carriage.

—

After putting Maria to bed, Nikolai boiled water and poured Kaethe a cup of tea. She sat at the table, frozen, staring at the wall with the carved notches that charted her growth throughout the years. Near the bottom was a fresh notch, Maria's first measurement, taken on her first birthday.

Nikolai sat down beside Kaethe. "Have a sip," he encouraged her. She turned her face slowly to look at him. Her eyes were bloodshot, and her cheeks wet from crying endlessly. Nikolai reached into his pocket and pulled out his handkerchief. As she took the thin, square fabric from his hand, there was a loud knock on the door.

Kaethe froze again and the handkerchief fell weightlessly to the floor. Her eyes showed the fear that both felt in that moment. Nikolai pushed his chair away from the table and walked steadily toward the door. He opened it and a tall man in military uniform towered over him, with a shorter henchmen in tow.

"Johann Warkentin," the large man bellowed. "Where is he?"

"He's not here!"

Nikolai turned around to see Kaethe standing just behind him. She was shaking. He gave her a look that said he would handle the soldiers, but she shook her head.

The officer looked past Nikolai at Kaethe and smiled coyly, enjoying his position and the fear he instilled in her. "Where is he, then?"

"He went to the train station," her voice was surprisingly steady.

The arrogant officer looked at the watch on his wrist, and turned to his henchman, "The train to Moscow doesn't leave for another two hours. We'll get the other man on our list first, and then get Warkentin at the train station."

With another coy smile the officer tipped his hat and bid them farewell. Nikolai closed the door behind him and Kaethe collapsed into his arms, the tears flowing once again. "Oh, Papa! They're going to get Papa! This can't be happening!"

Nikolai held Kaethe and rocked her in his arms, regrettably unable to reassure her.

—

Johann willed it all to be a dream, a nightmare. Surely he heard Ivan wrong, but he knew that wasn't the case. He had his suspicions it would eventually come to something like this, but he never thought it would actually happen. The memory of walking out of his home, for what he knew would be the very last time, unsure if he would ever see his daughter and her family again, plagued him.

He went from feeling afraid, to sad, to angry, berating himself for not having left for Moscow sooner. They could have made it easier, less urgent and heartbreaking. They could have held an auction and sold their belongings. But he knew it wouldn't have changed the inevitable. They still needed to get out of Russia, out of the hell they were experiencing, and into freedom. Regardless how inevitable it was, Johann felt guilty, that it was in some way his fault.

The train station was surprisingly busy for that time of night. Instructions were called out to passengers, and whistles blew erratically. Johann waited impatiently in queue at the ticket booth with the other passengers, keeping an eye on Anna and Paul who stood off to the side. He looked around anxiously as he waited, though he wasn't quite sure who, or what, he was looking for, or who, for that matter, was looking for him. There were many officials in uniform wandering around the platforms, smug expressions plastered on their faces. It disgusted Johann to see them getting pleasure out of their misery.

When he finally stood in front of the clerk, he steadied his shaking hands and forced his voice to come out smooth, unnerved. He didn't want to draw any unnecessary attention to himself.

"Three tickets to Moscow, please."

He shifted his weight from the front pads of his feet to his heels and back again, swaying nervously as the clerk stamped papers. Johann grabbed the tickets, and hurriedly led Anna and Paul to the assigned platform. Paul stepped up into the car first. Anna followed, holding Johann's hand to steady herself. With his wife and son safely on the train, Johann tightened his grip around the handle of the suitcase and took a deep breath. He stepped into the train car and sat down beside Anna. He lowered the brim of his hat, feeling the need to hide his face.

This can't be real, can it? He berated himself again for leaving Kaethe's family behind, but felt God's presence, and His calm, steady voice assuring Johann he was doing the right thing. The words from Genesis 19 echoed in his mind, *"Escape for thy life; look not behind thee."*

Then the whistle blew, and the train was off.

—

When the officers arrived at the train station, they ran to the platform bound for Moscow. The steam, and the smell of coal and soot from the engine, still lingered in the air. The leader of the group threw his hat on the ground and kicked it as he cursed into the air. Johann Warkentin was gone.

4

October 1929

PETER STOOD BEHIND AGANETHA, HIS HAND RESTING HEAVILY ON HER shoulder. Kaethe stood silently beside Nikolai, her eyes a tavern of grief. Aganetha's hands covered her mouth as Nikolai spoke.

"Kaethe's parents and brother left for Moscow last night. Johann's friend, the one in Stalin's party, warned him that they were coming for him. Kaethe and I will sell as much as we can at the store, and on the farm, before we leave for Moscow to join her family. We hope to be gone by the end of the week.

"Please, Mama and Papa, you must go as well. It's getting worse here, and from what we've heard, getting the appropriate papers and documents in Moscow to leave isn't getting any easier, either. You're not safe here. We must all try to leave, together."

His parents' faces were wrought with concern and panic. Peter thanked Nikolai for coming and informing them of the situation Kaethe's family, and the rest of the Mennonites, were in. His face was stoic, though, and he made no assurance of joining Nikolai in Moscow.

"But, you *will* meet us in Moscow, yes?" Fear gripped Nikolai as he waited for his father to respond.

Peter stared at the floor. He wiped his cheek with his hand, and looked Nikolai in the eyes.

"We would love more than anything to join you in Moscow, Nikolai. I just don't want to make a promise that I can't guarantee I can fulfill. We've heard the rumours – it's growing increasingly difficult for families to acquire passports. It does not bode well for Stalin, or Russia, if thousands of citizens are leaving while he's building his 'Paradise'. The Reghers down the street tried to get their documents, but were denied – multiple times. As has your brother, Kornelius and his family. Do you know how much it costs to apply for passports? Two hundred rubles per person. And if the government denies your request, each request after that is twenty rubles per person. For a family of thirteen, that's more than we can afford."

"We'll help you pay for the applications, Papa," Nikolai insisted, desperate to hear his father agree to go to Moscow. "Whatever you need, we'll help."

"It's not that simple, son," Peter sighed. "Even if we did get to Moscow, we'd have a hard time finding somewhere to live. The rental rates are going up because the owners know the Mennonites have to pay whatever they ask, for they have nowhere else to go.

"Kornelius and Elizabeth, and their three children, are freezing, and nearly starving to death in Moscow. It is no better there. We received word from him that there have been secret meetings in the woods, at night, near Djangarowka. They've been trying to get in touch with higher rank officials. The GPU learned about their meetings and have started arresting men that they deem suspicious."

Nikolai frowned, "But, Papa."

"Nikolai, I promise you we will try, but you must go with your family, regardless. We trust God will protect you all. We will not stop praying for you, for safety, and that we will one day meet again."

Nikolai leapt forward and wrapped his arms around his father. His sobs were stifled in his father's shoulder. Peter stood thin-lipped, his emotions unwavering as he kept himself composed, and held his son tightly. Aganetha's reaction was a contrast to her husband's. Her tears flowed freely as she stood to join Peter and Nikolai's embrace.

Kaethe prayed it would not be the last time Nikolai felt the warm touch of his parents, but there was no guarantee. For now, she prayed they would be able to get out of Ebenfeld in time, and that they would find her parents in Moscow, though there was no guarantee in that matter, either. Kaethe felt her world collapsing, and if it were not for Nikolai and Maria, she didn't think she'd have the strength, or the will, to fight for their freedom.

—

Nikolai carried their suitcase while Kaethe clung to Maria. The train station was flooded with passengers, all seemingly in a state of urgency and panic. Russian and Plautdietsch words filled the space in a cloud of confusion. She couldn't make out one conversation from the next. Train whistles blew, and the smell of coal filled their lungs as they made their way to the platform.

Kaethe's legs felt weak as the gravity of their departure sunk in. She scanned the crowd. Most of the passengers were Mennonites. The women were more or less dressed the same, with long skirts, blouses with varying colours of floral prints, and shawls draped over their heads and tied under their chins. The men wore hats similar to her father's beloved brown pork pie, though some wore the more traditional Russian ushanka, along with black or brown knee length frock coats.

Amidst the sea of sullen, fear-stricken faces was the occasional GPU officer. Kaethe tried to avoid making eye contact with them, but she was keenly aware of their presence among the crowd, and her heart raced knowing they were near. They stopped to talk to passengers, and every now and then they watched as families were ushered out of the train station. As if the train ride itself wasn't enough of a risk on its own, now they had the added worry of the officers stopping them from getting on the train in the first place.

They knew this was no easy feat to begin with. Since September, Kremlin officials had made it increasingly difficult, even impossible, for Mennonites to enter Moscow. Most trains that travelled through German-speaking settlements were not permitted to stop and take on any passengers.

Nikolai and Kaethe had travelled further down the line to a train station outside of their village to increase their chances of boarding. They tried not to look suspicious, or obviously German, though they didn't really know what made them stand out among the others. Most of the other Mennonite passengers waiting on the platform didn't have any luggage, hoping to look as if they were only going on an outing, not running for their lives.

Kaethe clutched the handle of their suitcase tightly in her fist. Stalin was already forcing her to leave the rest of her life behind, but she refused to leave with nothing to call her own. She hid the case among the folds of her skirt, and successfully boarded the train. She tucked it under her legs, making sure her skirt covered every corner of it.

Kaethe softly lulled Maria to sleep as the train swayed side to side, gliding up the tracks. Tears caressed her cheeks as she watched the familiar sights and landmarks fly past her window. Home was behind her now. Her life, her house, her childhood – everything was left behind. One suitcase with a few of their belongings, and a handful of money, was all they had.

Time moved at a leisurely pace, unaware of their anxiousness to arrive at their destination. Her body had not felt settled since her parents and brother had left for Moscow. She hadn't slept, fearing every little noise she heard was the arrival of the GPU. She never let Maria out of her sight, or Nikolai, for that matter. All day, every day, she felt anxious and afraid.

Her thoughts were interrupted at one of the stops along the way. At the front of the car, a GPU officer held a man by the back of his jacket, forcing him to stand. The man's wife screamed at the officer in Plautdietsch to let him go. The officer seemed to be enjoying the turmoil he was putting the poor woman through, and smiled coyly at her.

"Take your family and get off the train," the official ordered in Russian. "Go back to your home."

"We have no home, sir," the struggling man replied, his Russian less refined as the officer's. The officer let go of the man and glared at him.

"What did you say?"

"We have no home. It was taken away from us, along with everything else we owned."

The officer's eyes were only small slits now as he stared down at the man. "You'll get it all back. Now return to your home."

"We don't want to get it back," the man avoided looking into the officer's eyes. "Please, we just want to get out of this country."

The officer waved his hand toward the door, and two more officials appeared. The three men scoured the family's belongings, confiscating any money or gold, anything of worth they could find. The wife pressed herself against the window, her four children gathered in her arms. Though she was obviously terrified, she showed no signs of it on her face, aside from the slight twitch at the corner of her mouth.

Kaethe tightened her grip on Maria and pulled her closer to her body. She moved her hand slowly toward Maria's face, and covered her ear with her hand. The officers tossed the family's belongings aside, mumbling and laughing to each other. Kaethe couldn't understand anything they were saying, aside from a few random words. She looked at Nikolai, who kept his gaze fixated on something outside the window. She knew he understood what the men were saying, but his expression stayed neutral. She looked back toward the commotion.

"Now we have all your money," the first officer said smugly. "How do you plan to leave without being able to pay your way?"

The man's voice shook with fear, but he didn't cry. "We'll do whatever it takes. We'll drag ourselves to the border if need be. Everything else will fall into place once we get there, by God's grace."

"Ha!" The officers laughed in unison. Their evil tones sent shivers down Kaethe's spine. "Why don't we see if God's grace can get you out of prison, shall we?"

And with that, the man was seized and arrested. The first official escorted him off the train, and the other two officials followed with the man's wife and children, herding them like cattle, and yelling insults as they stepped off the train.

Once they were gone, the train car was silent. No one dared to breathe, or lift a finger. Moments later they were moving again. Kaethe let out a deep sigh of relief, and wiped a tear that had made its way down her cheek. Nikolai reached for her hand, and placed his other hand on Maria's head.

"*The Lord is my light and my salvation; whom shall I fear?*" He whispered the comforting Psalm in her ear. His voice was so quiet, the words only audible to the three of them. "*The Lord is the strength of my life; of whom shall I be afraid? Though a host should encamp against me, my heart shall not fear: though war should rise against me, in this will I be confident.*"

—

Nikolai, Kaethe and Maria disembarked the train a few stations before Moscow to avoid the risk of running into more officers, and potentially Nikolai's arrest. Nikolai carried Maria on his hip and held on to Kaethe, their fingers tightly interlocked.

They stumbled as they walked in darkness, from the uneven ground and from their shivering bodies. The cool air pierced through their skin, and their breath lingered in thick clouds in front of their faces with each exhale. Every now and then, a branch scratched their faces, or snagged their clothes. Nikolai's frock coat covered Maria's body to keep her safe from the branches and the cold, but she still shook in his arms.

They followed a crowd of Mennonites toward the forest, and after walking for hours with only intuition to guide them, they saw the faint flickering of candles in the distance. Everyone froze, uncertain if they had reached allies or enemies. They prayed it was the former.

A couple of men in the group ventured cautiously toward the small cluster of cottages, and returned soon after with tentative smiles across their faces. They had found respite, for the time being. Those living in the *Datschas*, summer cottages, came out to greet the newcomers. They offered what little bread and water they had, which did little to quench the hunger pangs of the new arrivals.

Kaethe took her small morsel and passed it to Maria, who grabbed it eagerly and devoured it instantly.

"*Mea*, more?" Maria asked, her voice soft with fatigue and hunger. Kaethe's frown deepened.

"I'm sorry, Michi, that's all we have."

Maria closed her eyes. She had no strength to argue with Kaethe, and simply sunk into her mother's arms and fell asleep. Kaethe searched the grounds, looking quickly from one person to the next, but her parents weren't among the hundreds lodging in the camp.

Nikolai came up behind her and sat on the floor beside her.

"I have word on your parents and Paul. They're staying with friends in an apartment outside the city. We'll get in touch with them and tell them to meet us here."

"Really?" Kaethe sat straighter.

"Yes, really." Nikolai kissed her forehead.

The relief Kaethe felt in that moment was merely a spec compared to the overwhelming fear and anxiety that clothed her every hour of every day. "And Kornelius and Elizabeth?"

Nikolai shrugged his shoulders. "Nothing yet."

Kaethe nodded her head slowly. They knew Nikolai's brother and his family had made it to Moscow, and could only hope and pray that they were still there, together. The image of Herr Wieler being torn away from his family again flashed in her mind, as it did often these days, and she shuddered involuntarily.

When will the misery end? she asked herself again.

The debilitating knowledge that your life was in the hands of someone else, that you had no control over your outcome, was enough to drive one mad. There were days when she felt herself slip away, giving in to the fear, and doubting God's promises that He would always be with her.

All her worries played cyclically through her mind as she lay on the wood planks that served as their beds. They shared a cottage with another family – a husband and wife with four children, and one expected to arrive any day.

The cottages were designed to be summer homes for the locals, and so were made with no insulation. The nine bodies around the room shivered, huddled together to glean what warmth they could from each other's bodies.

Men left the cottages at night to congregate in the forest. Every night, they discussed the current situation in Moscow and what they could do to attain the papers needed to leave the country. Many attempts had already been made from Mennonites that had arrived in Moscow earlier, and though hundreds of families had managed to step outside the Iron Curtain, thousands still remained. They waited daily for news from Moscow to arrive at camp with new refugees, but sometimes days passed without any updates.

Not only did the men retreat to the forest at night to plot out their next move, it was also an attempt to hide from imminent arrest. The Russian police were constantly prowling the streets, surrounding suburbs and woods, looking for refugees to arrest. Occasionally, the police came into their camp and cottages, rummaging through trunks and dressers to find anything of value, and to find the husbands and take them away from their families. Without the men, they assumed the wives and children would be foolish not to return to their homelands where they could wait expectantly for their husbands to return. The government knew the family ties of the Mennonites were too strong – no wife would leave the country without her husband.

Kaethe heard footsteps outside and the hairs on the back of her neck stood on end. She moved her arm further around Maria's small body and unknowingly held her breath as the thuds outside her cottage grew louder. A moment later, the door opened slowly. Even in the dark, she could make out Nikolai's silhouette. She exhaled and felt her body relax enough to be able to move over so Nikolai could lie down beside her. He kissed the top of her head, and then Maria's, before laying his head back and closing his eyes.

Finally, when she was exhausted beyond her limit, she fell asleep, and dreamed of a life of freedom – freedom from being hunted, hated and wrongly accused; freedom from fear, worry, and anxiety about making it to the end of every day alive; freedom to worship God, and to have rights. More than anything, she dreamed of having a life again, complete with a home to call their own, where they could raise Maria without wondering if their land and possessions, or even their lives, would be taken from them without warning.

A life, that was all she yearned for now. Simply, life.

—

A few weeks later, Kaethe's parents and brother arrived at the summer cottages. Johann's hands were empty. Their only bag of belongings had been confiscated shortly after arriving in Moscow. Anna's normally plump figure had leaned out significantly, and her eyes were deep and sullen, with dark bags beneath each one. To Kaethe, her family was almost unrecognizable. Where once joy and passion shone, was now replaced with desolation.

"*Waut es met jie passieren,* what happened to you?" Kaethe said in disbelief as she cautiously raised her hand to her mother's shallow cheeks. Anna's lips twitched as she tried to force her muscles to smile, but it was as if they had forgotten how to move in that way. Instead, she put a hand over Kaethe's and stood silently while Johann updated them.

"There is not much good to share with you, I'm afraid. A few weeks ago, Canada closed its doors to new immigrants, which led Germany to announce they would not accept any more refugees into their country. There are still men working to appeal to the German government to take the rest of us, but that is still the least of our worries at this time. Even if we could leave, the original lists of groups of families that were eligible to leave is irrelevant now. Many of those families are no longer in Moscow. The GPU has been more forceful and rampant than ever, arresting men every night, right from their homes. They are either sent to prison or to some village that isn't even their own home. Even children have been separated from their families and sent to Siberia."

"Siberia?" Kaethe gasped. "But it's nearly winter!"

Johann took a deep breath, not wanting to affirm her thoughts. All those children, and the men sent there to work, would be dead before winter's end. "There is much to be thankful for, though," he continued. "Let us not forget the hundreds of families that have already gone through the Red Gate and into freedom. God has delivered them, and we will continue to pray for those of us still waiting."

For the next month, they woke everyday with fear and dread, and went to sleep every night with a ball of anxiety lodged in their chests. The days got colder and the nights got longer. Food was scarce, and there was little to be done to stay warm. Fires were limited, as they would only draw attention to themselves. Cold and fragile, their immune systems weakened, and sickness spread through the camp. Children were the most susceptible, and many died in their mother's arms. Hope tapered off like a dying flame having reached the end of the wick.

—

On Monday, November 25, the family sat together in their small cottage, which felt more like an icebox, fighting to keep themselves warm. Nikolai held Maria on his lap, closest to the small fire. Kaethe tried wiggling her toes, but she was too cold to know if they were actually moving.

A dog barked in the distance and everyone's heads went up and they sat frozen, looking at each other with wide eyes. More barking. It was getting closer. Maria started talking and Nikolai instantly put a hand over her mouth, which she tried to pull away. Suddenly, there was a firm knock on the door.

Johann stood slowly and adjusted his trousers before moving to the front of the cottage. His hand shook as he raised it to unlock the door. An officer stood in front of him, dimly lit by the lantern he held close to his face. Johann's shoulders lowered.

"Ivan?"

Ivan moved the lantern even higher and leaned forward.

"Johann? Well, I'll be damned."

The two men hugged and patted each other on the back. "You have no idea how glad I am to see you, Johann." Ivan's tone was serious.

Johann put his hand on Ivan's shoulder and squeezed it. "Same to you, my friend. We owe our lives to you, for warning us. We can never repay you for your loyalty." He lowered his arm slowly. "Are you here to arrest me?"

"Arrest you?" Ivan laughed. "No, no. Quite the opposite. I bring good news – everyone here has been granted permission to leave Russia. Germany has opened its doors again."

"Pardon me?" Johann asked. The others hadn't moved throughout the entire conversation, and still sat in silence, watching the two men.

Ivan's eyes glistened. "Johann, you and your whole family can pick up your passports in Moscow and make your way to Germany." A tear slid unexpectedly down his cheek and he wiped it away with the back of his hand.

"Ivan, thank you." Johann embraced his friend again.

"Thank President von Hindenburg. It was he that told Stalin to let you come over."

Svoboda. The only Russian word Kaethe cared about. *Freedom.*

She could see it coming, literally see their freedom approach them. The metal structure, painted red, with a five-point star on the top, marked their passage from terror to freedom. She craned her neck as they passed through the gate, and looked over her shoulder as it grew smaller and smaller in the distance as they continued driving down the tracks.

It had only been five days since they received the news from Ivan. That night, after he left to tell the others the news, Kaethe and her family praised God through tears and song. The next day, they made their way to Moscow and waited in line with the thousands of other Mennonite refugees eagerly waiting for their documents to be handed to them, hoping Germany wouldn't change its mind again.

With the Red Gate behind them, Kaethe turned in her seat and looked ahead. The future was all that mattered now, but doubt still lingered. She fingered the tag hanging around her neck. A small, round piece of white paper tied to a thin thread identifying who she was.

The original lists of families were amended to account for those families no longer able to make the journey. Kaethe's family was amongst the second group of families to leave Moscow. They boarded a train at Pushkino station, along with over three hundred other refugees.

They drove all day, and through the night, until they finally arrived at their first stop in Riga, Latvia. They were welcomed with warmth and compassion from the locals, and were served bread, milk and hot cocoa prepared in the outdoor kitchen set up on the platform. From there, they boarded another train. Sick passengers were separated from the others and placed in hospital cars, most of whom had contracted trachoma. Those that were too ill to travel were taken to the hospital, but did not survive the journey.

They rode through Latvia and Lithuania without stopping. The snow continued falling, and Kaethe shivered in her seat. Her shoes were still damp from walking in snow at the station in Riga. She couldn't feel her toes, though she couldn't actually remember the last time her feet had been dry and warm.

Kaethe woke to the slight movement of her body, and the sound of Nikolai's voice. "*Oppwakjen*, wake up."

Fearing the worst, she sat up, her heart beating strongly in her chest as she looked around the train car. Blackness was all around her, save for a few torchlights flickering outside.

"Everything's okay," Nikolai assured her and squeezed her hand. "We've arrived."

Kaethe looked out the window and read the sign on the large building - *Eydtkuhnen Station.*

Dietschlaunt, Germany. They made it.

The passengers stood nervously, their faces care-worn and creased with anxiety. A crowd gathered on the platform and Kaethe's heart pounded inside her chest. Despite the assurance that they were out of Russia and out of Stalin's grasp, she couldn't help but fear something might still go wrong.

"Ready?"

Kaethe turned at the sound of Nikolai's voice. He, too, looked apprehensive. Not able to reassure him with a smile, she moved her hand into his and tightened her grip. Maria's arms were interlocked around his neck, her face buried in Nikolai's shoulder. The pit of guilt and shame grew in Kaethe's chest as she looked at her daughter, only eighteen months old, hiding her face from the world. She had seen and experienced far too much horror in her short life.

There was no time to dwell on regret, however. The passengers slowly moved toward the front of the car and disembarked the train. Kaethe inhaled the fresh air deep into her lungs. Snow fell weightlessly, and she licked a snowflake from her lip before tightening the shawl around her shoulders. Nikolai removed his frock coat and wrapped it around Maria's body.

Kaethe looked at Nikolai, who hurriedly scanned the crowd once again. He did this often. At every destination, on every train car, and on every departure. He was always searching for his family. Kaethe felt his desperate need to find at least one person from his family, to know they were safe. She stood on frozen tiptoes and looked over the crowd of passengers.

"There are still fourteen other groups to leave Moscow," she rubbed his arm as she spoke, "I'm sure they'll be on one of them."

Nikolai nodded slowly, his gaze fixed on the passengers still disembarking the train cars. Kaethe rubbed her eye, it had been painful the last few days. She blinked a few times before a voice rose above the crowd.

Reverend Pauls called the refugees together, and the 325 passengers formed a circle on the platform. He thanked God for delivering them out of Russia, and shared a few words of encouragement and praise with them. Many women cried, grateful to have finally reached freedom. Even some of the men had wet lines down their dust-ridden cheeks. They closed their time of thanksgiving by singing a few songs. Harmonious melodies filled the air, though many could not utter the words through their emotion.

A hundred and fifty years earlier, their ancestors boarded the trains at this very station to immigrate their lives to Russia, the very place where this group of Mennonites had just fled for their lives. They lamented over their livelihoods, now behind them. Everything their grandfathers and great-grandfathers had built and established was now gone. They were back in Germany, where they had originated from, and for the time being, they would cling to that for comfort.

5

February 1930

KAETHE FELT THE FAINTEST FLICKER OF HOPE THE MOMENT THEY ARRIVED at the refugee camp at Hammerstein. But the momentary break in despair was short-lived. Uncertainty loomed over the camp like a thick fog. Those running the camp made every effort to make life in the camp enjoyable, or at least less burdensome, than the life they had become accustomed to.

Even Christmas had been an elaborate event, complete with real Christmas trees, decorated with strings of electric lights. The hall was lined with tables, and they sang carols and dined together, the men on one side and the women on the other. The refugees were grateful for the time and effort put into the day, but it did little to raise their spirits.

Their thoughts were constantly plagued with questions and prayers. Would there be a country that would not only accept new immigrants, but also accept their culture and beliefs, their way of life? They were not willing to sacrifice their faith, or religious practices.

Canada had been willing to make those assurances. Hundreds of families had settled there, sending positive reports of the villages they had settled in, but their conditions for approval were strict. Refugees required a clean bill of health, authorized by a medical physician.

Kaethe's eye discomfort had grown worse. It became swollen and she constantly wiped the liquid that accumulated at the corners. When the time came for her to meet with the physician, they diagnosed her with trachoma and she was refused immigration to Canada, which meant her family would not be able to go to the most desirable land. She felt guilty, and even though her family told her they didn't blame her, and all that mattered to them was that they all be together, she still felt sick about it. It was her fault, she believed. And if they couldn't go to Canada, then where would they go?

By the end of December, fifteen groups of Mennonites had arrived in Germany, and still there was no sign of any of Nikolai's family members. They waited and waited for the last group, but weeks passed with no new arrivals. Eventually, news came to Hammerstein that the final group never left Moscow.

It was a cool night in February. Kaethe, Nikolai, Maria, Anna and Paul were getting ready for bed. Kaethe sat on Maria's bed, stroking her fine, brown hair, and sung her favourite hymns softly. Anna hummed along as she sewed a patch on to Paul's trousers.

Johann suddenly barrelled into their small room, his breathing laboured from having run back to their barracks. He leaned against the door frame to catch his breath and removed his hat from his head, his damp forehead glistening in the faint light. He wiped his face with his sleeve, set his hat back on his head and stood straight.

"Paraguay has opened its borders," he explained, sounding neither excited nor upset.

"What?" Anna asked, moving closer to her husband. She eyed him suspiciously, trying to discern his tone. "What does that mean? What are you saying?"

Johann placed an arm around Anna's waist. "It means, my dear, that hundreds of families will be transported to South America."

"To live?" Kaethe asked, stunned.

"Yes, to live. To build new lives. To start fresh. We'll have a place to call home again."

Eighteen hundred Mennonites from Canada had already settled in the Paraguayan region called Chaco, and reported back to the Mennonite Central Committee that it was a decent place to live and colonize. Paraguay granted all their requests, and offered them tariff and tax-free living for ten years. No physical examinations were required before entering, either, which was unheard of.

"So, I can go there, too?" Kaethe was hesitant to believe him.

"Yes, Kaethe, anyone who cannot go to Canada for health reasons can go to Paraguay."

It was good news, Kaethe knew that, it was exactly what they were praying for, but she couldn't help feel guilty for being the reason they couldn't go to Canada.

"The first ship leaves in the middle of March," Johann continued, "but it's already full. We are on the list for the second departure. We leave April 16."

There were murmurs of delight throughout the small room. Kaethe tried to see the news as the answer to prayer they were waiting for, but fear gripped her nonetheless. Sadness swelled inside her. As much as she wanted to leave Russia, she didn't want to leave her home. Somehow, she assumed they would eventually return to Ebenfeld, that the political upheaval and the evil moving through the land would cease, allowing them to resume life as it had been before Stalin and his godforsaken Paradise. But that dream drifted further and further away every day.

Nikolai walked toward the window and leaned against the wall. He looked down from their second story window and rubbed his chin knowingly with one hand. Kaethe kissed the top of Maria's head, who was already fast asleep, and joined Nikolai by the window.

From their position they could see the wire fence that once separated the new arrivals from the disinfected refugees within the barracks. They had stood on the other side of that fence when they first arrived, and the memory unsettled Kaethe.

"Don't lose hope yet, Nikolai." Kaethe turned to face him. His breathing was shallow and his lips tense. He shifted his weight on his feet and moved his gaze upward, toward the stars.

It was a clear night. The Big Dipper shone bright right in front of them, level to the horizon. Nikolai pinched the top of his nose and cleared his throat. "I think I'll try to get some sleep."

He kissed Kaethe's temple and went to his bunk. Kaethe joined the others around the small table and watched Nikolai pull the covers over himself. She sat with the others but her ears were focused on Nikolai, and every now and then she heard sniffling, and prayed God would bring his family safely out of Russia. And soon.

—

A few weeks later, Kaethe's family transferred to the Mölln refugee camp, where they prepared for their transit to South America. There, shoes and clothes were repaired, hair was cut, and equipment was made for their settlement in the new land.

The night before their scheduled departure, Johann sat in the corner of their room, hidden in the shadows. The single candle in the middle of the room flickered and hissed. In the morning, they would make their way to the harbour to set sail across the ocean. The thought both relieved and burdened him at the same time. He was grateful that his whole family had made it out of Russia safely, but he couldn't free himself from the guilt that engulfed him. It was his store – his wealth – that put them in greater risk of danger in the first place.

Kaethe sat against the wall, staring at the floor. Her fear was visible through the creases on her forehead. She looked older than her twenty-one years. Maria toddled toward her and Kaethe smiled. For a second, Johann saw the familiar face of his daughter, and his own lips turned upwards. Kaethe always smiled – or she used to, until they left Ebenfeld – and it was one of Johann's favourite sights.

Johann sighed, his mouth relaxing into a weighted frown. Anna came to him and placed a hand on his shoulder. If she was afraid, she hid it well, Johann thought. He envied his wife's ability to trust God unconditionally. He trusted, too, but not to the same extent as Anna. Johann smiled at her, and placed a hand over hers. If only he could draw some of her faith and add it to his own.

Before they snuffed the candle for the night, Johann prayed over the family and their upcoming journey. Suitcases sat by the door, packed and ready for the next part of their journey. The room was heavy with worry and doubt. Even in the darkness, they felt the familiar weight of uncertainty that followed them wherever they went.

Kaethe was keenly aware of the cobblestone and dirt beneath her feet as they walked toward the harbour. It would be weeks before she set foot on solid ground again. The cool morning air blew softly around them. The hair on Kaethe's arms stood on end and she shivered. Nikolai closed his hand firmly around hers and pulled her towards him when she lost her balance on the curved stones. Johann walked in front of them, carrying Maria, her beloved doll bouncing against his back.

People scrambled all around them, reading signs for guidance on which queue to stand in, and frantically searching purses for documentation. Ships lined the harbour from one end to the other. Kaethe had never seen anything like it before. Their vastness made her feel insignificant in comparison. Kaethe looked over at the tickets Nikolai held in his hand. The name 'S.S. General Belgrano' was typed in large font at the top of the paper. Shielding their eyes from the sun, they searched the sides of the ships until Nikolai spotted it. The others followed the direction of his pointed finger.

They craned their necks to see the tops of the masts, but they were hidden in the clouds. The navy hull blended perfectly into the sea. The blood red of the keel exposed itself with the rise and fall of each wave. Large copper pipes emanated steam as they stood sure and erect around the ship. A row of white, circular windows lined the top of the hull. The decks were painted in a thick layer of cotton white paint, and surrounded by metal railings.

"*Namen und Geburtsort*, names and place of birth," a man behind a small desk asked bluntly. His eyes remained fixed on the cream coloured papers in front of him.

"Warkentin," Johann replied. "Johann, Anna and Paul Warkentin. Crimea."

The man moved his index finger down the paper, scanning the list of names. Kaethe watched her father. He stood motionless, but she sensed his nervousness. They waited with bated breath, praying there would be no complications – they needed to board that ship.

The man grabbed the pen from the table and with a few quick turns of his wrist they were signed in. He stamped their boarding passes and handed them to Johann, his eyes having yet to leave the papers. He pointed behind him with his thumb, and curtly informed them to follow the gangplank onto the ship.

Johann's family moved past the desk and waited. Nikolai and Kaethe moved forward, Maria now in Kaethe's arms.

"*Namen und Geburtsort*," the man said with the same monotonous tone.

"Pen-"

"*Goodendach*, good day," Maria interrupted Nikolai.

The man turned his gaze toward Maria.

"Good day," she said again. "*Groote Schepp*, big ship."

Her round little finger pointed at the General Belgrano. The man followed the direction of her finger, not understanding the German dialect she spoke. The faintest of smiles crept into his lips as he resumed his position behind the desk, staring down at the papers. His smile faded.

"Names and place of birth," he repeated in his usual tone.

"Penner. Nikolai, Katarina and Maria Penner. Crimea."

Nervous trepidation coursed through Kaethe as they waited. He found their names, made the same jagged scrawling beside each one, and stamped their boarding passes.

With his thumb, he signaled them to move behind him. They scurried together, eager to get on the ship. The six of them walked the gangplank together, gripping the railing to steady themselves as the rolling waves gently rocked the boat.

The ship seemed bigger, and far more intimidating, when they were actually on it. Crew members yelled instructions to each other, children played on the deck, adults huddled under canvas overhangs, clutching their belongings. Below them, passengers stood in line, waiting to embark the ship. Nikolai searched the crowds desperately, and she knew he was looking for his family.

His shoulders fell as he turned around and Kaethe wrapped an arm reassuringly around his waist. She wanted to tell him that they would make it, that he would see them again in Paraguay, but there was no way of knowing if that was actually true. They walked around the boat until they found their berths and settled in for the long journey.

6

April 1930

THE LIGHTS OF HAMBURG TWINKLED LIKE A CLUSTER OF FIREFLIES IN THE distance. Nikolai held Kaethe until her tears ran dry. She pulled away from him and wiped her mouth one last time. The wetness of the bile in her shoes disgusted her, yet Nikolai still showed no indication of being repulsed by her.

She tucked the soiled handkerchief into her pocket and looked beyond the metal railing again. Nikolai wrapped his arms around her waist. They didn't move or talk until the sky was blacker than ink, an endless well of nothingness. Any signs of land or civilization was unrecognizable at that point. Not even the moon was visible through the dense clouds.

Kaethe's wet stockinged feet grew colder by the minute. She shivered and Nikolai stroked her back to warm her. She looked up and saw the worried furrow in his brow.

"*Waut denkjes du,* what are you thinking?" Kaethe whispered.

He tightened his grip around her. His gesture was simple, but it was enough to make her believe she was his *Lieblinkja,* his favourite.

"I try not to worry," he confided. "I do trust God. It's just hard not to think about them and wonder where they are."

"That's understandable, Nikolai. They're your family. You can't help but be concerned. You love them. If you weren't concerned, I would be concerned about *you.*"

"I know that. I ... I just—." Nikolai's shook his head.

Kaethe pulled herself away from Nikolai and turned so she could look into his eyes. She cupped his face in her hands. His tears ran over her fingers, leaving a warm sensation on her skin. She wiped his eyes with her thumbs and kissed his forehead.

"God has a plan. That's all we can rely on right now. Though, it's easy for me to say that to you, even though my own faith is wavering these days."

"Aren't you glad we got out in time?"

"Of course I am. But I would have preferred if there hadn't been a reason to flee in the first place. I miss Ebenfeld, Nikolai. So much. I miss our home, my rocking chair, my shoes." She wiggled her toes again and let out a slow sigh. "Maria took her first steps on our porch. As did I. And what of Maria? Will she have any memories of Ebenfeld? Of where she was born? Of where you and I fell in love and married those three summers ago? What about Papa's store?" She looked down at the deck, the usual string of doubts and questions running through her mind again.

"And when we get to Paraguay, then what? What do we even know about this place, aside from the temperature being warmer throughout the year?" Panic rose in her voice. "I'm so afraid of what we might find on the other end of this journey.

"We have one suitcase, which contains all of our current belongings – for all three of us. We have no money, aside from a few rubles, and I doubt Paraguay will accept those. We have nothing, Nikolai. Absolutely nothing to our names. And this new country – what are we going to do there? Will there be homes and jobs waiting for us? Schools? Maria is growing every day, it won't be long before she needs new dresses, and shoes. Yet how will we afford those items with a handful of useless rubles?"

Her voice grew increasingly loud with each question. She hated her doubt. She wanted to trust God, and knew in her heart that His ways were perfect, and that He was always guiding them, but her head had a million excuses as to why she shouldn't believe any of it. Though she couldn't see it, she knew the distending ocean was in front of her, all around her. Her heart raced as panic set in again. For the first time in her life, she had absolutely no control, and no idea what to expect. She squeezed her eyes shut, and buried her face in Nikolai's chest.

"Don't worry, Kaethe. We're in this together."

"You have no idea how grateful I am for that. I wouldn't be able to do this without you."

"I disagree," he kissed the top of her head. "God is a greater, and more reliable companion than I am, and He will give you the strength you need to get through this. But I'm glad I'm here with you, and Maria, so you don't have to navigate the uncertainty alone. And you, my dear Kaethe – I wouldn't want to be here, or anywhere, with anyone else."

Nikolai turned Kaethe's body so her back was against him again. Her breathing slowed as he kissed her neck yearningly. She unwrapped her shawl and draped it around Nikolai and herself, holding the ends in her hands. Their bodies swayed together with each swell of the sea beneath them.

"That was quite a sight today, when our little Maria gripped the attention of all those crewmates and passengers, wasn't it?" Kaethe recalled.

"Indeed. If she's this outgoing at nearly two, I'm curious to see how many friends she'll have when she's a teenager."

"She's a special little one, that's for sure," Kaethe smiled affectionately. "She was reciting that poem you taught her a few months ago. I still can't believe she memorized all the words." Lost in sentiment, the worries of her current situation were tossed aside.

"She has a gift," Nikolai said with pride, "and not just for memorizing words, but for bringing joy into people's lives. I saw some pretty big smiles on those passengers' faces today. I'm willing to bet they haven't had a reason to smile in a very long time."

—

In the weeks that followed, Kaethe grew accustomed to the ship oscillating on the open sea, the whir of the propeller, and the constant prodding of feet outside their berth. The General Belgrano was the closest thing to a home she had experienced since they left Ebenfeld.

Connection and camaraderie occurred naturally aboard the ship. Everyone could relate with one another, and everyone shared a sense of unease over what lay in store for their future. Kaethe befriended many of the women, their vulnerability and bravery inspired her, putting her own struggles in perspective. They were mothers, too. They ached and worried for their children as ardently as Kaethe worried about Maria. Some women had reason to be angry, to resent God – they had lost children on this journey. The outbreak of measles while in Germany claimed the lives of many children, and others lost infants from a lack of sufficient nutrients to produce breast milk. The forlorn, lost faces of the parents that buried their young ones before leaving Germany haunted her daily.

Kaethe tried to drown the images, not wanting to cry again. She was alone in her room, though her thoughts always accompanied her. Her mind taunted her from the moment she woke, to the moment she fell asleep. Even then, she would toss and turn as nightmares plagued her throughout the night.

Kaethe inhaled deeply, her body relaxing with each breath. The afternoon sun was in direct line with the only round window in their room. She stood in its path, the warm rays caressing her face, attempting to melt her worries away.

The door opened suddenly. Nikolai entered, obviously excited.

"Come, Kaethe!"

He reached his arm into the room. Kaethe grabbed hold of it, curious as to what he would lead her to. They ran out together, leaving the door open, a rush of wind trailing behind them.

Passengers hoarded the deck, leaning over railings, clambering on top of each other. Kaethe and Nikolai searched the crowd for her family, a feat made easier by Maria's brown curls blowing wildly in the wind as she sat perched on Johann's shoulders. Maria spotted them and waved, frenzied by all the hype unfolding around her.

In time, the ship slowed and came to a halt in the harbour of Buenos Aires, Argentina – they had travelled halfway across the world. Crewmates ordered the eager passengers to calm down and arrange an orderly queue. Kaethe wondered if some might jump over the side of the ship and swim to land in their ecstasy.

One foot, then the other, stepped onto firm ground. Kaethe knew she was off the boat, but her body still swayed. Her legs felt like jelly as they accustomed to walking on land again. Kaethe called to Maria who ran ahead of them, the swarms of people were great, and the risk of losing a little one was equally as great.

Their time on land was short-lived. Like a herd of cattle, they marched along the docks, surrounded by hundreds of other Mennonite families waiting to board another boat that would take them up the river to Paraguay.

The air was warm and humid. Kaethe's dress clung to her skin as a thin layer of perspiration covered her body. She was told the seasons in South America were opposite than what they were used to in Crimea. She had expected to arrive to more frigid temperatures, like those of their winter months back home, but it was anything but cold. Kaethe wondered how high the temperatures would be in summer, if they were this warm in winter. There was no time to linger over the thought, though.

The queue moved quickly. They embarked a river steamer that would take them up the Paraguay River. The name on the hull read, "*Apipe*." The Apipe was nothing like the vessel they disembarked earlier. It was old and decrepit looking, and significantly smaller than the General Belgrano.

Nikolai led them into the sleeping chambers. Kaethe could not mask her horror as she looked into the long room where bunk beds lined both walls, with a row down the middle of the room, as well.

"At least we have a place to rest and sleep," Nikolai reassured her, sensing her disapproval.

He sat down on one of the woodchip-filled mattresses and winced. The pillows provided were also harder than they preferred.

"I'll sleep on the top bunk," Nikolai decided, "you and Maria can sleep together on the bottom."

His own spirit deflated as he looked at Kaethe's expression, clearly unimpressed. He willed the circumstances to change. He couldn't give her the answers and assurance he knew she longed hear.

Sensing his thoughts, Kaethe lifted his chin with one finger, and looked him in the eyes.

"It's perfect. Thank you," she feigned a smile and gave him a hug.

Maria climbed onto the bed and attempted to jump. The woodchips in the mattress left her bounce-less. Kaethe placed their bag under her bed before the three of them joined the rest of the family in the dining hall for supper.

—

The days spent on the riverboat trudged along slowly. They travelled on the Apipe for nearly a week, which was a week too long, in their opinion. With hundreds of passengers sleeping in close quarters, and no ventilation to move air through the boat, the odour inside the ship was foul, to say the least. Anna dreaded going to bed every evening. Not only was the stench of unwashed, sweaty bodies disgusting and more than she could stomach, the evening hours were when rats ran circles around the room, scouring for any remnants of galletas left on the floor. She heard their tails dragging behind them, and the scratching of claws across the wooden planks. Images of the vile rodents infiltrated her dreams as she slept, and she often woke in a sweat.

During the days, she tried to focus on more pleasant things. Though the air was warm and humid, Anna looked forward to her daily strolls around the deck with Kaethe and Maria. She loved her conversations with Kaethe. The two of them had often sat side by side on their porch on warm summer days, or across from each other at the kitchen table during the cooler seasons, talking nonstop about one thing or another. Kaethe trusted Anna, and Anna found pleasure in sharing her thoughts with her daughter. Paul usually kept his thoughts and opinions to himself. Even as a young boy, he was far more reserved than his sister ever was. Even if Kaethe wasn't speaking, Anna knew her well enough to know what she was thinking, based on the expressions she wore on her face, or the way she carried herself.

With those fond memories at the forefront of her mind, Anna laced her arm through Kaethe's and smiled softly at her. Kaethe tried to offer a smile in return, but her mother's empathetic touch released the tears she had been holding back.

"Come now, Kaethe, everything will be all right," Anna encouraged.

"That's what everyone keeps saying," Kaethe raised her voice, "but they don't know that for sure, do they? They can't. Did you hear about the woman who gave birth on this godforsaken boat yesterday? Who nearly died from bleeding because there are no doctors on this boat? Do you think she wanted to hear that everything was going to be all right when she was clinging to her life, and praying her baby wouldn't get sick from who-knows-what is lurking in those disgusting mattresses?"

"Calm down, Kaethe."

"They used a pair of rusted scissors hanging on the wall to cut the umbilical cord, Mama. And dirty, old towels to wrap the perfect newborn in. It's unthinkable!"

"You're right, it is," Anna's voice stayed calm, "but who are we to claim to know better than the Almighty One? Hmm? If we can praise Him in our joy, we must also praise Him in our sorrow, for both circumstances come from God. I don't know why that woman had to give birth in such poor conditions, but I trust God. Jesus wasn't born in pristine conditions either was he? But it was part of God's plan, and God's plans cannot be thwarted."

Kaethe steadied her breathing and wiped her cheeks dry. "You're right, Mama. It's just, I can't imagine how scared she must have been, and still is – having a newborn in such a filthy place."

"You're a mother, Kaethe, and all mothers long to provide the best for their children, to keep them safe and healthy." Anna stopped and turned to face Kaethe. She wrapped her arms around her daughter and held back the emotion caught in her throat. *Just as I long to keep you and your family safe, my sweet Kaethe,* Anna thought.

—

Once disembarked from the river steamer, Kaethe held on to Nikolai's arm as the family followed the other passengers. The heat from the sun instantly caused their bodies to perspire. They were guided to the train station where they climbed into cars, and waited for the trains to take them to their next destination. Kaethe had once found travelling to be enchanting, the stories her father told her from his younger years piqued her curiosity of the world, and what lay outside their small village. She no longer felt the desire to travel after the last few months of constant transportation to somewhere.

Somewhere. The fact that she had no idea where they were actually going made the trip that much more burdensome. Maria reached her arms up toward Kaethe, who gladly welcomed her daughter onto her lap. The weight of her body against hers kept her thoughts grounded to the present moment, subsiding her fears temporarily. She hoped they would be off the crowded train soon. Personal space was considered a rarity these days.

Kaethe took in the landscape all around her. Everything was dry and arid. Trees grew endlessly, but they weren't trees she had seen before. The forest was filled with stunted trees, though fully grown, and scattered throughout the brush, one species of trees stood erect, towering above the others.

The end of the line was visible in the distance. As the train slowed, mosquitoes festered around them once again. Kaethe waved at them. Her arms began to itch where small red bumps began to swell. The bites were irritating, but she her only thought now was to get off the train and stretch her achy legs.

Kaethe held Nikolai's hand as she stepped down. She adjusted her dress and wiped a few dirty spots on her skirt with her hand. Strange sounds hovered around her, animals or insects she had never heard before. Dust wallowed around their feet as they walked toward a group of men standing by some wagons. A cactus scratched her leg and she bent to pull out a needle, letting out a long sigh. This country would be their new home. Her heart clenched at the finality of it. Panic and sadness set in. She longed to be home, to where everything was familiar and comfortable.

Nikolai gently touched her shoulder.

"Kaethe? Are you okay?"

She turned to meet his gaze, then closed her eyes and shook her head, hoping the motion would wake her from this nightmare. When she opened her eyes, she was exactly where she hoped she wouldn't be. Sweaty, itchy, hot, tired, overwhelmed. A tear curved its way down her cheek.

"Yes, I'll be fine," she lied.

They were finally on the last leg of their journey. A rickety wooden wagon with four equally unreliable wooden wheels drove them to their new home. Maria cried, begging to be released from Kaethe's tight grasp around her body. She grew restless as the hours passed and Kaethe's frustration escalated. Not only was she adjusting to the idea of settling into a new land, but she also had a daughter who still needed constant care and attention. At this point, their little girl was hungry and desperate for a nap.

Maria coughed, her lungs full of dust. Kaethe gathered the hem of her skirt and tried to hold it over Maria's face. The dust settled in the air like a thick fog, stinging their eyes and burning their lungs. Their clothes, shoes, hair and skin were covered in a fine layer of dust. The midday sun only intensified their discomfort. Kaethe twitched as drops of sweat ran down her back and chest. She didn't know how much longer she could go on like this.

The oxen suddenly came to a halt in the middle of nowhere. Kaethe assumed the wagon was in need of repair, but upon further investigation, she realized that was not the case. The driver stepped down from the wagon and tied the oxen to a nearby tree. The wagons ahead of and behind them also stopped. Passengers dismounted and unloaded their belongings. The wagon wasn't broken, after all. They had merely reached their final destination.

Nikolai and Johann followed the other men who were congregating a few yards away. Kaethe strained her ears to pick up any of their conversation, but Maria's cries were too loud. Kaethe cradled her daughter in her arms, holding her close to her body. She tried to console Maria, though it felt like she was trying to console herself. The shock and realization that the nothingness around her was meant to be their new home paralyzed her. Eventually, her heart's rhythmic beat soothed Maria to sleep. In that moment, Kaethe distinctly heard God's voice tell her, *Everything is going to be fine. Trust me.*

After some time, the crowd of men dispersed, like the ripple of a drop in the sea. Each man returned to his own family and relayed the information they had just been given.

"This is our new home," Johann informed his family, with hesitation in his tone.

Kaethe wasn't sure where, exactly, he was referring to. Only grassland, trees and thorn bushes stood before them. There was no sign of a house, or village, anywhere, aside from one lone well standing off in the distance.

This was Friedensruh No. 6 – the sixth Mennonite settlement in the Fernheim Colony.

There was no time to dwell in despair, or disappointment, at the barrenness of the land. The men got to work immediately, using the few tools and supplies the Mennonite Central Committee had provided for them. Nikolai grabbed a shovel and looked at his chosen ballot. The men decided where the main street would be built, which would run down the centre of the village, and cleared the way from all the brush by hand. They were left with a long stretch of dirt, roughly a kilometre in length, with the land on either side of the street divided into lots for each family to build their homes and farms on.

Nikolai shoveled for hours, burrowing into the ground. Across the street, Kaethe's father did the same, her brother helping beside him, shovel in hand. By nightfall, Nikolai had dug a hole for them to sleep in. It was roughly three feet deep, and long and wide enough to fit their three bodies. He found branches in the forest at the end of their lot and hammered them into the dirt on all four corners of the dugout. With Kaethe's help, they pulled a tarp over the branches and secured it to the ground.

They stood beside each other as they scrutinized the final product. Nikolai's arm held Kaethe's waist, his shirt stained with sweat and dust, and the smell of body odour lingered around him. He knew she was not keen on their new abode, though she didn't verbalize her disappointment.

"I know it's not quite like our home back in Ebenfeld, but it will do for the time being, until I can build us an actual house. We'll stay cooler at night, too, being a few feet below the ground," Nikolai tried to console her.

"No, it's not like our home in Ebenfeld," she whispered to herself. She wrapped both arms around his waist. "But, it could be worse. We have a roof, something to eat, and our health. God has provided everything we need for this moment." She looked at him and forced her lips into a smile. He smiled in return and leaned down and kissed her.

Kaethe could not fall asleep that night. In the distance, she heard strange songs, or chants, she wasn't quite sure, with the consistent beat of a drum. The rest of Friedensruh No. 6 was as quiet as the nights on the open sea, save for Nikolai's snoring.

Maria lay still beside Kaethe. Her eyes fluttered every so often as she dreamed. Kaethe could feel both Maria and Nikolai's bodies against hers, the space too small to allow any room between them. She was grateful for their presence, though. They kept her grounded when her thoughts ran rampant. Kaethe watched the slow rising and falling of her daughter's chest in the moonlight.

Kaethe laid on her back and looked up at the tarp. Tears streamed down her cheeks but she was too defeated to wipe them away. She felt so very conflicted. On one hand, she trusted God and knew He was guiding them, and that He was with them, but on the other hand, she longed to be anywhere but here. She was, after all, sleeping on the ground, in a hole. Her daughter's face was covered in dirt, her husband's hands calloused and bleeding from the strenuous labour he had endured that day. Her own clothes began to tear, snagged from greedy thorns as she walked through the bushes behind their lot.

It was hard to see the purpose in it all, until an image of Herr Wieler being taken from his wife and children flashed in her mind, and she realized what their alternative would have been.

"He makes no mistakes," she reminded herself, then slowly cried herself to sleep.

7

October 1930

THE MENNONITES OF FRIEDENSRUH NO. 6 BUILT A VILLAGE, A LIFE, FROM nothing. They worked tirelessly from first light until night, when they could barely see their hands in front of them. In the weeks that followed their arrival, the vast, uninhabited land took semblance of civilization. Each family's lot was marked with a fence around the perimeter. Some families acquired horses and oxen to aid with farming, while others had cows and chickens. With very few resources available to them, everyday common tasks were substantially more difficult to accomplish.

Fields were plowed with makeshift equipment. A portion of seeds had been provided by the Mennonite Central Committee, and were divided among the residents and planted in the fields. Cotton, peanuts, corn and sorghum eventually sprouted in lines, though no one really knew anything about these crops, or the best techniques for growing them. Everything was new for them.

They were warned by other Mennonite settlers that the dry spell they were in the midst of would eventually end. Downpours were common in late spring, and could flood an entire village within an hour. Mud would find its way onto every surface and into every hole, making their in-ground homes less than ideal for such weather conditions.

Nikolai was intent on getting his family out of their underground haven and into a proper room with walls and a roof. He set to work a few weeks after arriving, molding dirt and clay into large rectangular bricks, and waited for days until they were dry.

Once hardened, he stacked them, one on top of the other, until four walls stood erect. The little room, only slightly larger than their dugout, would keep the worst of the rain and dust storms out. He laid some branches across the brick walls and covered them with straw to make a roof.

With the remaining bricks, Nikolai built a stove outside the shack. A cast iron plate was set on top of the structure, with four holes cut out of it, which opened into the hollow stomach where they burned the wood. With the final brick in place, their new home was complete, though Kaethe was reluctant to call it such. It was more of a shack, in her opinion. A far cry from the lavish estate they left in Ebenfeld.

Despite its lack of space and aesthetic appeal, Kaethe was eager to leave their humble hole in the ground and sleep under a roof. Never had she considered a roof over her head a luxury before. She was desperate to have a sense of normalcy again, even if that meant being the one to gather the bovine manure for the brick sealant.

Kaethe mixed the manure with dirt to create a paste-like glue. She tore the bottom few inches of one of her more tattered skirts and placed it over her nose and mouth. She tied it in a knot behind her head and adjusted her hair around it. Scattered rays peered through the straw roof where she stood looking into the bucket of cow feces and dirt. The cloth covering her face was far from capable of warding off the stench of the repugnant concoction. She gagged as she looked down at the brown mixture. Flies swarmed around it, unexplainably attracted to the smell. If not for her immense desire to sleep under a roof, she would not have found the strength to proceed.

She reached her bare hand into the bucket. Her eyes stung from the odour and she shut them tightly, turning her head away. This was her life now, she bemused, plastering cow dung on walls. But there was no other option. If the bricks were not sealed, they would wash away with the first rainfall. The foul stench never lessened, and her eyes watered from gagging so often behind her mask.

Kaethe distracted herself by thinking of Nikolai's dedication to building this modest home. She had watched him while she washed laundry in the shade of the big bottle-like tree growing at the front of their lot. The curves of his strained muscles had caught her attention as he placed the first brick on the ground. Upon placing the next brick, a piece of the first brick chipped off from the impact. He didn't notice, though. She could tell by his curved eyebrows that he was concentrating on his job. She loved the way he prided himself in his work. When he had completed the four walls, he combed his moustache with his fingers as he stood back to look at his progress. He hadn't realized she was regarding him with fondness, until he glanced her way and met her gaze. She blushed, and he smiled, flattered she was still so obviously attracted to him.

Kaethe finished sealing the bricks and also the straw scattered on the floor of the shack. Finally finished, she stood outside and looked at the finished product, wiping between each finger with a towel. Nikolai walked up and hugged her from behind, dramatically sniffing the air around her.

"*Du rikje waut schrakjlijch,* you smell awful," he teased. Kaethe gasped, turning sharply on her heels, a look of shock and dismay on her face. She hit him with her towel. Nikolai flinched and laughed as he ran away from her. Kaethe crossed her arms and shook her head emphatically at him, but couldn't pretend to be angry with him. If anything, she was grateful for the change of mood he brought. He had a way of always helping her find good in every situation.

—

Nikolai carried Maria to their shack and placed her on the sheet spread across the floor. The sun dipped beneath the horizon, casting an iridescent glow over the land. From her spot by the stove, Kaethe heard Nikolai and Maria playing and laughing inside until it suddenly grew very quiet. Curious, she walked to the doorway and leaned against the frame. She kept her body out of sight, but listened keenly to hear their conversation.

"What are you thankful for today, my little Mariechen?" Kaethe loved it when Nikolai called Maria by his nickname for her.

"Hmm … *miene Popp,* my doll!" Maria replied excitedly, holding her doll in Nikolai's face.

He laughed, lowering Maria's arms, and the doll with them, so he could see her sweet face. Her cheeks were rosy and her eyes were so rich, like looking into a cup of freshly brewed coffee.

"Ok, we'll thank God for your doll. Again," he said with a hint of feigned exasperation. "Do you know that God loves you very much, Mariechen?" She nodded vigorously, her doll moving with her. Nikolai laughed again, swept Maria into his arms, and fell back onto the bed. Her head rested on his strong chest as her little fingers stroked his moustache.

"Yes, Papa," she said, "and God loves you very much, too. And Mama. And Oma and Opa. And Onkel Paul!"

"Time for bed," Kaethe announced as she walked into the room.

Nikolai kissed Maria a few more times before lifting himself off the floor and kissed Kaethe's cheek as he walked out the door. Kaethe lifted Maria into her arms and rocked her in her lap. She sang a few lines from a familiar lullaby, soothing Maria to sleep within minutes. She placed Maria on the floor, covering her with the blanket. After kissing the top of her head, she whispered, "I love you," before walking out of the room.

"She's already asleep?" Nikolai asked as Kaethe gently closed the door behind her.

"Yes, she was clearly very tired."

Kaethe moved a chair across from Nikolai. The sky had turned an azure-blue, speckled with a myriad of stars. She could tell he had been contemplating something while she was with Maria.

"Are you thinking about your family?" she asked him sympathetically.

"It's hard not to think about them," he cleared his throat and shifted his body.

Nikolai rarely mentioned his family. The questions he wanted to ask could not be answered. He hoped they made it out of Ebenfeld, but Nikolai knew that was an unlikely outcome. He assumed they had been killed, but he couldn't think about it without feeling ill.

Nikolai wiped his palms on his trousers and stood up, clearly burdened by his thoughts.

"Maria has no shoes," Kaethe changed the subject. "The pair she has don't fit anymore."

"And, what of it?"

"What of it?" Kaethe asked with surprise. "Doesn't it bother you that our daughter is running around all day with nothing to protect her feet?"

"Many of the other children don't have shoes, either."

"That's the point. This isn't okay. Children should have shoes that fit. The problem is that we can't actually afford to buy her shoes. Not even one pair, Nikolai."

"The crops will be ready for harvesting soon," she could hear the guilt and shame in his tone, "and then we'll have some money in our account. At least, I think that's how it works."

"How *does* it work, anyway?" Kaethe asked.

"The Cooperative in Filadelfia, Fernheim's capital, buys our harvest, and adds the money to our account. Whenever we buy anything from the Cooperative, we give them our account number and they take the amount from there."

"Sounds confusing."

"It does. But apparently it's been working really well for the other villages. The Cooperative has everything we would ever need, even fabric," he nudged her, hoping the news would alleviate her worries for a moment.

"Fabric we can't afford."

Nikolai sighed and reached for Kaethe's hand.

"You've seen how happy Maria is here, though, haven't you?" he asked.

She looked over Nikolai's shoulder toward the main street, though there was nothing but darkness to be seen. Earlier that day, she watched from a distance as Maria gaily ran with her friends, dust rising around her bare feet, a smile fixed on her lips. Maria had adjusted to Chaco living with ease. It was a far simpler life compared to Ebenfeld, as far as possessions, but the daily chores and effort needed to survive were far greater.

"Perhaps," Nikolai continued, "it's a blessing that she will have no memory of Ebenfeld and how things used to be. She may have already forgotten what shoes are, and that before we left she had two pairs available at any given time. It will be easier for her to see God's hand in her life than it is for you and I. We've been given much in our lives, and now we have nothing. Can we say that we are happy, truly happy? I'm not sure that I could. I rarely thank God for providing us our small ration of dry baking ingredients, or a forest of trees that we can cut down and use to build our homes."

"I envy Maria, and the other children," Kaethe sighed, "and I pray daily for God's forgiveness for my selfishness and lack of faith to see His hand in all of this."

"Aren't you the one who always reminds me that God doesn't make mistakes? That everything happens for a reason?" Nikolai covered her hands with his. "There are no coincidences, my love. I do believe that."

Kaethe sighed. He was right. Everything he said was right, and she was ashamed for her inability to see the blessings God had lavished them with in spite of the difficult situation they were in.

"You're right, Nikolai. I'm being selfish. Maria may not have shoes, but she has not gone hungry, Nor have we, which is more than many families can say. It's just so hard to not feel resentful or bitter. I'd rather be home."

"You'd rather be home when home was still safe. This village is an answer to prayer. Many were not so fortunate as us to make it out of Russia." His voice trailed off. As much as he wanted to think positively about his family's where-abouts, the thought of them always distressed him.

Kaethe leaned forward and kissed Nikolai. His lips tasted of salt, remnants of his arduous labour. They leaned back in their chairs and looked at the star-filled sky until they could hardly keep themselves awake and went to join Maria on their bed made of straw. Tomorrow held another day of endless tasks.

—

Kaethe and Nikolai's relationship continued to grow despite their circum-stances. They saw little of each other during the day, each preoccupied with their own chores and projects, but even while apart, Nikolai made Kaethe feel loved and noticed. Whether it was in the way he admired her from across the yard as he led the oxen, or the swift, gentle graze of his hand on her arm as they crossed paths. Butterflies stirred to life inside her with each of his subtle advances.

Kaethe counted the black marks in her notebook, one for each day since they had left Ebenfeld. If her markings were accurate, Nikolai's twenty-sixth birthday was that day. For a moment, excitement grew inside her – she loved celebrating birthdays. In the next moment, disappointment washed in. She had nothing special to offer Nikolai. She couldn't bake a cake without an oven, and she had no money to buy him a gift. Last year, they had celebrated his birthday with all their usual traditions for the very last time, only days before the police came looking for her father.

The memory sent shivers down her spine, but Kaethe was determined to do something special for Nikolai, though she struggled to think of ideas. Finally, she thought of it, and she set to work.

—

Nikolai wiped his brow at the end of the day and stopped at the well at the end of the street to collect their daily bucketful of water. More wells had been dug, but few actually resulted in potable water. From one hole to the next, the water that poured through the earth varied greatly. One hole would be sweet, and drinkable, whereas the next hole, even a few feet away, would yield salty water.

As he approached the yard, he saw Maria running toward him. The sight of her small body barreling down the lot, brown curls bouncing wildly around her head, was enough to erase every worry from his mind, at least for that moment. He crouched down, setting the bucket of water on the ground, and opened his arms. She fell into them and he held her tight, kissing her forehead.

"*Froo Je'burtsdach*, Papa, Happy Birthday!" she shouted the newly learned phrase with pride.

"*Danksheen*, thank you!" he balanced himself as he stood up, holding her on his hip. He grabbed the bucket with his free hand and walked up to the shack where Kaethe welcomed him with a bright smile.

Nikolai set Maria and the bucket down, and put his arms around Kaethe. He pulled her toward him and kissed her. When their lips parted, they kept their faces close, and looked into each other's eyes.

"Happy Birthday," Kaethe's breath lingered on his lips, stirring desire within him.

Nikolai smiled back, looking longingly at his wife.

"Thank you."

He kissed her soft lips again and held her hand as they walked across the street together. Maria ran ahead and was already bouncing on Paul's lap when they arrived. As he moved his legs up and down, he recited a familiar children's poem.

"*Hoppa, hoppa Reiter, wenn er fällt dann schreit er. Fällt er in den Graben, fressen ihn die Raben, fällt er in den Sumpf, macht der Reiter plumps!* Hop, hop, rider, if he falls he will cry. If he falls in the ditch, he will be eaten by the ravens, if he falls in the mud, the rider makes a splash." Paul emphasized the final word by spreading his legs apart and lowering Maria to the floor. Maria laughed hysterically and urged him to do it again as she climbed back onto his lap.

Conversations flowed easily throughout the evening. Supper consisted of the usual stovetop, over-baked buns, like the galletas served on the Apipe steamer, with a side of fried eggs. Birthday suppers in Ebenfeld were much more elaborate than this modest feast, but it would have to suffice for this year, at least. If Nikolai was hoping for more, he hid his disappointment well, she noted.

They stayed seated around the handmade wooden table outside after the dishes had been cleared. Johann shared tips he had heard from some men in Filadelfia that morning about how to increase your chances of a good corn crop. When there was a break in their exchange, Kaethe placed a small object wrapped in a handkerchief in Nikolai's hands.

"Happy Birthday," she wished him again.

Intrigued, he slowly lifted the four corners of the handkerchief outwards, exposing a small piece of clay. He smiled dutifully. He didn't know what he was holding, but didn't want to risk disappointing her with a less-than-enthused reaction.

"Thank you," he said as genuinely as possible.

"Do you know what it is?" she asked him, eyes sparkling.

"I'm sorry, I don't," he furrowed his brow as he admitted it.

Kaethe smiled and quickly explained, "It's a piece of the first brick you laid as the foundation of our shack. I saw it fall off when you placed the second brick on top. When you had left to fetch a tool, I grabbed it. I don't know why I felt the need to keep it. Perhaps I was feeling sentimental in that moment."

Nikolai looked at the dark mound as he turned it in his hands. He never noticed the first brick chip.

"That brick," Kaethe continued, "is the beginning of the next chapter of our lives. To me, it's a symbol of hope, of change, and of positive things to come!" She clapped her hands together, and placed them in her lap, waiting for him to respond. After another paused moment, he reached out his hand to touch hers.

"I love it," he assured her.

They spent the rest of the evening dancing, laughing, telling stories, and singing into the wee hours of the night. When stars dotted the night sky like ashes blown from a quenched fire, Nikolai thanked and hugged his in-laws. He gathered Maria's sleeping body off the floor and into his arms and they walked toward the large swollen tree on their lot.

With the light of the moon guiding their steps, they made their way back to their shack. Nikolai opened the door and lay Maria down on the blankets. He laid beside her for a few minutes until he was sure she was fast asleep. Kaethe waited outside and placed the small piece of brick beside the stove.

She walked over to the bottle tree and sat down beside it, leaning her back against its round trunk. It was a comical looking tree, with its trunk bulging near the ground, narrowing toward the top. The branches grew sparsely at the top of the tree, leaving the trunk completely visible. She thought it looked like a vase filled with flowers, or like a glass bottle spraying liquid out the top of it.

Nikolai joined her soon after under the star-filled sky.

"We're nearly out of sugar and beans," Kaethe informed him. "Any chance we could make a trip into Filadelfia tomorrow?"

"I think that should work. I need some more nails, too. We'll plan to leave right after breakfast tomorrow."

That was the last they spoke until Kaethe announced she was going to bed and Nikolai followed her to the shack.

While Nikolai secured the horse to the wagon, their neighbour, Herb, called to him from the fence separating their lots. Nikolai went to greet him and Herb handed him a piece of paper. Nikolai's lips moved as he read each word silently. It informed them that Peter Braun had passed away during the night. The letter contained all the details for the funeral, which would take place later that morning behind the school.

Peter was one of Nikolai's closest friends, even though Nikolai was only twenty-six, and Peter was in his forties, they developed a close friendship. Shortly after arriving in Fernheim, Nikolai and Peter often worked side by side, chopping wood for their fences.

He thanked Herb and brought the letter to Kaethe before walking across the yard to their other neighbour. He handed the letter to Fritz, who then passed it on to his neighbour, until the letter had been read by everyone in the village.

In such a small community, no one was a stranger. You knew everyone by name, including their wives names, and each of their children's names. You knew their stories – which cities they were from, and what their lives in Russia consisted of before they fled. Relationships were built, and friendships formed naturally – it was unavoidable.

Nikolai walked to the bottle-like tree at the front of their lot and lowered himself onto the ground beside it. It had all happened so fast. A few weeks earlier, Peter's eldest son fell very ill – first complaining of headaches, which quickly developed into a fever. Peter and his wife, Martha, assumed it was a typical cold, or influenza, and suggested he rest as much as possible. A few days later, a rash appeared on his chest, which spread rapidly to the rest of his body. The village nurse, Frü Doerksen, came to see him and confirmed their worst fears – it was typhus.

Peter's son wasn't the first victim of the fatal illness. Typhus moved rapidly throughout the surrounding villages, claiming the lives of many. The disease spread via lice, which made everyone in the colony susceptible to contracting the illness. With only a handful of wells dug throughout the small village, baths and laundry were not regarded as a necessity, which meant filthy bodies lay inches apart in their small shacks as they slept.

A few days after Peter's son was diagnosed, another one of Peter's children came down with a fever, followed by a rash. A week later, another child was infected. By the time Peter's fifth child was diagnosed with typhus, his eldest son had passed away. And so the vicious cycle continued, until all but one of Peter's eleven children were dead.

Everyone in the colony gathered around the grave that afternoon. The minister stood in front of them, reading words of encouragement from the Bible. Martha stood near the hole in the ground, wailing uncontrollably. She clutched a handkerchief in her right hand and brought it to her cheeks every now and again. In her other arm, she held her six-month-old son, John.

Kaethe's tears glimmered in the sunlight. Her chest tightened as she watched Martha mourn the loss of her husband of nearly twenty-five years. Kaethe and Martha became instant friends soon after they arrived. It was Martha that delivered her baby, John, on the river steamer. And now, in a span of three weeks, Martha and John were the only members left of their family of thirteen.

The minister uttered the final *Amen*, and the crowd slowly dissipated. Martha didn't move, though. She stood frozen, looking at Peter's body lying in the hollowed trunk of one of the bottle trees. Her tears had ceased, leaving her stained cheeks opalescent against the sun. Her eyes remained fixed on the coffin in the ground, in which lay her beloved husband.

Nikolai pulled Kaethe close, almost too forcefully, fighting back his own tears. He wished he could hold on to Kaethe and Maria like this for the rest of their lives, keeping them away from harm. He knew he didn't have that power, but he prayed that God would not take his family away from him. He couldn't bear the thought of losing them.

—

The wagon bounced wildly as they moved down the uneven dirt paths, through the forest. Nikolai led the horse, his grip tight on the reins. His other hand draped over Kaethe's shoulders, gently stroking her arm. Her insides fluttered at his caress and she smiled. She could tell he still felt unsettled over Peter's death. The funeral earlier that day affected him more than he was expecting it to.

"*Waut es daut, w*hat is that?" Maria asked. She sat on Kaethe's lap and pointed to everything along their route, her eyes filled with wonderment. Kaethe turned her attention to her daughter and answered her to the best of her knowledge. When Maria pointed to one of the bottle-like trees that grew everywhere and asked what it was, Kaethe looked to Nikolai for an answer.

Nikolai shrugged, "*Flaschenbaum*, bottle tree." It came out more as a question than an answer but Maria didn't sense his uncertainty. Satisfied with his response, she pointed at the next foreign object.

They continued that way for the entirety of their drive into Filadelfia. Nikolai stopped the horse in front of the Cooperative and waited outside with Maria. Kaethe wandered through the aisles, a wire basket hanging in the crook of her elbow. She noted the way the clothes were folded and how the canned goods were stacked on shelves, comparing them to the way items were arranged in her father's general store. She stared at various displays, lost in nostalgia. A reel of memories played through her mind as she thought back to all the days spent helping at the store.

She turned a corner and found the baking section. She placed a bag of sugar in her basket, along with a small container of yeast. She continued on to the sewing section and found a rather small selection of rolls leaning against the wall. Kaethe was used to a vast spread of fabrics available at her father's store, and found herself comparing her new life to her old life yet again.

She placed a corner of each fabric between her fingers, analyzing the texture of each one. She wanted to make a new dress for herself and Maria, and use any leftover fabric to make a new apron. Her current apron had caught on a nail along the fence and ripped in half. She moved to the thinner cottons. A white one with small, sky blue floral arrangements scattered throughout caught her eye.

She set the roll of fabric on the counter to be measured, and greeted the young woman who stood in front of her. The woman cut the fabric with precision. Kaethe hoped Nikolai wouldn't be upset that she purchased new fabric, but she couldn't bear the thought of sitting in the church pew with her stained, broken, navy dress again. It wasn't that the other women donned more refined dresses than herself – they were all in the same position. Kaethe knew her appearance was the least of anyone's concerns. But she could only add so many patches to one piece of clothing before it looked like a quilt. And she was sure Nikolai wouldn't want her to wear a blanket to church.

The woman folded the cut fabric and handed it to Kaethe, along with a small piece of paper marked with the price of the material. Kaethe thanked her and made her way to the clerk. A man stood behind the desk and asked Kaethe for her account number. He wrote the cost of each item in a notebook and removed the sum from their account. Kaethe grabbed her bag of goods and turned for the exit, feeling rather odd not having to physically pay for her items. She still wasn't used to the new system.

She walked back into the blazing afternoon sun – another change she still wasn't accustomed to. Once her eyes adjusted to the brightness, she looked around for Nikolai and Maria. They saw her, and Nikolai scooped Maria up and lifted her onto his shoulders. Kaethe put her items in the back of the wagon and stepped onto one of the large wooden spokes of the wheel, raising herself onto the hard wooden bench. Nikolai untied the horse, holding the reins tightly in his hand as he climbed onto his seat next to Kaethe and Maria.

Maria fell asleep minutes after their departure. Kaethe took advantage of the time with Nikolai and leaned into him, resting her head on his shoulder. Every now and then he would kiss the top of her head or stroke her arm. She knew she was very much loved. He showed it in the way he worked, not only building their home, but farming their land, and helping others in the colony when they needed it. The strenuous labour had aged him, she noticed. Strands of grey hair dusted the hair at his temples. His moustache had lightened, as well, and his skin was dark and leathered from the sun.

She didn't mind his physical changes, though. As the wagon bounced down the path, Kaethe tried to picture what he might look like in fifty years. A smile spread across her face. Regardless what he looked like, she knew it would have little effect on her attraction to him. In her opinion, he was the most handsome man she had ever met, and she was sure that would always be the case, wrinkles and white hair, and all.

8

December 1930

KAETHE SAT IN A CHAIR OUTSIDE THEIR SHACK. SHE WORKED A NEEDLE AND thread through a patch on the sleeve of one of Nikolai's shirts. The sun rose slowly, painting the sky pink and orange. Nikolai moved effortlessly up and down the field, turning up dirt with the plow as he pulled the oxen along. Kaethe watched him every now and then, and wondered why he kept scratching his head.

She placed the needlework on the chair and walked toward the shack. An apron hung on a nail by the door. She tied the strings around her neck, moving her hands down the sides until she felt the straps by her waist and tied them in a bow behind her. As she tucked a few loose strands back into pins, she caught sight of Maria across the street, running circles around Kaethe's mother as she collected eggs from the hens.

A bucket sat beside the door, and Kaethe bent down to grab it. She looked back at Nikolai. He wasn't himself these days. His overexertion must have worn him out. She wished she could get him to rest, to take some time away from the fields, and the digging, and the other incessant tasks that needed to be done. It would never – could never – happen, though. He was too dedicated and there was far too much work still to be done.

"*Lord, give Nikolai strength. If he cannot physically rest, please fill him with Your rest,*" Kaethe prayed as she approached their cow.

Kaethe moved the small wooden stool from the fence closer to the cow. She lowered herself onto the stool and positioned the bucket directly beneath the cow's udder. She rolled her shoulders to loosen her dress and leaned forward.

She held a teat between both thumbs and forefingers. Slowly and methodically, she massaged each one, encouraging the milk to flow. She pulled and worked each teat until the udder was empty and her bucket was nearly full. The stool was returned to its spot by the fence, and she thanked the cow for her diligent service, patting her on the rump. Kaethe wiped her brow with her apron and headed for the house with the bucket in hand.

They continued with their morning chores until the midday sun was at its fiercest. All the men, women and children returned home to replenish their bodies with food, water, shade and sleep. Kaethe prepared the usual meal of buns and eggs. Maria was already eating her portion when Nikolai came in from the field. He looked flushed, his cheeks red.

"You don't look well, Nikolai. Are you feeling all right?" she asked him, with obvious concern in her voice. She set his plate down and sat across from him, eyeing him.

"Oh, I'm fine, Love. Just a little overheated, is all," he said as he wiped his face with a handkerchief, hoping to reassure her.

Kaethe wasn't convinced. She went to the water basin beside the stove and saturated a rag. She wrung it out, and folded it into a rectangle. Her concern grew as she stood behind Nikolai. His head was lined with open wounds where he had scratched, his hair covered with both fresh and dried blood.

Not wanting to frighten Maria, Kaethe stayed silent. She placed the wet cloth on Nikolai's head and sat back down. She knew something wasn't right. Nikolai had been having trouble focusing all day. If it wasn't his itchy head interrupting his work, it was the dizzy spells that came over him intermittently. Even from a distance she could tell that it took all his strength to keep working.

Kaethe's forehead creased as she tried to discern what was wrong with him. He looked at her, trying again to reassure her with a smile. He cut a piece of egg with his fork and pierced it. The egg was nearly to his lips before he lowered the fork back to his plate.

"I think I'll go lie down for a little while before I need to head out again," he said as he pushed his chair away from the table. Again he smiled at Kaethe. He kissed the top of Maria's head before walking into their shack, closing the door behind him.

Kaethe sat at the table and stared at her plate until Maria threw a piece of bread in her face. Maria waited anxiously to see if her mother would scold her. But Kaethe's thoughts were elsewhere. Instead, she gathered the plates and scooped Maria out of her chair, holding her on her hip.

Kaethe walked briskly to the edge of the yard and across the street, Maria still in her arms. Her family was surprised to see her. Kaethe placed Maria on

Johann's lap and asked if they could watch Maria for her. Kaethe didn't wait for their answer. Turning on her heels, she headed back to their gate without an explanation, leaving her family to worry in her absence.

Kaethe ran from home to home in search of Frü Doerksen. One family suggested she look in on the Kroekers, someone had seen her there. Kaethe thanked them and ran down the street and into the Kroeker's yard. Frü Doerksen was there, dining with the family.

"I'm so sorry for barging in like this, but I need Frü Doerksen to come with me. Right away. Please," Kaethe's words came out quicker and more urgent than she had intended.

Frü Doerksen wiped her mouth with her handkerchief and followed Kaethe. They walked at a quick pace beside each other, Kaethe sharing all the details of the last few days with Frü Doerksen, including Nikolai's itchy scalp, fatigue, and lack of appetite.

When they reached her yard, Kaethe led the nurse to their shack. She opened the door slowly. The room was bright. The scattered straw above them allowed the sunlight to stream in, highlighting all the dust that lingered in the air. Kaethe looked at Nikolai lying on the floor, his eyes closed. He was drenched with sweat, as was the pillow under his head and the sheets he lay on. His body shook as shivers coursed through him. Kaethe sat on the ground next to him. She took his hand in hers and leaned close to his ear.

"Nikolai, Frü Doerksen is here with me. She's going to examine you."

Her voice was steady, but her stomach tossed within her. She willed herself to keep her composure. Nikolai didn't respond. His eyes remained closed as he shook. Kaethe turned to Frü Doerksen and nodded, inviting her come closer to Nikolai.

Frü Doerksen walked to the other side of Kaethe and sat down. Gently, she lifted his eyelids with her fingers, examining his pupils. With the back of her hand she felt his forehead. She lowered her head onto his chest and placed her ear right over his heart, listening to the rush of blood.

When she finished her examination, Kaethe led Frü Doerksen to the shade of the Flaschenbaum.

"He has a bad viral infection, but from what I can see, it looks like it's just influenza. He needs to rest, and drink lots of water."

Relieved, Kaethe exhaled, and realized she had been holding her breath the whole time. She thanked her for coming to see Nikolai and promised she would call for her again if his condition changed. She walked Frü Doerksen out to the street.

Kaethe was relieved to know Nikolai's illness wasn't anything more severe. She could handle influenza. She filled their bucket at the well before going home to nurse Nikolai back to health.

—

The next few days consisted of tending to Nikolai, all day and all night. Maria spent her days with Johann and Anna, coming home every evening to sleep. She required no explanation for her daily separation from her parents. The novelty of spending countless hours with her oma and opa delighted Maria, which Kaethe was grateful for. It was one less thing for Kaethe to worry about.

The days were monotonous in structure. Wet rags were continuously wrung and placed back on Nikolai's head; his body wiped down; a cup held to his lips as she slowly poured drops of water into his mouth. Yet his fever would not subside. Rather, new symptoms appeared.

It wasn't until one afternoon, when Nikolai opened his eyes and looked at Kaethe through a cloudy film, that she instantly knew something was terribly wrong. She ran to find Frü Doerksen. Fear drove her as she ran frantically through the colony. All logic and reason ceased to matter at that point. She found Frü Doerksen and grabbed her arm, pulling her the whole way back to their shack.

Frü Doerksen sat on the floor beside Nikolai and felt his forehead. It was noticeably warmer since her last visit. She looked in his eyes, a milky film covered them. No wonder Kaethe had come looking for her, she thought. Then she noticed red spots on his neck. Frü Doerksen reached for the buttons on Nikolai's shirt and looked at Kaethe for permission to unbutton them. Kaethe nodded her approval. They were both shocked to find his chest and stomach covered with red, blotchy bumps.

Kaethe hadn't noticed the spots before. His skin had been clear the day before when she wiped the salty layer of damp sweat from his body. The rash had occurred overnight. Everything was happening too quickly.

The nurse covered Nikolai with the sheet and walked outside. Kaethe followed her. Johann stood outside, waiting. He had seen Kaethe and Frü Doerksen run down the street and into the shack and came to see what was happening. When Kaethe saw her father, she moved to his side. They stood with their arms around each other, staring at the nurse, waiting for her to speak.

"Kaethe," Frü Doerksen began, hesitant to meet Kaethe's gaze. Kaethe waited with bated breath, her eyes wide with worry and anticipation for what she might hear next. "Kaethe, I wish there was an easy way to tell you this," she paused again, rubbing her chin with her hand. "I'm afraid Nikolai has typhus."

The world fell silent. The ground beneath her sank away and Kaethe's legs went numb. Johann caught her before she fell to the ground and moved her to a nearby chair. She could hear the faint, distant sound of her father calling her name. She assured herself she was dreaming. It was all a dream, a nightmare. It had to be.

Slowly her father's voice grew louder and Kaethe turned to him, then to Frü Doerksen. Tears ran down the nurse's face. Kaethe looked at the shack, and the gravity of the news forced her to the ground.

She screamed as she lunged for the door, but fell to the ground. Johann lowered his body next to his daughter and gathered her shaking body into his arms. Her wails were deep and loud, resounding throughout the entire village. Tears marked paths down both of their dust ridden cheeks. He held her tight, knowing there was nothing he could say to comfort her in that moment.

—

One day followed another, which followed another, leaving nothing but blurred memories in its wake. Kaethe spent her days by Nikolai's side. She cried over him as he slept, and gave him water to drink when he was awake. She talked to him, even tried having conversations with him, as if he was coherent and well. But mostly, she talked to him as he slept.

Nothing made sense. From the moment their lives were at stake in Ebenfeld, to this moment with Nikolai fighting for his life – she couldn't understand the purpose of any of it. She couldn't fathom why God was punishing her. Her anger ebbed and flowed with each passing hour that Nikolai's health declined. Between moments of anger and defeat, when God's love enveloped her, she prayed for strength and faith for herself, and healing for Nikolai. But his symptoms never lessened.

Gangrene covered his nose and ears, the result of blood circulating slower through his body. His breathing was laboured, and he gasped for air every few minutes. He looked so weak. The strong, lively man whom she knew, now lay in bed, weak and unable to move.

"*It's not fair,*" she whispered into the night air. And when her rage took over, she yelled. "IT'S NOT FAIR!"

Tears poured onto her dress, her breath short from the rage and the fear that overcame her.

"I don't understand," she prayed, as she rocked her body back and forth. "Why did You bring us here, to this godforsaken land, if You only meant to take my husband away from me as soon as we got here?" Her voice grew louder and firmer as her anger intensified. "Why couldn't You have left us alone in Ebenfeld? Why couldn't You have sent Stalin away, instead of casting us off? Nikolai would be fine if we had stayed! He would be fine."

She cried harder as she looked down at Nikolai, and laid down beside him on the sweat-soaked sheets. Her head lay right next to his, and she stroked his cheek.

"You would have been fine," she whispered.

"Kaethe," Nikolai forced himself to speak, his voice quiet and hoarse. Startled, she propped her head up and moved even closer to his body.

"Oh, Nikolai. I'm so sorry."

"For what? Kaethe, this isn't your fault."

"I know," Kaethe whispered through tears, "but I wish I could make you better."

"Me, too," he lifted a weak hand and placed it over hers. "Kaethe, look at me." She turned her head up to meet his cloudy gaze. "I'm going home," he said apologetically. A tear creeped off the edge of his eye and fell onto the pillow.

Kaethe buried her head into his shoulder and screamed at him, "*Heare opp,* stop! Don't say that! You can't leave me! You're not going anywhere! How could I live without you? And Maria, how would I raise her all by myself? You can't leave us here all alone, Nikolai."

She sat up, moving herself closer to his head. She cupped his face in her hands and pleaded, "Nikolai, do not leave me. You cannot leave me!"

Nikolai clenched his eyes shut as tears rolled down his cheeks and over Kaethe's fingers. He willed the circumstances to change. This was not how it was supposed to be. He grabbed Kaethe's arms as firmly as he could, and looked into her brown eyes again.

"Kaethe, God will take care of you. I'm going home," his voice shook.

She lowered her forehead onto Nikolai's, both of them allowing their tears to flow without restraint. Her tears streamed down her cheeks onto his. She stayed there, her face on his, until Nikolai's eyes closed again.

Kaethe made herself comfortable beside him, stroking his hair. She regarded him as he slept, his chest rising and falling as he struggled to breathe. Every time he gasped for air, fear radiated through her veins. He would catch his breath eventually, and then his body would lie still again. He was oblivious to the panic he roused in her, and she prayed every breath would not be his last.

—

Kaethe preferred to be alone with Nikolai. She knew others meant well when they brought meals and their support, but she was not interested in conversing with them. She cared little of the goings on around the colony, or of others' predictions of the next rainfall. She sat quietly anytime someone came to visit and added their food offerings to the pile of other food on the stove.

She sat beside Nikolai, the straw beneath her grooved, indented from the weight of her body. Hours passed both quickly and laboriously. The quietness in the room engulfed her, blending her dreams with reality. Her eyes were closed when she heard a faint tapping on wood. Kaethe didn't have time to analyze the source of the knock before a stream of amber light pierced the room.

The silhouette of a woman stood in the doorway. Kaethe strained her eyes to identify the visitor, her eyes slowly adjusting to the light.

"Martha," Kaethe said, followed by a sigh of relief.

She stood and moved toward the dark figure with her arms extended and embraced her friend. She hadn't felt emotional in the moments before Martha's arrival, but her tears flowed heavily as her body folded into her friend's arms.

"*Ekj weete,* I know," Martha whispered, stroking Kaethe's head. "I *know.*"

Others offered the same words of encouragement, but they only irritated Kaethe more than anything. How could they possibly *know* how she felt, when their husbands were out working the fields, healthy. But Martha actually understood Kaethe's grief. She had cradled her own husband in her arms as his body slowly failed him.

Martha ushered Kaethe to a pair of chairs in the shade. She laid a parcel in her lap and unfolded the linen to reveal a freshly baked loaf of bread. She tore a piece and handed it to Kaethe, who waved her hands in refusal. Martha insisted, sternly ordering Kaethe to eat the small morsel of bread to gain strength – if not for herself, then for Nikolai and Maria.

Kaethe obliged. The bread was light and delicious. She couldn't remember the last time she ate and devoured her mouthful. Martha offered her more until she was satisfied. They stared at the ground for a long time, neither one feeling the need to speak. The silence was comforting to Kaethe. After some time, she gained enough strength to verbalize her thoughts, processing out loud what she had been struggling with internally for so many days. Martha listened intently, nodding every now and again to validate her friend.

Kaethe's tears cascaded down her cheeks and she made no attempt to stop them. The freedom to speak honestly brought a lightening she didn't realize she needed. When Kaethe's words ceased, her skirt was nearly soaked through from where her tears had pooled as they fell from her face.

Once Martha was out of sight, Kaethe returned to the shack, resuming her place in the cushioned straw beside Nikolai. She talked to him for the rest of the day, until the scattered light shining into the small space glowed with the soft reflection of the moon.

She drifted into a light sleep at some point as the seamless hours passed. With her eyes closed, her hearing sharpened, and the sound of footsteps plodding toward the shack roused her and she went outside. Her parents, along with a few other men from the village, stood in front of her.

Maria pulled herself away from Johann and reached for Kaethe. Kaethe wrapped her arms around her daughter, grateful to hold her. Maria was Kaethe's driving force. Without her, Kaethe feared she would crumple entirely.

"*Papa bätre,* all better?" Maria asked through a yawn.

Kaethe fought to keep her tears back. "No, Maria, Papa's not better yet. Why don't we go in and say goodnight to him?" Her voice shook as she spoke. Maria nodded and the two of them stepped into the shack.

Kaethe placed Maria on the sheets beside Nikolai before lowering herself on the other side of him. A soft groan emitted from Nikolai and he opened his eyes slightly.

"Mariechen? Is that you?" His voice was barely audible.

"Hi, Papa!" Maria said excitedly and Kaethe shushed her immediately. She tried again, this time whispering, "Hi, Papa."

A faint smile spread across Nikolai's face. The curve of his lips defined by the soft light illuminating the room. Not able to see through the film covering his eyes, Nikolai envisioned Maria's features – her dark curly locks springing from her head, the roundness of her cheeks, and her deep brown eyes that pierced his soul. He felt her soft skin as he touched her arm and suddenly realized he may not have the opportunity to hold his daughter again. The gravity of the realization gripped him and his body convulsed as he wrapped his arms around Maria.

Kaethe covered her mouth with her hand, muffling her own sobs as she watched her husband's tears fall. She knew what he was thinking, of all the moments he wouldn't get to experience – Maria's first day of school, her first love, her wedding – all the milestones and experiences he and Kaethe had dreamed of since the day she was born.

"Mariechen, never forget that I love you," Nikolai's voice was broken yet stern. "You might not always remember, but know that I loved you, and that God will always take care of you and Mama. I'm going home soon, but I'll see you again, all right?"

"Okay, Papa. I love you, too," Maria was confused by Nikolai's words, but she felt the tension in the air and tears started rolling down her cheeks. She wrapped her small, chubby arms around Nikolai's neck and held him tight. Kaethe joined their embrace.

They stayed huddled together until Maria's soft, rhythmic breathing brought Kaethe back to reality. Nikolai slept peacefully with Maria's head on his chest, moving up and down as he breathed. Kaethe remembered the visitors waiting outside and moved away slowly.

"Maria's asleep, so is Nikolai," Kaethe told her parents.

"Kaethe," Johann began, "Nikolai's friends would like to sit with him tonight so you can get some sleep."

"No, no, that's not necessary."

"Yes, Kaethe, it is necessary," Anna insisted.

She hadn't slept in days, and her energy waned. She thought of Maria, and with that she obliged her parents' request. She needed her strength to be the mother Maria needed her to be. She set a blanket on the ground beside the shack and moved Maria onto it. The men entered the room and sat on the floor or leaned against the walls. She made the men promise to wake her at even the slightest shift in Nikolai's health.

Kaethe looked into the vast dark sky as Maria slept soundly beside her, unaware of the turmoil Kaethe felt in her heart. Her blood pulsed loudly as her anxiety increased. She prayed, reciting the soothing passage from Psalm 23 until her body relaxed and her mind went blank.

—

Kaethe's heart raced as she sat on the blankets in the darkness, her eyes wide with shock from the sudden awakening.

It was just a dream, she assured herself, and lowered her body back to the ground.

She couldn't remember the dream, only that someone was calling her name. Her heart was still pounding audibly in her chest as she lay beside Maria.

"Kaethe!"

Kaethe's eyes sprung open. It wasn't a dream, after all. A man came out from the shack, horror in his eyes.

"Kaethe, come now. It's Nikolai."

She stumbled to her feet, lungs tightening, fear and adrenaline coursing through her veins. Inside, Kaethe fell beside Nikolai and touched his face with her warm hands. Even before she felt him, she could see the lifelessness in his body in the dim light of a candle that now filled the room.

"Nikolai? Nikolai!"

Kaethe reached for his limp hand.

"NIKOLAI!" She screamed into the night as tears descended her cheeks and fell onto Nikolai's chest. "Nikolai, wake up! Don't leave me! You can't leave me!"

Her grief drowned her and she fought to breathe. She pulled at Nikolai's shirt, crumpling it between her fists, grappling for any sign of life, though there was none to be found. Nikolai was gone.

For a moment she thought she was going to die from the pain she felt in her chest. The emptiness she felt in that moment when she held Nikolai's dead body in her arms was like getting the wind knocked out of her. She couldn't breathe. She couldn't see straight. All she could do was scream in short, breathless intervals, until the gravity of the situation muted her sounds, and she gasped, clinging to her chest.

The room slowly cleared until she was alone with Nikolai, but her pain only intensified.

—

Kaethe cried freely, without restraint. Every tear carried a memory of Nikolai. She knew she was alone in the shack, though she didn't know when the men had left, or how long they'd been gone for. Somewhere in her state of semi-consciousness, she heard Maria's small voice, groggy with sleep, coming from outside.

"Oma? Opa?" she asked, obviously confused by their appearance in the middle of the night.

Johann's voice followed with much effort to remain steady, "Maria, *Papa es met Jesus nu*, Papa is with Jesus now."

Maria poked her head into the shack and looked at her father's body. "No, Opa, he's sleeping on the floor."

Maria's words sent another dagger through Kaethe's stomach. She thought she might vomit as she stood and walked toward the door. She lowered herself with outstretched arms and wrapped them around Maria's innocence. Kaethe struggled to breathe, and fought the overwhelming feeling that her lungs might collapse, taking her life as well.

—

Kaethe sat motionless as her mother brushed her hair. Time suspended around her, the hours since Nikolai's death sank away like anchors in a bottomless sea, pulling Kaethe down with them. Every now and then, Kaethe gasped, jarring from her seat, gulping for air. With each episode, Anna laid the brush down and placed a weighted hand on Kaethe's shoulder, which only reaffirmed to Kaethe that she wasn't dreaming.

Her eyes were fixed on their shack across the street. Small bumps rose on her skin and she shivered. Two weeks ago, life was relatively normal, given their circumstances. Nikolai was healthy, able and strong, working the fields while Kaethe did her share of chores around the house and yard. That little shack was their home, where the three of them rested and slept in the safety of each other's presence before facing another day, together.

But now – *what now?* Kaethe dropped her chin to her chest as tears fell straight into her lap.

Anna's fingers moved like a soft wind through her locks as she pinned Kaethe's hair in place on top of her head. Kaethe wiped her cheeks with the back of her hand. She took a deep breath and lifted her face and saw her father and Maria across the street.

Johann moved a saw methodically through a Flaschenbaum tree, while Maria balanced on fallen logs. The end of the tree had been cut off, leaving seven feet of trunk that he arduously sawed in half lengthwise. The wide centre of the trunk, and the softness of the sapwood made it ideal for use as a coffin. The thought of Nikolai's body lying in the hollowed tree trunk churned her stomach. She turned to her side and vomited on the ground beside her chair, turning the dust an even darker shade of brown.

Anna moved around the chair and crouched down in front of Kaethe so their faces were inches apart. Anna cupped Kaethe's face in her hands as tears ran over her plump knuckles, swollen from arthritis. She knew there were no words she could say, and no wisdom to impart, that could possibly lessen the pain Kaethe was experiencing.

Kaethe lingered in her mother's familiar touch. Soon her comforting voice crooned, calming Kaethe, until the words of the song registered in her mind and her body convulsed with sorrow once more.

Be not dismayed, whate'er betide, God will take care of you;
Beneath His wings of love abide, God will take care of you.
God will take care of you, Thru ev'ry day, O'er all the way;
He will take care of you, God will take care of you.
No matter what will be the test, God will take care of you;
Lean, weary one, upon His chest, God will take care of you.
God will take care of you, Thru ev'ry day, O'er all the way;
He will take care of you, God will take care of you.

Nikolai's final words to Kaethe repeated through her mind, *God will take care of you.* Kaethe's quivering body sank into her mother's comforting embrace. When the shaking stopped, Anna lifted Kaethe from the chair and half-carried her into the shack.

A dress lay draped over a chair in the corner of the room. Anna went to it and gathered the fabric in her arms. She took a deep breath, composing herself. Kaethe stared at the wall as she slowly unbuttoned her dress and let it fall to her feet. Anna stood behind her with the clean dress and lifted it above Kaethe's head and over her arms. She moved in front of Kaethe and buttoned the front of the dress. Kaethe stood placid the entire time.

Fully dressed, with a black handkerchief tied around her neatly pinned hair, Kaethe looked in Anna's eyes. Anna teared up in response and gripped Kaethe's shoulders.

"We'll get through this together," she promised.

Kaethe nodded slowly as she reached for Anna's hand, and together they walked out of the shack and down the street to the school.

—

The hollowed out Flaschenbaum sat empty and waiting behind the small building. Kaethe stared blankly at the tree, lined with a white sheet, and the unearthed hole behind it. Oblivious to the perspiration forming on her forehead, the wet drops quickly trickled down her temples and cheeks, though she made no effort to wipe them away. Her focus was on the coffin in front of her, and the body that would soon inhabit it.

Footsteps came around the side of the building, and heads turned to watch as Johann and his friends carried Nikolai's corpse. Kaethe turned at the sound, her knees weak at the sight. *This is a dream, a nightmare,* she kept telling herself, but the plodding feet continued to move past the crowd that had gathered for the funeral.

Her body and mind went numb as Nikolai's body was lowered into the coffin. Johann crossed Nikolai's arms before taking his place on the other side of Kaethe. Maria was safe in Paul's arms, and Johann and Anna stood with their arms around Kaethe's waist as the preacher began to speak.

Kaethe's chest suddenly collapsed as she looked at her husband's still body. She screamed and her legs gave way from beneath her. Her parents caught her limp body before it hit the ground. A few people flinched, and others began to cry from the raw, agonizing shriek of a woman calling out to her soulmate.

Kaethe fought to free herself from her parents' grip, but failed. Eventually she gave in to their firm embrace and her screams quieted. When her breathing slowed, and Johann was sure she would be all right, he nodded to the preacher to continue.

Johann and Anna kept their arms around Kaethe throughout the entirety of the ceremony. When the preacher had said the final *Amen,* the crowd slowly dispersed. Kaethe kept her gaze locked on Nikolai, unable to acknowledge the condolences offered to her. As the last of the guests walked out of the school yard, her parents and brother followed them with Maria, giving Kaethe time alone with Nikolai.

She didn't move or say anything for a few minutes. The air around her was eerily quiet and still. When she approached the coffin, her heart sank, and she began to mourn, loudly and painfully. She knelt beside Nikolai and reached for his cold hand, stroking it with her thumb. Her tears fell onto his greying skin as she leaned over him, touching his cheek with her other hand.

"I'll see you again, my love," she promised him.

She leaned further into the coffin and kissed Nikolai for the very last time.

—

The skies were painted in golden hues as the sun dipped below the horizon. Kaethe stood behind the school, looking at the mound of dirt covering Nikolai's coffin. She had come back to the grave after everyone finished eating supper. She hoped it would be easier to walk behind the school now that his body was buried, but it wasn't.

She fought against the urge to move the loosened dirt so she could see him again, but she knew that wouldn't change the fact that he wasn't alive. Instead, she sat on the ground and recalled every memory she had with Nikolai in an attempt to preserve their memories.

A soft weight on her shoulder roused her and she turned to see Johann standing behind her. Maria was fast asleep in his arms. Kaethe looked up at the sky – the golden strokes replaced with unending blackness. She stood reluctantly, not sure how late it actually was, but knowing Maria needed to get to bed.

Johann walked them both back to their shack and lowered Maria on the freshly washed linens on the straw bed. Kaethe couldn't enter the room, the memory of Nikolai lying dead in her arms on that bed haunted her.

Johann joined her outside the shack and embraced her, "You should try to get some sleep, too."

He kissed her forehead, but Kaethe didn't respond. She shut her eyes and clenched her hands into fists as he walked away. She was all alone now. It would be her and Maria from this point on. Kaethe's body began to shake. Not knowing what else to do, she forced herself into the shack and laid on the floor beside Maria's small, warm body.

Maria's chest moved up and down effortlessly as she breathed, the way Nikolai's had refused to the night before. Kaethe wrapped an arm around her daughter. The sheets beneath her were crisp from drying in the summer's heat. The room felt like it was enclosing around her, suffocating her. Kaethe bustled out of the shack, breathing heavily. She groped in the dark for a chair and sat down, cradling her head in her arms as she leaned onto her knees until her heart settled.

She saw a candle sitting on the table in front of her and stood to look for a match. Feeling around the stove, she felt the familiar form of the matchstick box and struck the tip against the igniter. A spark caught and a flame grew on the wooden stick. She held it against the wick and the space illuminated with a dull orange glow.

In the dim light, she caught sight of the small brick fragment she had gifted Nikolai for his birthday. It sat innocently on the stove, leaning against the outside of the shack. All the sadness and grief she was feeling instantly turned to rage. Her brows furrowed and her neck flushed red with anger. She reached for the grey slab of hardened clay and brought it to her face and scowled at it. She screamed, releasing all of her anger and bitterness and confusion. She threw the brick as hard as she could against the shack. The brick crumbled from the impact, leaving nothing but dust and smaller fragments of brick on the ground.

Maria cried, woken by the sudden noise. Defeated, Kaethe blew out the candle and walked into the shack to comfort Maria. All the hope and promise of a positive future the brick once held was lost forever. In the stillness of the shack, Kaethe cried until her tears ran dry, and her jaw hurt from silencing her despair. Eventually, she drifted off, Nikolai's face the last image she saw before the nightmare-filled sleep began.

—

Kaethe massaged a teat between her fingers, expressing the milk into the metal bucket beneath the udder. She couldn't shake the emptiness she felt since Nikolai's death the day before. Her sleep had been restless, plagued with nightmares. She woke drenched in sweat, unlike Maria, who had slept peacefully the whole night.

Kaethe looked toward the other side of the yard where Maria gaily chased the chickens, feathers drifting around the frightened hens. She seemed to be relatively unaffected by Nikolai's absence, not yet comprehending the finality of his death.

"*Es Papa boolt Hüss*, is Papa home soon?" she had asked that morning over breakfast, with her mouth full of fried eggs. It was all Kaethe could do not to fall into a puddle of sorrow at her daughter's feet. She took a deep breath, avoiding eye contact with Maria, and answered her gently, "We'll see Papa again soon, my dear." She ran a hand through Maria's frazzled curls before turning toward the stove, wiping her eyes on her sleeve.

Maria now laid on her stomach in front of a hen, her feet moving like scissors, bending at the knee as she waited patiently for an egg to appear. With the cow's udder emptied, Kaethe placed the stool beside the fence and started walking toward the shack, the bucket of milk swinging in her hand.

She looked across the street and spotted her mother bending over a large basin, moving a wet shirt vivaciously over a washboard. In their field, Paul walked behind the plow, guiding the contraption as her father led the oxen.

Kaethe came to a sudden halt. The bucket she held fell to the ground, the contents soaking instantly into the dry ground. A pit formed in her stomach as she regarded her brother with fear. It was an image that brought back the memory of Nikolai from a few weeks ago.

Paul let go of the plow often, and was scratching his head profusely.

Nikolai Penner in his early twenties, taken in the mid-1920s.

*A group of men outside the Mölln refugee camp in March 1930. Johann Warkentin,
second from the left. Nikolai Penner, far right.*

Johann and Maria Warkentin, sitting, and Kaethe's brother, Johann, standing behind his parents.
Photo likely taken in Ebenfeld in the late 1920s.

PART TWO

9

May 1935

MARIA STOOD BY THE FENCE, WAITING. THE SKY WAS LIT BY A SLIVER OF light from the waking sun. The morning air clung to her skin, forming small beads of sweat around her temples. She could vaguely make out the figures of the two cows in the distance, their large bodies moving side to side as they ambled towards her. Beside her, two calves chewed their breakfast loudly, their noses stuffed into the buckets filled with sorghum. Thick saliva hung in long strands from the sides of their mouths. Maria dreaded this time of day. She wasn't sure if her perspiring brow was caused by the heat or from the anticipation of what would shortly ensue.

The cows were smart, despite the dopey expression they donned. Their udders were taut, filled with milk, but they would not come to the fence to be milked when they were supposed to. Instead, they waited. Eventually they made their way to the fence, clouds of dust rising around them as their hooves bore their weight into the ground. Rather than head to the part of the yard where Kaethe was waiting to milk them, they walked toward Maria, and their calves.

The calves lifted their heads simultaneously, the aroma of their mother's milk reaching them at the same time. The cows quickened their steps and stopped when they reached the fence and rubbed their thick hides against the wood planks. Instantly, the calves moved their noses toward their mother's udders. They latched onto a teat and began sucking.

Maria wrapped her arms around one of the calf's necks and groaned as she attempted to detach the calf from its mother. The little cow weighed more than she did and her feet buckled beneath her as he dragged her closer to the fence. She wrestled with the calf until she had him securely pinned beneath her body.

There was a rush of wind beside Maria as Kaethe came to her aid. She grabbed hold of the other calf and unlatched her from the cow's udder and pinned her to the ground beside Maria. It was too late, though. The calf had emptied the udder, leaving no milk for the family. The cow bounded off, back into the distant field, satisfied with her little scheme.

Kaethe loosened her grip on the young calf beneath her, milk dripping from his mouth. She grabbed a stick as she pulled herself off the ground. The remaining cow still stood by the fence and Kaethe tapped her hind legs with the stick, commanding her to move toward the milking bucket and stool. Maria let go of the calf, sweaty and dirty from moving around on the ground. The calf returned to the bucket of sorghum and plunged his nose into the grains, unphased by the whole ordeal.

Maria sat on the ground for a few minutes, catching her breath and rubbed her leg where the calf had kicked her in his struggle for freedom. She watched as her mother placed the stool by the cow's hind legs. She placed a tin bucket beneath the udder and began the familiar procedure of massaging and releasing the cow's milk. Maria looked beside her at the two calves, their noses shoved into buckets, finishing their meals.

"Next time," she assured them, and herself, before jumping to her feet and brushing the dust off her dress.

—

Kaethe's face reflected the sunrise as it kissed her skin and she dabbed a drop of perspiration as it wandered down her cheek. She watched Maria carry the two empty buckets toward the house. It was a modest upgrade from their tiny shack, but an upgrade nonetheless The original shack stood just in front of the house they now lived in with Kaethe's parents.

Kaethe's brother, Paul, passed away two weeks after Nikolai. Typhus took his life, along with the lives of so many others in their village, and surrounding villages. Life went on, though, out of necessity. Kaethe's family could not grieve for days on end, work still needed to be done. Their survival depended on it. If they didn't work, they didn't eat.

The daily tasks were strenuous and required effort beyond Kaethe's ability. In the weeks after Nikolai's death, she attempted to manage the farm and the domestic duties on her own. Johann came to help as often as possible, but his own farm required his attention, and without his son to help, there was even more work for him to do. Johann and Anna's aging bodies grew wearier by the day and Kaethe could see the burden they carried from the arduous work.

Shortly after Paul died, Kaethe and her parents decided it would be wise for them to live together on Kaethe's lot. Kaethe and her father had worked tirelessly on the bricks for weeks. One balmy night in January, the heavens opened without warning and rain fell to the ground in sheets, blanketing the land with water. They ran to the side of the lot where the bricks laid spread out on the ground to dry. Even in the dark, it was obvious that there was nothing but a pile of mud and clay left. The rain completely disintegrated their weeks of labour. They remoulded the bricks and eventually had a sufficient amount to begin constructing the home.

The house they now lived in was larger than their shack, though still small for a family of four. On either end of the house was a bedroom, with a small window on two of the outside walls. Kaethe and Maria shared one room, and her parents the other. In between the rooms was an open area that served as both living and dining room. A low wall, nearly three feet high, stood on either side of the room with two doors, one opening to the front of the lot, and the other to the back.

"*En Ei*, an egg! Mama, can you cook me an egg?"

Maria ran toward Kaethe, interrupting her memories. Kaethe looked at her hands. Milk no longer fell from the teat in her fingers and she wondered how long she had been distracted. Maria nearly lost her footing as she reached Kaethe, a silky brown egg in her hand.

"Michi, slow down or you'll break the egg," Kaethe instructed. "Go inside and ask Oma if she can cook the egg for you, and then ask Opa if he needs help with the plowing today."

Maria turned on her heels and ran toward the house, bustling through the door. Kaethe watched from a distance. Anna placed her mug on the table and took the egg from Maria's hand, leading the way to the shack outside, which now served as their kitchen. Kaethe moved the bucket out from under the cow and returned the stool to its place beside the fence.

"*Wajch*, go," she urged the bovine with a pat on its rump. The cow plodded off toward the other cow in the distance. She felt like it was smirking at her, satisfied with their plan to reach their calves before Kaethe could milk them. Kaethe moved her hair off her sweaty face with her apron. She frowned as she looked into the bucket – only half the amount of milk they needed.

—

After breakfast, Kaethe moved with effort toward the field with a bucket of sorghum seeds. Her body leaned to one side, pulled by the weight of the bucket, accentuating her curves. Her hips swayed with each step. She thought she must look like their cow, walking into the field, rump bouncing from side to side. The image made her laugh out loud.

Kaethe handed the bucket of seeds to her mother and went back to the house to grab a large basin from beside the house. She filled it with a few inches of water from the well they now had on their lot. The water rippled where drops fell as she pulled the bucket up. Kaethe looked into the well and calculated how much water remained, based on the distance of the glimmering liquid below. They hadn't had any rain in months, and their water supply was running low. Instinctively, she looked up to the sky and shielded her eyes. Nothing but blue above her. Not even a thin cloud. No hope of rain anytime soon.

She dragged the basin closer to the field and ran back to the house to fetch the washboard, soap and the dirty laundry. Despite her best efforts, she couldn't help but worry that they may run out of water, and constantly questioned why their lot yielded only one potable well, while other lots around her had multiple. It didn't make sense. She set the bucket of dirty laundry on the soft dirt and prayed under her breath. If God chose to limit their water source, He would have to sustain them until the next rainfall.

Kneeling beside the basin, she held one of Maria's frocks in her hands. The dress was filthy, with dirt so deeply embedded into the fibres of the fabric that even soap and water couldn't remove the stains. She dipped it into the shallow, soapy water and ran it up and down the ridges of the washboard. The water turned brown instantly, but getting fresh water for each garment was not possible. The rest of the laundry would be washed in the same dirty water. Kaethe wondered why she even bothered with the laundry if the clothes never came out clean anyway.

Once all the laundry hung on the line, Kaethe grabbed another small bucket of soiled fabric. She looked around, making sure no one was near her, and pulled the laundry basin behind the house, brown water splashing onto her dress from the movement.

She glanced back one more time to make sure no one was coming, and dumped the contents of the bucket - the strips of fabric she used while menstruating – into the basin. Red streaks infused the brown mixture as the cloth strips saturated with water. There were no sanitary napkins available at the Cooperative, and even if there were, she couldn't afford them. Instead, she took scraps of fabric, usually old shirts of Nikolai's, and tore them into strips, which she used to contain her flow. It was not ideal. She felt exposed and vulnerable every time she menstruated.

She rinsed the last of the strips in the basin as best she could and hung them to dry behind the house where they would be less visible.

—

Kaethe sat behind the communal village sewing machine that evening. A candle flickered on the table and Kaethe squinted as she threaded the needle. Tattered clothes lay piled beside her, all needing to be mended over the next few days before the sewing machine would be passed on to another family.

"*Dreie,* turn," she instructed Maria, who stood slouching beside her. On cue, Maria slowly turned the flywheel and the sewing machine hummed to life.

"Are you almost finished?" Maria sighed.

"Stop," Kaethe said without taking her eyes off the presser foot. Maria stopped turning the wheel and waited. Kaethe lifted the presser foot and pulled the shirt toward her. "I'll be finished when there are no more clothes on the table."

Maria sighed melodramatically.

Kaethe cut the loose ends of thread and placed the patched dress on the table. As she reached for the next garment, loud gunshots resounded through the village. Maria screamed and covered her ears, automatically curling her body into itself. Kaethe jumped in her seat and looked over the low wall toward the sound.

Another round of gunshots followed. And then another. Kaethe moved her chair back and pulled Maria onto her lap, closing her arms around her daughter's small body. She could feel Maria's heart beating strong and fast against her, matching the pace of her own heart.

They sat together until the gunfire subsided. Kaethe's chest was damp from Maria's tears and she stroked her daughter's fine, silky hair.

"Why do they have to fight so much?" Maria's voice was muffled, but audible.

"I don't know, Michi. Hopefully they'll be done soon."

Kaethe looked outside again and saw smoke rising beyond the trees. Her hope that the war would be over was dwindling quickly. It had been nearly three years since the war between Paraguay and Bolivia began. A fight for Chaco, both countries wanting to claim it for themselves. Some said the land sat over valuable oilfields, which they claimed was the reason for the war, yet others argued it was the river that ran through Chaco that held the most worth for the countries, both of which were otherwise landlocked.

For three years they had listened to that awful, ear-piercing sound of guns going off in the distance, though close enough that they could feel the reverberations in their bodies. Many nights, Kaethe or Maria, or both, would wake in a fearful sweat. They spent many nights together on Kaethe's bed, with their arms wrapped tightly around each other while the guns fired in the deserted lands around them. Kaethe tried to stay positive and comfort Maria as best she could, but she was afraid, too.

One positive outcome the war had on the colony was their access to the military's doctor. Whenever the army was stationed nearby – which was infrequent, and never for long periods of time – the doctor generously came through the Mennonite villages offering aid. The Mennonites were weary of the Paraguayan soldiers, and the presence of the soldiers in their small villages was unsettling. Their dark skin was unlike anything Kaethe had ever seen before, but it was their iniquitous eyes, and lustful desires, that sent shivers down Kaethe's spine. Word spread like wildfire in their small communities, and it was said that a few Mennonite women had been raped and harassed while soldiers meandered down their streets.

When the soldiers weren't around, Kaethe relaxed into the day-to-day tasks with relative ease. She had eventually adjusted to life in Paraguay, and though life was not easy, and the workload was intense, she came to feel at home in No. 6. Until the war began, and all sense of home was replaced with same overwhelming fear that had gripped them when they fled Ebenfeld.

No one knew all the details of the Chaco war, and what the outcome would mean for the Mennonite colonies within the area. If Bolivia won, would they be forced to uproot their lives yet again and find somewhere else to build and live their lives? Kaethe's lower lip quivered at the thought and she closed her eyes tight and pulled Maria closer to her chest. She kissed the top of her head.

Oh, Nikolai, Kaethe thought, *I wish you were here.*

Kaethe moved her legs side to side, rocking Maria until she fell asleep, and prayed over her silently before carrying her to their room.

The war ended the following month, a few days after Maria's birthday, with a victory for Paraguay. Relief washed through the colonies. They finally had assurance that they wouldn't have to relocate again after all.

10

March 1936

MARIA WOKE WHILE THE ROOM WAS STILL DARK. KAETHE WAS STILL ASLEEP in her bed on the other side of the room. Maria felt her way across the room and nestled in next to her mother. Kaethe stirred and opened her eyes slightly. She draped her arm around Maria's middle and closed her eyes again.

"Mama, it's time to wake up! It's time to get ready for school!" Maria whispered with excitement. Kaethe moaned and turned to face the other way. Maria sat up and rolled her mother onto her back. "Wake up! Wake up! I don't want to be late!"

With that, Kaethe wiped the sleep from her eyes and sat up. "I'm coming, I'm coming," she said with a yawn.

Maria didn't wait for her mother to get up before she jumped off the bed and ran into the living room. Johann sat at the table reading the *Mennoblatt*, the local village newspaper, and Anna poured their morning prips, the closest drink to coffee they could muster up, into mugs.

Prips was Anna's invention – a desperate attempt to recreate their favourite morning ritual. She would gather seeds from the harvested sorghum and boil them slowly in milk. Then she laid them out on pans, made from salvaged scrap metals from the aftermath of the Chaco war, until they dried. She placed the pans in the oven - another advancement to their minimal kitchen quarters – and roasted the seeds, just as she would her coffee beans, adding a dab of butter and a pinch of sugar. Every morning she walked to the shack and ground the roasted seeds and steeped them in hot water. The taste of watered down sorghum was incomparable to the satisfying taste of freshly-brewed coffee. However, with no coffee to be found in Filadelfia, prips was the best they could do as a replacement.

Kaethe joined them when she was dressed and held her mug of steaming prips in both hands. Maria sat next to Johann, smearing a thin layer of butter on her *tweeback*, bun, for breakfast.

"It's time to plant the sugar cane," Johann began. "I need to finish harvesting the rest of the corn and then I'll start seeding the sugar cane. I need to make a trip into Filadelfia with the corn as soon as I finish." He folded the newspaper and placed it on the table.

"So, Michi, are you excited for your first day of school?" Anna changed the subject and looked at her granddaughter.

"Yes!" Maria mumbled through a mouthful of bread before Kaethe scolded her on her lack of manners.

Maria had been looking forward to her first day of school for so long. Every day, she would stand by their gate and watch with envy as the older kids walked to and from school. She had been counting down the days until her first day of Year One for nearly a year in anticipation. Finally, March arrived and she would be amongst the children walking to school.

With a small canvas bag slung over her shoulders, Maria made her way to the gate. Kaethe followed closely behind her. At the rickety gate, Kaethe bent down to look Maria in the eyes. She straightened out the collar on her daughter's dress.

"Remember to be respectful to the teacher," her throat was thick with emotion. "Use your manners and be kind to the other students. If you can't see the writing on the blackboard, ask to move to a table closer to the front." She paused, still holding on to Maria's collar. A tear sat on the precipice of her eye. She thought of Nikolai and how much he would have wanted to be here with them right now. He loved learning, and always told Maria stories about his own school days, and about his father as his teacher. She took a deep breath, composing herself. "And most importantly – have fun!"

"I will!" Maria bounced with excitement.

"I love you, Michi," Kaethe said, as she pulled her daughter into her arms and held her tight.

"I love you, too, Mama. But I'm going to be late if you don't let go."

Kaethe released her grip and watched Maria run down the street, the bottoms of her feet brown from the dirt. She stood by the gate until Maria turned into the school, out of sight. Kaethe felt an ache as she walked back up to the house. She chided herself for being so silly – Maria would only be gone a few hours, not for eternity.

The void lingered throughout the day, though. Kaethe and her parents resumed their usual daily duties, but a cloud hovered over Kaethe as she worked. It took all her might to focus on the task at hand, and she was easily distracted with thoughts of Maria, turning often toward the gate to see if she was coming home from school.

—

Promptly at noon, Kaethe waited by the gate. The village was quiet and empty as everyone finished off their morning chores. She kept her gaze down the street until a stream of children walked and ran in every direction. She spotted Maria, who waved her arms frantically, a huge smile spread across her face. She came barrelling down the street toward Kaethe, jumping from one shaded patch to the next, allowing her feet to cool before streaking to the next tree's shadow. Before she even reached Kaethe, Maria was talking a mile a minute, recalling every minute of her day.

Kaethe laughed as she listened to Maria, dramatically moving her arms at the same time.

"Then, during recess, Peter – he's in Year Three – dug a hole and put a raw egg into it and covered it with dirt, and after school he dug the egg out, and guess what? The egg was cooked! He cracked it and the shell peeled off and the egg was cooked!"

"Is that so?" Kaethe was thoroughly amused. Maria didn't hear her and continued on with her next thought.

"And Hertha, Susa and Adeline are in Year One with me. They're so nice. Hertha even shared her *tweeback* with me. And we played Tip-Tip during recess, too. I almost made it to the can, but Viktor tagged me before I could kick it, so I was in jail the rest of the time. But so was Susa, so we talked about our dolls."

They walked into the house together. Maria was still divulging every minute of her day as she changed out of her school clothes. Kaethe smiled as she placed four plates on the wooden table. The looming unsettledness she felt all day lifted with Maria's return, leaving Kaethe feeling whole once again.

Slowly, Kaethe adjusted to Maria's absence during the days. She didn't like it, but she grew to accept it. Her chores distracted her thoughts, and eventually the hours whiled away quickly as Kaethe worked around the house. Maria's return from school was always the highlight of Kaethe's days.

"Eins, zwei, drei, vier, fünf. One, two, three, four, five." The students chanted in unison. Maria leaned on her desk, squinting to minimize the fuzz of the chalked numbers their teacher, *Lehrer* Ratzlaff, had written on the blackboard.

"Sehr gut, very good," he encouraged them.

Maria sat in the front of the room, a row of 1's scrawled on the lined paper in front of her. She enjoyed learning *Hüagdietsch,* High German, and grasped new concepts quickly, as she did with every subject. Lehrer Ratzlaff saw her potential, even at the young age of eight. Her poor eyesight didn't slow her down either. She was determined to learn, and stayed in her seat after the final bell rang to copy the notes from the teacher's book into her own.

There were six classes in the school at the same time, from Year One to Year Six. Seven students made up Maria's Year One class – four girls and three boys. Her excitement for school never diminished. She thoroughly enjoyed it. Not just for the endless knowledge she was taught, but for the constant company, as well.

Maria had a special connection with a girl in her class – Susa. Bonded instantly by their shared love of dolls, they became fast friends. The two girls spent every free moment at school together, and as often as possible throughout the week. There was one similarity that connected the girls on a deeper level – Susa had lost her father a few years ago during the typhus outbreak, as well.

"Kinder, children," Lehrer Ratzlaff clapped his hands together to get their attention. "We have a special visitor today, all the way from *Deutschland,* Germany!" He extended his arm to the back of the room and the children followed his gaze. Two men and a woman walked between the desks to the front of the room. The two men carried a large box.

"Guten morgen, Kinder! Haben sie viel spaß in die Schüle heute? Good morning, children! Are you having a good day at school today?" The woman's German was beautiful. Each word rolled eloquently off her tongue. "My name is Renate, and these are my friends, Simon and Klaus."

Maria strained her ears to understand as many words as she could. The expressions on her classmates' faces indicated she wasn't the only one struggling to translate the perfectly enunciated words that flowed from the woman's lips. Lehrer Ratzlaff explained to the children that the box the guests brought with them contained gifts for all the students. Inside the box were an assortment of toys and games, including dolls and miniature cars.

Maria's ears perked at the mention of dolls. She was fond of her beloved *Poppsche*, but had desperately wanted another one. Her back straightened as she listened to the rest of the instructions. Klaus held a white porcelain vase, which held small folded papers numbered from one to twenty-five. He walked up and down the rows of desks and each student reached into it, eager to find a low number.

Finally it was Maria's turn. With bated breath she reached her small hand into the jar and stirred the remaining papers with her fingers. She grabbed hold of one and slowly unfolded it. She stared at the number written in black ink – "12." There were only five dolls in the lot, and twice as many girls in the school. Her shoulders slumped. There was no way she would walk out with a doll.

Renate called number one and Viktor went up to the front. She continued to call the numbers in order, and one student after the other chose their prize. A few girls were called in a row after that, each returning to their seats with a brand new doll in their arms. Susa was one of the lucky ones. She sat down next to Maria and held the doll out for Maria to see, her face beaming. Maria returned a forced smile.

She wanted a doll. She *needed* a doll, she told herself. There was only one doll left now, and two numbers ahead of her yet. She was losing hope.

"*Zehn*, ten," Renate continued. Helmut happily chose a toy car, and Maria's hope grew ever so slightly. "*Elf*, eleven."

Maria prayed that whoever held the eleven would be another boy. Her heart sank as Hertha rose from her seat and moved toward the front. Deflated, Maria slumped further into her seat. She watched Hertha rifle through the box and pull out a set of Dominoes. Maria couldn't believe it. Still in shock, she didn't hear her number called the first time.

"*Zwölf*, twelve?"

Maria jumped out of her seat, moved around her desk, and rifled through the remaining toys in the box until she found what she was looking for. She held up the small, rubber doll. The brown hair was set in two plaits that hung on either side of her head. Maria went back to her seat and cradled the doll in her arms, and the shining brown, glass eyes disappeared under the doll's eyelids.

"Susa, look! Her eyes close!"

"I know! Mine too!"

After school, the two girls skipped together all the way to Maria's house. They scrambled through the gate and up the yard. Maria waved to Kaethe, who was helping Johann cut the sugar cane stalks. Susa waited under the Flaschenbaum as Maria ran inside the house and reappeared moments later with a cotton blanket and a tin tea set. She unfolded the blanket and held one end with both hands. The blanket soared weightlessly in the air like a ship's sail before slowly lowering to the ground. The girls pulled each corner so it lay flat.

Small, dusty footprints marked the steps the girls took as they excitedly placed four hand-painted teacups on matching saucers. Smiles reached across their faces and their giggles carried out to the fields. They propped their newly-acquired dolls up with blankets, and Susa and Maria held their cups quaintly, with pinkies pointing up to the sky as they sipped on air.

They sat on the blanket for a long time, drinking tea and caring for their babies whenever they cried. Their conversations revolved around their dolls, and the excitement and nervousness of the visitors at school that morning. After some time, Susa grew quiet, the gap between her brows narrowing.

"What is it, Susa?" Maria asked her friend.

"Do you ever wonder what it would be like to have a mum *and* a dad?" Susa asked, a hint of longing in her tone.

"Yeah," Maria confided, "sometimes I wish I had a dad."

"Me, too."

Maria paused for a moment, stroking her doll's hair. "Mama doesn't really talk about my dad very much. I think it makes her too sad. But Oma and Opa always tell me how much he loved me, and that he called me 'his little Mariechen.' But I don't remember him myself. The only thing I remember, though it's not really a specific memory, is that he made me feel safe."

"The only memory I have of my dad was when he was dying," Susa kept her eyes on her empty teacup. "He looked a little scary – all pale, and his eyes were covered with something that made him look funny. It's not a very nice memory to have of him, but that's all I have."

"I'm glad I don't have any memories of my dad dying. I think it would scare me, too."

They played silently for a few more minutes, their friendship deepened by their vulnerability.

"A little higher," Kaethe instructed Maria, who held one end of a sugar cane stalk. Kaethe turned the crank of the press and the stalk moved slowly through the metal rollers. The stalk flattened and sweet juice dripped into the bucket, strategically placed right underneath it on the floor. The work was monotonous and unending. A tower of stalks still remained after hours of labour. Maria dreaded September every year – she loathed pressing the sugar cane.

"Bring the bucket out to Oma, and then come straight back."

Maria bent and grabbed the handle of the bucket with both hands. The weight of its contents surprised her again, despite the many trips she'd already made out to the fire that day. She grunted as she hobbled out of the house, the bucket sloshing between her legs. Sharp pains radiated up and down her back with each step. She closed her eyes as a gust of wind blew through the yard, lifting the light dirt off the ground and into the air.

"*Pauss opp*, be careful, Michi!" Anna grabbed the bucket from Maria before it tipped over.

Maria's chest moved up and down as she breathed heavily. She stretched her arms as high as she could. Her back cracked and another stabbing pain shot through her, though it felt somewhat pleasurable as it relieved some of the built up tension.

Her back was a constant source of discomfort. A slight curve at the top of her spine seemed to be the culprit, often leaving Maria bedridden for days at a time, though never long enough to fully heal. With Johann and Anna getting on in years, and Kaethe's own physical condition ailing her, they needed Maria's help.

Everyone had a role in running the farm and maintaining the home. Maria helped Johann with the farming, riding their horse, *Growa*, with the farm equipment trailing behind him. *Growa*, aptly named for his luscious grey fur, was a stubborn old stallion. He was temperamental, and Maria didn't trust him.

Anna did all the baking, making sure they always had a supply of buns and galletas for themselves. She also baked bread every week that she sold to the *Guaraní*, the local Indians. Kaethe was swift with a sewing machine and used her skills to earn an income by making and selling shirts to a store in Filadelfia. And when they weren't in need of shirts, she would clean houses or seal bricks with manure. Laziness was not an option for any of them, back pain notwithstanding.

Maria's moment of relief was short-lived. The bucket, now empty, was placed back in her hands and she ran back to the house, shielding her eyes from the dust with her free arm. Kaethe was waiting for Maria with another stalk in her hand. Maria grabbed it begrudgingly and held it level to the floor, with one end touching the metal rollers, as Kaethe's arms moved in rapid circles.

From her spot by the press, Maria watched her oma heat the sugar cane juice outside. A large cast iron plate with high ridges sat on four metal legs over a roaring fire. Anna stirred the contents of the oversized plate with a long wooden spoon. Drops of sweat ran down her cheek, winking in the light every time the sun hit the side of her face.

The surface of the syrup eventually bubbled sporadically in slow motion. Like lava, the thick syrup began to boil. The liquid thickened and darkened the hotter it got, requiring more strength than Anna had to stir it. Johann came to her aid and stirred until it reached a rolling boil, which was when a layer of foam settled on top. Anna scooped the syrup into the empty buckets lined up beside the fire. When the large pot was empty, she poured the buckets of freshly pressed sugarcane juice into it and started the process all over again.

"Michi? Maria!" Kaethe raised her voice to get Maria's attention. "Grab another stalk; this one's almost done."

"Why do we have to make all this syrup, anyway?" Maria exhaled.

"You know very well why, my dear," Kaethe moved the end of the stalk into the metal rollers.

"I know that we eat it more at the end of winter, but why?"

"The rains have stopped for the winter, and we'll only have enough water in our wells for a couple of months."

"Can't we get water from other families that have more wells on their lots?"

"Yes, and we do, but there's only so much water to share. The cane syrup will fill us up when water is at its lowest."

"But why does it have to take so long?" Maria coughed as a wave of dust blew through their home.

"Because it does. Now hold that end up a bit higher, please."

―

Johann and Anna squeezed their bodies into the tiny desks. The school building was used for both school and church, including Saturday evening prayer meetings. After the meeting, conversations flowed out through the doors and small groups lingered outside. Anna stood in a circle with a few other women, talking about the new items recently brought to the Cooperative. The winter's icy touch brushed her shoulders, sending chills down her spine, and she pulled her shawl tighter around her body.

Johann stood on the other side of the school with a group of men, seemingly in deep conversation. Anna watched him as he stroked his long moustache with forefinger and thumb, his face expressionless. Some of the men's voices rose above the others, but their words weren't clear, and she wondered what they were talking about.

Eventually the groups dispersed, and Johann fell in step beside each other as they walked silently most of the way home.

"What were you and the other men talking about tonight? It looked quite serious," Anna finally asked.

After a moment, he replied. "Some families are planning to leave No. 6. Leave Fernheim, actually. They want to move further east."

"What?" Anna's mouth hung open in shock. "Why would they want to do that?"

"They think the land will be wetter out there, they think it rains more there."

"That's ridiculous! Where are they getting this information from?"

"I'm not sure. I didn't ask because I didn't want to add fuel to the fire. They seemed to be pretty firm in their knowledge. They plan to leave in a week's time, and from the sounds of it, their plans are unlikely to be thwarted."

"And what if they're wrong?" Anna's voice fell to a mild whisper. Her initial disapproval changed to concern for the families. "What if they get there and it's no different than here? Or, what if it's even worse?"

"Those are all questions I cannot answer. We can only pray for them, that God will give them wisdom regardless of the outcome."

Johann held the gate open and waited for Anna to walk through. He closed it behind them and saw Kaethe and Maria sitting outside.

"How was the meeting?" Kaethe looked up from the seam she was stitching back together as they approached them.

"It was encouraging. Many reasons to praise God," Johann answered, turning up the corners of his mouth. "Did you get the last of the cotton planted?"

"Yes, just finished not too long ago. I was sad to miss the meeting. Did anything important come up?"

Johann didn't make eye contact with her. "Yes, actually. It seems quite a few families from around Fernheim, including a fair share from No. 6, are moving next week. Further east."

Kaethe and Maria looked at him with astonishment.

"Surely you're mistaken, Papa?" Kaethe asked.

"I'm afraid not."

"But, why would they move?"

Johann repeated the information he heard from the men that were leaving. He tried not to sound cynical as he spoke, though he still couldn't rationalize their decision.

"Which families from Friedensruh are planning on leaving?"

"The Toews, Baergs and Klassens, are among them. Those are the only ones that were mentioned tonight."

"Which Baergs and Klassens?" Maria dropped her book into her lap and looked at her opa with concern in her eyes.

"I'm sorry, Michi," Anna comforted, "Adelina and Hertha's families will be moving."

Maria's lip quivered as she searched her grandparents' faces for any trace of jest or humour. One tear descended her cheek, and then another, until she was sobbing heavily into her mother's apron. Adelina and Hertha were the other two girls in her Year One class, and though she wasn't as close to them as she was to Susa, they were still two of her dearest friends.

Kaethe gathered Maria onto her lap. The adults sat silently, listening to Maria cry. Kaethe wondered if they were right, those families that believed they would find better living conditions east of Fernheim. The thought was enticing, and for a moment she wanted to consider leaving with them, but something assured her it would be no different elsewhere. Yet …

No, she chastised herself. Men had travelled around the colonies before, and neither Menno Colony nor Neuland were any better off than Fernheim. It would be the same wherever those families decided to settle, and Kaethe would not put herself, or Maria, through such uncertainty. Let alone rebuilding their lives and village once again. The first time had been long, arduous and incredibly painful. Kaethe's back pained her all the time, and she could see Maria wincing as she moved heavy objects. And the emotional pain, losing Nikolai from the poor hygienic conditions – she couldn't imagine losing Maria, or her parents.

Maria's tears quieted, and the four of them sat in silence, staring at the sky. Stars streaked from one end to the other. Kaethe wondered if Nikolai's parents were looking at the same night's sky as her. She knew it was unlikely that they were still alive, yet every time she looked at the stars, with their vibrancy and aliveness as they twinkled above her, she felt hope that they may still be alive.

Suddenly she frowned, realizing that if they were still alive, they had no idea that their son was not. Her stomach turned and she felt ill at the thought. But still, she longed to know one way or another.

—

Johann snored softly beside Anna when she woke. She moved as quietly as possible around their small room as she slipped out of her nightgown and into her dress. Johann stirred once, but didn't seem to rouse from his blissful sleep.

Anna reached for a shawl as she walked out of her room, and down toward the shack. Though the air was still mildly frigid, she could feel the impending presence of spring as the temperatures rose slightly every day. A breeze danced across the yard, the dust following in its wake like a beautiful ball gown twirling across a dance floor. The sky was still mostly black, with the faintest light brimming over the trees.

When she reached the stove she screamed, instantly covering her mouth so as not to wake the others. Curled around itself on the stove lay a rattlesnake, savouring what little warmth emanated from the previous day's fire. Anna reached for the nearest poking device, which happened to be a large wooden spoon. She held it out in front of her body and squealed as she jabbed the snake, its tail rattling from the disturbance. Her first attempt failed and she leaned over once more and pushed the spoon harder against the shiny skin. The snake fell to the ground with a thump and slithered away in the opposite direction.

She watched the snake until it was out of sight and she could be sure it wouldn't come back to haunt her again. Her shawl fell off at some point during the episode and she went back to retrieve it. Covered in dust, she shook it and used it to wipe the dust covering the remainder of the stove around the circle of the snake's body.

Anna placed fresh wood in the stove and lit a fire. While the flames grew and the element heated, she grabbed a bucket and walked toward the well, cautiously looking for anymore snakes. She heaved on the rope until the small basin appeared. A measly two cups of water was all it held. Anna sighed and poured the water into her bucket. It may not be much, but it was enough for a few cups of coffee.

Real coffee beans were finally brought in to the Cooperative earlier that year. It had been a joyous day for the family. Steam slowly billowed out of the saucepan on the stove. Anna stood by the table, turning the small crank of the grinder. The smell of freshly-ground beans wafted into her nose and she inhaled deeply. She never tired of the smell of coffee, and had gained a deeper appreciation for it, having gone without real coffee for their first years in Paraguay. Prips was tolerable, simply because there had been no other option, but nothing could compare to real coffee.

As the water rolled to life, Anna added the ground coffee beans and removed the saucepan from the hot element to let them steep. She grabbed three tin mugs off the shelf inside the shack and dusted them off with a nearby towel. When she walked back outside, the sky was dimly lit with shades of coral. Anna memorized the picturesque view before slowly pouring the velvety liquid into mugs, holding back the grounds with a spoon. Later, she would discard the grounds in the garden, amongst the flowers, like she used to do in Crimea.

Anna reminisced on the beautiful variety of flowers that had bloomed around their house in Ebenfeld. Though she spent most of her days at the shop, she looked forward to going home to swing on the porch surrounded by a rainbow of fragrant flowers. Her garden was often the talk of the town.

Anna looked at the arid ground around their home. There was a small garden, with a handful of wild flowers. The cacti in the back forest produced gorgeous blooms in the spring, but they were short lived. Even shorter lived was the *Königin der Nacht,* Queen of the Night that she had only ever heard about. It bloomed once every few years for merely minutes before the silky petals fell to the ground. Some said they heard stories that the flower was magical, revealing insight to your soul if you were so blessed as to witness the short-lived beauty.

Johann was awake and reading his Bible at the table when Anna reached the house. She placed the mugs on the table, hung her shawl by the window, and wiped the surface of the table with her arm to clear the dust.

"You'd think after six years I'd get used to all this dust, but I haven't," Anna sat down across from Johann and took a sip of her coffee. "Are Kaethe and Michi awake yet?"

Johann closed his eyes and inhaled the sweet aroma from his mug. "Hmm? Oh, yes, I think so."

The door to the other bedroom opened and Maria bounced out, kissing Johann and Anna on their cheeks.

"*Morje*, morning!" she sang rather chipperly. "Oh! My hen is laying!"

She was out the door before either Johann or Anna had a chance to say anything in return. They chuckled to themselves and continued sipping their coffees. Kaethe stepped out of the room, rubbing her forehead. She sat down beside Johann and reached for her mug.

"Everything all right?" Johann asked her.

"Ugh. No," Kaethe sighed heavily, "the store needs more shirts but I can't get the sewing machine today, and I'm cleaning the Neudorf's house today, and they asked if I could seal the bricks for them while I'm there. I don't know how my back will be after that. I'm in more than enough pain after cleaning. And there isn't enough water to wash the clothes…" Kaethe paused. "I'm sorry, I don't mean to complain."

"Don't apologize, Kaethe," Anna reached a hand across the table to reassure her daughter. "You have reason to feel weary. We all do."

"I know, that's why I shouldn't be complaining. We're all doing more than we're capable of."

"Yes, by God's grace."

Kaethe's mouth lifted slightly on one side and she raised her mug to her lips. "Where's Michi?"

Johann pointed a crooked finger toward the back of the yard. Kaethe followed his direction and saw Maria lying on the ground on her stomach in front of the laying hen. The hen stood and revealed a smooth, lightly browned egg. Maria grabbed the egg and ran back to the house.

"Mama! Mama! *En Ei*, an egg! Can I have it for breakfast? *Bitsheen*, please?"

—

Kaethe stood beside the stove, waiting for the opaque liquid of the egg to turn white. She berated herself for complaining to her parents. They, too, had their share of ailments and issues. At least she was still able to work, and they had enough money to eat and survive. Yet, she couldn't help but long for an easier life, for all of them. Even Maria worked beyond what an eight-year-old should be required to do. She felt responsible for the curve in Maria's back, and the constant pain she was in.

Maria never complained, though. Kaethe's heart swelled with pride as she thought of her daughter. If only she could give her more. She deserved more.

Kaethe exhaled slowly, overwhelmed with defeat and shame, and gently lifted the egg out of the pan and onto a plate.

The yard was covered with dirt, even the sides of the house, and the leaves on the trees, donned a thin layer of fine dust. The wind unravelled strands of hair from the pins on Kaethe's head. Another big gust blew and she turned her body and shielded her eyes. When it passed, she brushed the dust off her skirt and went inside. She placed the dust-laden egg on the table in front of Maria who ate it with delight, seemingly unphased by the added texture.

Kaethe picked up the recent *Mennoblatt* and leaned back in her chair. Johann and Anna sipped their coffees in silence. Another gust of wind picked up the dust outside and blew it through their house. They covered their faces and heard a thud behind them. When the wind subsided, they turned toward the sound and saw Anna's shawl swaying in the opening of the window.

"NO!" Kaethe yelled as she threw her body off her chair, onto the floor behind her. Their last bucket of sugar cane syrup that had been sitting on the ledge now lay on its side on the straw floor. The deep amber liquid glimmered in the morning light. Kaethe cupped her fingers in the sticky syrup, but it fell through her fingers, and weaved its way through the layers of straw.

Kaethe let out a raging scream and stormed out of the house. The others watched her leave in silence. Syrup dripped from her fingertips as she moved hastily toward the gate. Her neck was visibly red, even from a distance. She slammed the gate behind her and continued down the road.

"Is Mama okay?" Maria looked bewildered and her eyes begged for an explanation.

"Yes, Michi," Anna assured her, "Mama is fine. She's just upset that the syrup is ruined. Finish your egg, you don't want to be late for school."

Anna stroked her granddaughter's uncombed hair. She, too, felt responsible for their current situation. And with her health slowly declining as she aged, she was of far less use around the house as she wanted to be.

11

December 1940

IT WAS THE FIRST SATURDAY OF DECEMBER. THE ROOM WAS STILL AS DARK AS the depths of the sea when Kaethe woke. She pried her nightdress off her sweaty body and hung it on a nail in the wall. A brassiere hung on the back of the door and she silently slipped her arms into it, closing the hook behind her back. She quietly pulled her dress off the door of the wardrobe. She set it out the night before so she wouldn't have to open the squeaky door in the morning, and risk waking Maria.

She slid into the familiar dress, her Sunday best, and moved the buttons at the front through their designated holes with ease. She twisted her thick, brown hair into a ball and pinned it into place on the top of her head. Kaethe wiped the sweat from her forehead and brushed the skirt of her dress before leaving her room.

The gate clicked shut behind her and she took a deep breath. A few candles flickered through open windows of the houses on either side of the street, but for the most part, the village was still asleep. She walked at an even pace, but her heart raced in anticipation. It was only a five minute walk to the school, but that day it felt like years.

She faced the school building and looked down the path that led to the back. With another deep breath, she willed her legs to move forward until she was standing over the spot where Nikolai's body lay. There were no stones or posts marked with names to indicate who was buried underneath each grave, but Kaethe didn't need anyone, or anything, to tell her where her husband lay.

It had been ten years to the day since Nikolai left her. Every year, on the anniversary of his death, she woke early and visited his grave. She knew it would seem ridiculous to others, if they knew, but she needed to be with him, even if only to touch the earth that covered his bones.

She straightened the collar on her dress and knelt down, placing both palms on the ground. Her breath caught in her throat. The knowledge that Nikolai was beneath her sent a chill down her spine. She felt him, somehow, though she couldn't explain how, exactly. A tear slid off the curve of her cheek, darkening the dirt where it fell. Soon more tears fell as she allowed herself to feel the weight of her grief.

Absence was supposed to make the heart grow fonder, but in her case, absence only made her long for his presence even more. She missed Nikolai immensely. There was a hole in her life that had not been filled in all those years. She brushed the dust over his grave and lowered her body so she lay parallel to the ground.

"Du fälst mie sea, I miss you," she whispered, not able to control the sobs that escaped her. She tried to hug the ground beneath her. It was the closest thing to comfort she felt, when she was there with him, lying as close to him as possible. She felt him there with him. Whether it was actually Nikolai she felt, or God, she didn't know, and frankly didn't care. She laid on the ground, motionless, for a long time.

"Mama and Papa want to move to Filadelfia," Kaethe eventually whispered. "I agree with their reasons. I know the farm work is too much for Papa to do on his own. We haven't told Maria yet. I'm terrified to, honestly. She'll be devastated to leave her friends. I'll miss my friends, too, but I know a few people in Filadelfia, so at least I have that to look forward to."

Kaethe moved her hand back and forth over the dirt, the fine granules moving smoothly between her fingertips. "If I'm being really honest, I don't know that I can leave you, Nikolai. I know what you're thinking – you're not actually here anymore. But, you are – here, beneath me. The thought of moving somewhere else, where we haven't made memories together, feels so unsettling. Just knowing that you're buried here brings me comfort in a way I can't explain. I know I sound ridiculous, but it's true. I can't count how many times I've walked past this building on days when I've felt so overwhelmed with Maria, or life. I just—"

The tears came again, and Kaethe hid her face in her arms.

After some time, a rooster crowed in the distance and roused Kaethe. She opened her eyes, squinting at the sudden brightness. The sky was alive with pastel hues blending into each other like a watercolour painting. The bustling sound of families starting their morning chores resounded through the small village. Cicadas sang in unison, the comforting sound of summer approaching.

Kaethe wiped her eyes and looked at Nikolai's grave one more time. She brought her hand to her mouth, kissed it, and softly touched the dry earth.

"*Ekj sie die goot,* I love you, Nikolai. Good-bye."

—

Johann listened amusingly as Maria recounted the many dreams she had the previous night. She spoke with such speed he strained to catch every word. She took another bite of the eggs on her plate, and continued speaking until she looked out the window and stopped mid-sentence.

"Where was Mama? And why is she wearing her Sunday dress? It's Saturday."

Johann looked over the low wall and regarded Kaethe as she neared the house. Her eyes were red and swollen, her dress and cheeks covered with dust.

"I thought we weren't allowed to get our Sunday dresses dirty?" Maria was confused by her mother's disheveled appearance.

"Michi, can you bring the sorghum out to the calves, please?" Johann urged her. Maria obeyed, though somewhat reluctantly. She shoveled the remainder of her eggs into her mouth and went out the back door, with one final questioning glance toward Kaethe.

Johann wasn't surprised to see Kaethe in such a state. He had seen it before. In fact, he had seen it ten times before. Every year, on the anniversary of Nikolai's death, he heard the faintest movement on the straw in the living room before the first light of day.

The first year, Johann had been curious as he saw Kaethe's silhouette in the moonlight, moving toward the gate. He followed her out of concern. He kept his distance, hidden in the shadows of the night. When he reached the back of the school, he saw her lying on the ground, crying over Nikolai's grave. He watched her silently her for a moment, his heart aching as she mourned her husband. He had left almost immediately after, giving her the space and privacy she desired.

Kaethe didn't make eye contact with her father as she went to her room. He looked at the closed door with compassion.

"*Morje, Schatze,* good morning, sweetheart," Anna came out of their bedroom, her voice still hoarse with sleep. "Where is everyone?" She kissed Johann and sat down across the table from him.

"I sent Maria to feed the calves, and Kaethe…" he pointed his chin toward her closed door. "It's the seventh of December," he whispered.

"Ah," that was all the information Anna needed to understand what was going on.

—

"But why? I don't understand," Maria bounced on the seat of the wagon beside Kaethe as they rode into Filadelfia. "I don't want to move."

"I know it'll be hard to leave your friends, but the work is becoming too difficult. Oma and Opa are getting old, and I can't run the farm and the house all by myself."

"But … but …" Maria tears fell into her lap.

"I know, Michi. I'm sorry." Kaethe wrapped an arm around Maria's petite frame. Her body quivered as she cried silently. "We'll come back to visit your friends, okay? And you'll make new friends at your new school."

"I don't want to go to a new school! I want to go to *my* school, with *my* friends."

"I know you do. It will take time for all of us to adjust. But know that we prayed about it for a long time and we all agreed that it is the right thing to do."

There wasn't much Kaethe could say to comfort Maria just then. They rode the rest of the way in silence, until they pulled into the Cooperative. With Christmas just over a week away, Maria needed to choose the fabric for her new dress. It was the highlight of the year for Maria. She lingered over each fabric, running her hands up and down each roll, until she found a silk material – red as crimson – she fell in love with.

Kaethe started working on the dress as soon as they arrived home. She measured Maria and drew the pattern accordingly. She cut the delicate silk and sewed the pieces together with Maria's help, who turned the flywheel at Kaethe's request.

The final piece, a lace collar, was sewn on by hand. Maria had longed to have lace on her dresses for years, but was always told it was too expensive. The plentiful harvest of the year had enabled them to purchase a few extra items that year, including the small amount of lace. In the grand scheme of things, a few inches of lace did little in providing the necessities of life. For Kaethe, however, as a mother, even such trivial items were worthwhile investments every now and then, if they would bring joy to her daughter.

Kaethe smiled as she tidied her workspace. Maria's excitement seeped out of their bedroom where she was trying on the dress. Another squeal of approval and she jumped out of the doorway, twirling for Kaethe.

"I love it, Mama! Thank you so much!" Bits of straw stuck out between her toes and she continued twirling.

"*Sea schmock,* it's beautiful, Michi, but it's missing something."

Maria froze and looked down at the shimmery frock. Her eyebrows wrinkled together with confusion. "What?"

Kaethe reached toward the back of the low shelf on the other side of the room.

"Here, these are from Elvira Wall," she presented a pair of brown canvas shoes to Maria, whose eyes lit up at the sight of them.

"For me? Really, Mama?"

"Yes, their youngest daughter outgrew them so she asked me if you would want them. I said you'd be thrilled. But I can always give them to someone else if you don't want them." Kaethe couldn't hide a smile as she started to turn away, the shoes still in her hands. Maria's hand grabbed Kaethe's elbow and pulled her back.

"No! I want them! Thank you!"

Maria took the shoes from Kaethe's hand and sat on the nearest chair. She slipped her dirty feet into the shoes and tied the laces with minimal difficulty. She stood, admiring the simple shoes.

"They're perfect!"

—

Christmas Eve arrived without trumpets and horns. It came silently, almost forgotten amongst all the preparations for their upcoming move. With the women in their new dresses, and Maria wearing her new-to-her shoes, the four of them walked down the dust-laden streets together, until the not so surprising moment when Kaethe exclaimed she forgot her purse.

Maria knew the scheme well by now, but humoured her mother nonetheless. Kaethe turned back toward the house to supposedly fetch her purse, but Maria knew she used this time alone at the house to place the gifts under the tree. Johann, Anna and Maria continued walking to the school. Maria's lips moved as they walked, quietly rehearsing the lines to the poem she was to recite that night.

Maria was often chosen to recite poetry during the Christmas Eve service. Memorizing came naturally to her, and she loved being asked to say them. Maria beamed from the stage as she said the final line, before sitting back down beside Johann. He squeezed her shoulder, his own pride radiating from his upturned lips. The pastor led the congregation in singing *Stille Nacht*, Silent Night, Maria's favourite carol, before blessing them with a benediction.

Once home, Anna brought the oil lamp to the counter. With a spoon, she poured peanut oil into the bowl, not quite filling it to the brim. A jar of scrap fabric strips sat on the shelf beneath the counter and she placed a strip into the bowl and waited for it to saturate with oil. Once soaked through, she pulled the slick, wet fabric through the glass top and made sure it was secure. With a match, she lit the fabric, illuminating the room with a dull glow. *Tweeback* and cold cuts were placed on the table, and all four of them found their seats.

Maria eyed the small box under the tree throughout their entire meal. Until a few years ago, she had unwrapped the same gift every Christmas – her beloved handmade doll, washed and mended. Much to Kaethe's chagrin, she hadn't been able to afford anything else for Maria. However, having lost interest in playing with dolls in recent years, the doll no longer sufficed as an acceptable Christmas gift.

Anticipation stirred in Maria's chest as she opened the small rectangular box wrapped in a pillowcase. She slowly unfolded the linen, and reached inside. Her hand felt a wooden box and she pulled it out.

"Dominoes!" she exclaimed as she read the writing on the box.

The four of them sat around the table and played Dominoes until well into the night, laughing constantly. Of all the things Kaethe could not offer Maria, love was not one of them. Emotion welled in her throat as she looked around the table at the three people she loved more than anything in the world, and who loved her and her daughter just the same.

—

A few weeks later, the family sold everything they owned, save for their clothes, some of their furniture, and their hens. The house they moved into in Filadelfia was of comparable size to their home in No. 6. Maria and Kaethe shared a bedroom inside the main house, which was just off the kitchen. Outside, a covered walkway separated the main house from the other bedroom where Johann and Anna slept. The yard was much smaller, but at least they didn't have to work the fields anymore, and they had their own cistern to store water. They sold their wagon to another family in No. 6, not wanting the responsibility of caring for a horse, and no longer having need for one, as everything in Filadelfia was within walking distance.

The town was divided by a long, wide street, Hindenburgstrasse – named after President von Hindenburg. The Cooperative was located on that street, along with most of the other shops and businesses. The streets that crossed the main road were divided into lots, each one a hectare in size, with a small house in the middle of each lot. There were a few workshops off the main street, and the school Maria would attend was a few blocks from their new home, past a woodshop, and down another block.

Maria was nervous to start Year Six in a new school, but her teacher, Lehrer Stahl, was smart and engaging, and she loved learning from him. She sat at the front of the class, and quickly fell in love with German history. Lehrer Stahl brought history to life. The way he connected with his students made even the *Deutscher Bund*, German Confederation, sound exhilarating. He had quite the sense of humour, and Maria laughed often during class.

The sound of her laugh was contagious – free-spirited and loud, with no shame or fear of judgement. It wasn't only her laugh that drew people to her, though. Within a few weeks, Maria befriended most of the girls in her class, and quite a few boys. She was particularly fond of a girl named Tina. They lived a few streets apart and waited for each other every morning just past the main road to walk the rest of the way to school together. By the end of the school year, Maria had a busy social life, always visiting someone, and life in Filadelfia was beginning to feel normal.

—

Pages of notes were scattered across the ground. Tina leaned against the fence of the school yard, her knees bent. A notebook rested on her lap. Their final exam was next week, and if they passed, they could move on to *Zentralschule*, high school, the following March.

Maria wasn't worried. She consistently scored ones, the highest grade, in all her years at school. Learning came naturally to her, but that was not the case for Tina. Tina worked hard to maintain her high grades. She studied for hours, toiling over facts and equations until they finally made sense, at least somewhat.

"You know, I used to be the smartest in the class before you came around," Tina's tone was jovial, but Maria sensed a hint of resentment.

"I'm sorry," Maria winked at her friend and took another bite of her bun. "Aren't you going to eat your snack? Come to think of it, you didn't eat your lunch earlier, either." Tina's lunch bag lay open, its contents uneaten.

"I'm not hungry. I can't eat when I'm nervous."

Maria shrugged and continued eating while she read over her notes on the Habsburg Monarchy of Germany. She knew she should review some of the mathematics exercises, but she was too fascinated by Habsburg. She reread it now out of sheer pleasure, having already memorized everything there was to know about the topic.

The bell rang, signalling the end of their morning break. Maria and Tina gathered their notes and walked back into class.

—

It poured on the day of the exam. Tina and Maria ran with their backpacks over their heads. Their white stockings were soaked through with mud by the time they reached the school. They stopped to catch their breath under the overhang at the doors, wiping the wetness from their skin. Tina leaned against a post, her eyes closed.

"Tina? Are you ill?" Maria touched her friend's shoulder.

"I'm fine. It's just the nerves, I'm sure," she tried to sound reassuring and forced her lips to curve into a weak smile. The dark circles under her eyes, and the paleness of her skin, led Maria to believe otherwise.

"What was the name of the first ruler of Habsburg again?" The brows over Tina's eyes morphed into one as she pinched the bridge of her nose and wracked her brain to find the piece of information she had lost.

"Ferdinand I," Maria replied, incredulously scanning her friend.

"Right, I knew that."

When they walked into the school, some of the desks were already occupied. Papers rustled loudly in the classroom, last minute attempts to ingrain every piece of information into their minds. Maria recognized a few familiar faces from her class, but the others were unknown to her. Every Year Six student from all the villages in Fernheim gathered at the Zentralschule of Filadelfia for the exam.

Someone called her name as she hung her dripping backpack on the hook in the hallway.

"Viktor!" Maria reached out her arms and embraced her old classmate and friend. She hadn't seen Viktor since they left Friedensruh No. 6. "How are you doing? Is Susa coming, too?" She peered over his shoulder, searching the crowd for signs of her friend.

"No, I'm the only one coming from No. 6," he replied. Maria's heart sunk, but she smiled despite her disappointment.

"Never mind, then. How are you doing? Tell me everything that's happened since I left!"

They found two empty desks beside each other and sat down. Tina sat a few desks in front of her, clearly not doing well under pressure. Lehrer Stahl appeared at the front of the class and ordered everyone to sit before relaying the instructions for the exam. Viktor tapped his foot nervously, and Tina scratched her head with her pencil. Maria felt calm, she was confident with her efforts in preparing for this day.

The teacher walked around and placed an exam face down on each desk. When he returned to the front, he looked at his watch with his forefinger raised in the air in anticipation.

"You may be—"

A loud thud interrupted his words. He looked down in front of him where Tina's body lay bent over itself. A few students screamed. Maria hurried to her friend's side, holding her head in her lap. It was only a matter of seconds before Tina's eyes opened wide, full of shock and embarrassment. They fetched her some water and Maria held it to her lips as she drank.

"I'm okay now," Tina assured them, pushing herself off the ground.

"You need to eat something, Tina," Maria urged her. She looked at the teacher who nodded in agreement. Maria went to Tina's bag and placed a guava on Tina's desk. Tina took a bite and waved Maria aside, but Maria refused to leave.

"Tina, you haven't eaten or slept in days. You shouldn't be here."

"What are you talking about? I'm fine." She lingered on the "I" in fine, and Maria rolled her eyes.

Lehrer Stahl agreed that Tina was not fit to take the test that day and sent her home, making her promise to eat and sleep as soon as she got home, and told her she could take the test the following day.

Once everyone had settled back into their seats, Lehrer Stahl looked at the clock again and the exams commenced.

—

The rest of the exam was uneventful. Maria finished first, and left the building right away. When she got to the end of the street where the woodshop was, she turned left onto Hindenburgstrasse instead of right. She walked to the Cooperative to buy a few items Kaethe had scribbled on a piece of paper for her that morning.

The weight of the basket made Maria limp as she walked down the aisle. She scanned the items on her list – flour, beans, white thread, and other dry goods. The only thing left to add to her basket was milk. She walked toward the back of the store and placed a jar of milk in her basket.

As she stood in line, she thought about Viktor, and the others still writing the exam. Maria was excited to go to *Zentralschule*. Her thoughts wandered to what the next few years of school would entail as she waited to pay for her items. Maybe she would become a teacher, herself, but that was unlikely. She frowned. Teachers were mostly men. A nurse? She smiled at the thought, but it quickly faded. Nursing school was too expensive.

Her daydream was interrupted by a sudden warmth between her legs. She froze, frantically deciphering what was happening. Maybe it was nothing? No, it was definitely something. The slow trickle of some kind of liquid ran down her thigh. Fear shot through her veins and her cheeks flushed with terror. She placed the basket on the floor and ran home as quickly as she could.

When she was finally inside the house, she was breathing heavily. Kaethe sat at her new automatic sewing machine, and jumped at Maria's abrupt entrance.

"Michi! Is everything all right?" She draped the shirt over the back of her chair and came to Maria's side.

Maria told her what had happened, and began to cry. Kaethe smiled.

"Oh, Michi, it's nothing to worry about. You've simply started your monthlies."

Maria looked her mother in the eyes, relieved that she wasn't dying, and dried her eyes. She felt instantly ridiculous for crying about it. She should have known. All her friends were starting to bleed, it was only a matter of time before she did, as well. Then her chest puffed up slightly – this meant she was a woman now. She felt a strange sense of accomplishment. In her mind, she had reached a new level in society, in life. She wasn't a child anymore. Perhaps next she could get a new pair of leather shoes, with a bit of a heel. The thought made her smile, and her mother's proud stare brought her back to the present moment, and she blushed.

When she had fully regained her composure, Kaethe brought Maria into their bedroom. She opened a drawer in the dresser and explained how Maria would need to keep herself clean. In the drawer was a stack of fabric, cut in long, wide strips. Beside it was a bowl filled with cotton. Kaethe laid a fabric strip along her hand.

"Grab a handful of cotton and put it on top," she explained as she went through the motions. "Then, grab another strip of flannel and place it on top, like so."

Maria watched in wonderment. She noted the way her mother, well-practiced, made it look easy and natural. She wanted to model the same sureness and femininity that she saw in her mother. Maria listened to the rest of the instructions, and did as she was told.

Family portrait taken around 1923. Maria age five or six.

Maria (7) on the left. Holding the doll she got at school from the German visitors.

Kaethe (28) and Maria (9), wearing her favourite red dress with lace collar.
Photo taken around 1938.

Their home in Filadelfia. The building closest to the camera was an addition built in the 1960s.

PART THREE

12

May 1943

MARIA WALKED AT A LEISURELY PACE TOWARD THE END OF HER STREET. SHE squinted her eyes and read the blurred white letters of 'Hindenburgstrasse' and turned right. She did a mental review of the notes she would be tested on that morning. North American history was not as interesting to her as German history, but she preferred any history over mathematics or science.

She saw the familiar shape of the woodshop approaching on the next corner. Once there, she would cross the street and walk another block to the school. The building's four walls and roof were all made from wood planks. A large opening on either side of the shop allowed the workers to enter and exit, but there were no doors or shutters on any of the openings. As she neared the woodshop, she saw someone leaning against a doorframe beside a stack of wooden wagon wheels.

Not wanting to be impolite and stare, she kept her eyes on the road in front of her. The figure was obviously male, and tall, with a lean body and long limbs. There was a sort of haze or cloud around his face. She couldn't make out the colour of his eyes, but knew his hair was blond from the few strands peeking out from beneath his cap.

Maria felt his gaze fixed on her but she refused to look at him. She crossed the street sooner than she usually would, and quickened her pace. The man whistled, one upturned note followed by a lower one – a catcall if she'd ever heard one. Caught off guard, Maria stopped walking but didn't turn around.

It took all her will not to give the man a piece of her mind, and also not to run the rest of the way to school. Tina noticed her agitation when she reached Tina's house, but Maria was too furious to speak. She felt violated somehow. Why did that man think it was appropriate to whistle at a young woman? Clearly he was no man, at all. Merely an immature boy acting on natural impulses rather than respect. Her heart was pounding.

The rest of the day dragged on as Maria's mind replayed the morning's event over and over. Her thoughts were consumed by the pompous mystery man who had the audacity to whistle at her. Rudeness aside, she couldn't understand why he would whistle at her. Tina, she could understand. Her body was slender and delicate, her bosom full and her hair thick and a luxuriously rich brown. Maria possessed none of those qualities. She was short, not yet fully developed like her friend, and her hair was a dull shade of brown, and very thin. Was he making fun of her, perhaps? The thought made her frown.

After parting ways with Tina on their walk home from school, Maria pulled her book out of her bag and began to read. Distraction would help ease her mind. She had been anxious about walking past the woodshop after school. She reread a paragraph, not able to focus on the words. A small wet drop appeared out of nowhere and fell on a 'S'. The defined curves of the letter slowly merged into one blob of black ink, drawn to the centre of the droplet. The sky above her was dark; angry clouds hovered close to the earth. A soft rumble moved across the sky and a raindrop fell on Maria's nose.

A loud crack startled her and echoed throughout the town. She flinched as another drop landed on her face, and then her book. Within seconds, the clouds gave way and rain fell with fury. Maria ran as fast as she could back to the house. She ran right past the woodshop, too concerned to get out of the rain to be bothered with the mystery man.

She found shelter in the passageway between the house and her grandparents' room. The book she had been reading was ruined. The pages soaked and unreadable, the ink running into one black mess. She loosened her hair from the pins that kept the fine strands in place and shook her head like a wet dog. Her clothes clung to her skin, and she shivered, desperately wanting to find dry clothes.

Her mother and grandparents were huddled around the kitchen table, their heads close together. Maria stood behind them, peering over their shoulders. They didn't hear her come home, and seemed to be oblivious to the torrential rain falling outside the window, despite the racket it produced. The object of their attention lay on the table in front of them. Maria craned her neck to get a better view.

"*Waut es daut?*"

The three adults jumped at the sound of her voice, moving for the first time since Maria came home.

"Michi!" Kaethe exhaled, her hand over her pounding heart. "You scared us half to death!"

"What is that?" Maria ignored her mother's melodrama.

"*Ne Birn*, a lightbulb," Johann answered. He picked up the glass ball and moved toward the middle of the room where a cable hung over a wooden beam from the ceiling. He stood on a chair positioned underneath the cord and turned the metal end of the bulb into the opening of the cord.

"How does it work?" Maria asked, intrigued. The Cooperative was equipped with electricity, so she had seen lights before, but never this close. Johann stepped off the chair and walked to the counter where the other end of the cord was attached to a small box with a toggle switch.

"Ready?" he asked them.

The women nodded silently. He flicked the switch with his thumb and instantly light appeared above them. They cheered and clapped as they looked at the magical invention illuminating the room.

"We can only use it from Monday to Saturday every week, from morning until ten o'clock in the evening."

Maria held the small box in her hand and pulled the toggle switch toward her with her finger. The light disappeared. She tried it a few times, and was amazed every time the light turned on and off. No more holding books beside a candle flame to read at night, or squinting while sewing, hoping the seams would actually line up. *This simple little addition to our home will significantly improve our lives,* she thought.

"Well," Kaethe interrupted Maria's thoughts, "now that that's sorted out, we need to go to the eye doctor, otherwise we'll be late for your appointment."

Maria quickly changed into dry clothes. The sun was already shining but the roads were still covered with mud and puddles. The ground absorbed her feet with each step, like a vacuum. By the time they arrived at the doctor's office, her shoes were covered in thick mud.

―

Maria could tell the sign was white, but that was as much detail she could give. That, and that the doctor wore a white cotton jacket that was a few sizes too small for his protruding midsection. And he smelled of body odour, though that much could be confirmed without sight.

"What letters can you read from here?" the doctor asked her from across the room.

"Nothing," Maria replied. He took a few steps closer, intensifying the strength of his body odour. She held her breath and tried not to make any rude facial expressions. She focused on the board in front of her. Her nose scrunched up like a rabbit.

"E?" It was more of a question than a fact. The black letters blurred into each other, formless. "I think it's an E. And then, um, another E? Maybe a T?"

The doctor took another step forward and Maria gagged as a waft of his scent went in her nose. He stood a few feet away from her now.

"E, F, P, er, T? O, Z, L, F? E, D. The rest of them are just black smudges"

"Well, it's obvious, Miss Penner, that your eyesight is very poor."

Maria scrutinized the plump man in front of her. *How long did he have to go to school to make that diagnosis,* she wondered.

"I'll do my best to fit you with a pair of glasses that should clear things up a bit for you." He snorted at his own joke, making his stomach bounce up and down. Maria wasn't amused and regarded him flatly.

The frames of her new spectacles were round and made from black metal. She held them delicately in her hands, afraid to break them with her calloused fingers. Uncertain of what to expect, she slowly raised the glasses to her face and placed them on her nose, tucking the curved ends around her ears. She looked up and started at the sight of the doctor's face. She backed away, surveying him and the small office. Crisp, clear objects came into view – a stark contrast to the fuzzy, muddled shapes she was used to seeing for so many years.

Emotion caught in her throat like a knot. She thanked the doctor and walked outside while Kaethe paid for the glasses. She knew her mother worked long hours to afford them, and she had felt guilty about her mother spending that much money on her, but now that she wore the glasses, and could see every-thing around her, she was beyond grateful.

The sky was clear and the sun sat directly above her, highlighting every tree, house, and wagon in the near vicinity. It felt as if she was seeing the world for the very first time, and she didn't know whether to smile with excitement, or cry from the beauty she beheld.

She could see children kicking a ball at the end of the street, and the clear, white letters of the Hindenburgstrasse sign at the corner of the intersection.

"Ready?" Kaethe touched Maria's shoulder. Maria turned around and hugged her mother.

"*Danksheen*, Mama."

"You're welcome, Michi."

⸺

"Aren't you special now?" A boy in her class teased Maria the following day after school. "First, some fancy new glasses, and then what? A refrigerator?" An uproar of laughter followed from the group gathered outside the school.

"You don't have to brag about how much money your family has, you know. It's not very *kjristlijch*, Christian-like," another boy chimed in.

Maria's neck and face went red as she listened to their juvenile comments.

"You think I'm bragging?" she retorted. "Do you think I would spend my mother's money on a pair of glasses if I didn't need them?" The pulse in her neck throbbed as her volume and fury rose. "I don't need to prove anything to you."

With that, she slung her backpack over her shoulder and stormed off. Dust billowed around her feet as she stomped down the street. She kept her head down until she got to the intersection where the woodshop was. That man had been there every morning for the last few weeks, and every morning he whistled at her, without fail. Every now and then he would see her walking home from school and take the opportunity to whistle at her then, as well.

Inhaling deeply, she crossed the street, hoping he wouldn't see her today. She exhaled when she was a few steps passed the shop and hadn't seen him. Then she heard the familiar whistle, followed by a deep voice.

"*Schmock Brell*, nice glasses."

Maria stopped walking. Her hands clenched into fists at her sides. Her chest heaved as she tried to control her temper, but failed. She turned on her heels and walked right up to the man. When she reached him, he stood mere inches away from her, and towered over her. Seeing him clearly for the first time, she suddenly forgot what she was going to say.

His eyes locked on hers and drew her into him. Pools of blue sapphires, stirring her soul in a way she had never experienced before. She stared at them and her fists relaxed, as did the folds between her eyebrows. With a start, she pulled herself together and pushed a pointed index finger forcefully on his chest as she spoke.

"I've had enough of your whistling! That is no way to treat a lady! Have you no respect?"

With that, she turned on her heels, not waiting for a response, and walked away from him, fighting the urge to turn back and look at his eyes once more. Focused on her steps, she prayed she wouldn't trip and make a fool of herself in her grand exit. At the next street, she glanced back toward the woodshop, but the man with the beguiling eyes was gone.

—

Maria sat on her bed, holding a mirror in front of her. Nearly half a year later, the mysterious woodworker continued harassing Maria with whistles every morning and afternoon. Though it irritated her fiercely, she struggled to think about anyone, or anything, other than him. They hadn't exchanged words with each other since Maria's outburst the day she had gotten her glasses. She knew nothing about him, not even his name, yet his image plagued her thoughts.

Tired of the reflection looking back at her, she placed the mirror back on the nightstand. She tightened a few pins in her hair and shifted the white cotton dress so it sat evenly on her waist. The morning sun glistened her skin and she reached for a handkerchief in the drawer and dabbed her forehead. She fastened the buckles on her white leather sandals and hung her purse in the crook of her elbow.

The family walked together, two by two, toward the church. Johann walked beside Maria. His weathered skin drooped slightly on his face, and the coarse, grey whiskers above his lip sat unruly, despite his efforts to comb them before they left. His eyes were dark, shaded from the sun by the brim of his favourite brown pork pie hat. Kaethe and Anna dabbed their necks with handkerchiefs, and fanned themselves as they walked.

A large crowd gathered outside the church, and Maria found her place at the front with the other girls dressed in similar white frocks. The boys wore white shirts and trousers, and stood at the end of the line. Those were all the candidates that would be baptized that day. In front of them, a small pool dug into the ground was filled with water. One by one, each candidate stepped into the pool, where the pastor stood waiting, clothes wet from the waist down.

As she waited for her turn, her mind wandered again to the whistler. Her eyes searched the faces behind her. She found herself looking for him, for whatever reason. She had never seen him at church before, and she chided herself for thinking he would be amongst the congregation today. And why did she even care? He made her blood boil every morning, and she had no desire to meet him or know him.

Then she saw them – those gem-like eyes that made her feel completely exposed and vulnerable. She looked toward the pool of water, hoping he hadn't seen her staring at him. Her heart pounded in her chest as she felt a rush of blood move up her neck.

Get a hold of yourself, Maria, she told herself.

When it was Maria's turn, she handed her spectacles to her mother and descended the stairs into the pool. She gripped the makeshift railing as she felt blindly for the next step under her feet. The water was warm, heated by the sun the previous day, but Maria still shivered when she reached the bottom.

"Do you believe that Jesus is the Son of God, that He died on the cross, and on the third day rose from the dead for the forgiveness of your sins?" The pastor recited the obligatory questions.

"I do," Maria replied confidently. Another shiver moved down her spine, this time from the keen awareness that he was watching her, whoever he was.

"And do you desire the fullness of God's Holy Spirit in your life, that you may live a life that is pleasing to God in every way?"

"I do."

"Then it is my pleasure to baptize you in the name of the Father, of the Son, and of the Holy Spirit."

Maria raised her arms out of the water and crossed them over her chest. The pastor placed one hand between her shoulder blades, and the other on her folded hands, and dipped her into the pool so she was fully immersed. She winced as he bent her backwards, sending a shooting pain down her back, into her legs.

When she emerged out of the water, she wiped her eyes with wet hands, grabbed hold of the blurred railing on the other end of the pool, and pulled herself out of the water. Her mother was waiting for her there, and Maria positioned her glasses on her nose and around her ears. Her mother's face beamed, her eyes glistening with joyful tears. Kaethe wrapped a towel around Maria and ushered her into the building to change.

Donning fresh, dry clothes, Maria made her way through the crowd after the service to find Tina. There was little room to move, bodies bounded into each other as they searched for friends or family. She could see Tina through the sea of people, but before she could make it to her, someone walked by her, bumping her on the shoulder. She tripped and fell to the ground.

"Ow!"

"I'm so sorry," a deep, soothing voice apologized as he instantly offered his hand. Maria accepted and placed her hand in his. He pulled her to her feet easily. Maria brushed the dust off the back of her dress with her hands.

"It's okay, it's not your—" she adjusted her glasses and looked at the man responsible for her fall. He was tall, towering at least a foot above her five-feet-two-inches. The sun hid directly behind his head, casting a warm, ethereal glow around his blond hair. She looked into his sapphire eyes, intently locked on hers, and equally as shocked to see her, as she was to see him.

"Oh, h-hello," he stammered.

"Hi," her mouth was dry and she wasn't sure if her greeting had been audible. His shock quickly turned to delight, and his lip turned up on one side. His eyes sparkled even more when he smiled, she noted.

"I don't think we've officially met," he offered his hand to her again, "I'm Jacob."

Jacob held a measuring stick against a piece of wood. He drew two lines and removed the ruler. With a saw in his left hand, he moved the sharp metal teeth back and forth over the markings. His hair fell forward, bouncing wildly as he moved his arm. The piece of wood fell to the ground and he wiped his brow with his sleeve before moving to the next marking.

He was having a hard time concentrating on his work. As usual, his thoughts revolved around the girl from up the street. He still didn't know her name. He hoped his chance encounter with her after the baptism the day before would have started something between them, but she ran off right after he introduced himself to her. She had looked utterly terrified, possibly even disgusted – he didn't know enough about women to differentiate their facial expressions.

Maybe he should just move on and forget about her. Clearly nothing was going to happen if it hadn't already, and there were still plenty of other young women in the village he could pursue. He shook his head. He didn't want another young woman, he wanted the girl with the bright smile and deep, soulful brown eyes. The girl who made his heart palpitate every time she walked by. The girl who wasn't afraid to speak her mind and put him in his place. The girl who made him lose all reason and logic and caused him to involuntarily whistle at her.

Jacob let out a deep sigh. He honestly didn't know what had possessed him to whistle at her the first time he watched her pass by his work. It was his first day at his new job, having just moved to Filadelfia from Kleefeld No. 2, another village in Fernheim. He arrived at work early that day and was smoking a cigarette while waiting for his boss to tell him what to do. That was when he saw her in the distance.

She hadn't seemed to notice him, but there was no denying the fact he was attracted to her. Her hips danced as she walked toward him and he smiled. She was about to cross the street, still oblivious to his existence, when he caught himself whistling, but it was too late to stop it. He cringed instantly, berating himself for acting so immature, and equally as surprised at his forwardness.

Why he didn't end the whistling after that first episode, he still didn't have an answer for it. Somehow, her disapproval of it amused him, in an endearing way. Her cheeks reddened every time he whistled, and if her hands were free, they curled into small fists. He laughed at the thought of her ever trying to hit him, but then flushed at the thought of her touching him. Even their brief encounter the day before, when their hands touched momentarily, sent a spark through his veins. It made him think that maybe he should start going to church, after all.

The few Sundays his parents dragged him to church, he searched for her, but he always left as soon as the benediction was finished. He knew if he wanted more opportunities to see her, he could go to the *Jügent Owent*, youth nights, where she was sure to attend. But his aversion to faith, and his need for authenticity, kept him away from any church-related functions. If he didn't believe he needed to have a personal relationship with Jesus to live a good life, then he wouldn't go to church. And that wasn't an option. He would have to find another way.

If he couldn't get to know her outside of their brief encounters when she walked by the shop, he would have to come to his own conclusions about her, based on his observations. What he did know was that she walked past his work at a quarter-to-seven every morning, and just after noon every afternoon, except

Sundays, which was also his day off. From the backpack slung over her shoulders, he figured she was heading to *Zentralschule*, which was in the same direction she walked to and from every day. If that was the case, she was anywhere between thirteen and seventeen years old. Her body was somewhat developed already, which made him blush to think about, and her hair was always neatly pinned on top of her head. She must be at least fifteen or sixteen, he guessed. He would be nineteen next week, so fifteen wasn't too young, in his opinion.

He turned his attention back to his work, keeping an eye on the street behind him. It was nearly twelve o'clock, which meant she would be walking home soon. He hoped today would be the day he could finally talk to her, maybe even start a friendship with her. But he didn't want to get too carried away in his expectations. Consumed for a moment with the wheel spoke in front of him, he nearly missed his opportunity. By the time he looked up, the back of Maria's head passed by the window. He ran out the door with a sense of urgency.

"So, we meet again!" The words came out louder than he intended and startled Maria. The textbooks she carried fell to the ground. She bent to pick them up and he rushed to her side, reaching for a book. "I'm so, so sorry. I didn't mean to scare you."

Jacob felt terrible. He could tell she was angry. If only he hadn't looked up and seen her pass by, then none of this would have happened.

"Well, if you didn't want to scare me, then maybe you shouldn't have jumped out behind me and yelled at me!" She glared at him.

"I really am sorry," he tried again. Not wanting the moment to pass by, he added, "Please, tell me your name."

The genuine sincerity in his voice seemed to have softened Maria's hatred for a moment. She looked into his eyes, and he swallowed hard. He had never met anyone that could unravel him with one glance. She grabbed the last book out of his hands and blew the dust off its cover. They stood in front of each other, though Maria kept her eyes fixed on the books in her hand.

"I have to go," she whispered and began walking.

"At least let me walk you home?"

"I can find my way just fine on my own, thank you."

She moved past him and he watched her walk away. He lowered his head and resigned to leave her alone, she clearly wanted nothing to do with him. He kicked the pile of wagon wheels, irritated at himself for handling the situation the way he had. Never again would he whistle at a girl, he consigned, but he doubted he'd ever come across another girl whose attention he would want to attract the way he longed for Maria's.

—

The next morning, Maria left earlier than usual for school, hoping to avoid running into Jacob. The sky was awake, bright colours blending into one another above her. Cacti were blooming, and she stopped to smell a few of her favourites along the way.

She was nearly at the woodshop when she saw him. He was leaning against the stack of wheels, one foot crossed over the other. A cloud of smoke lingered around his head. Why couldn't she get away from him? She straightened her back and pulled back her shoulders. The last thing she wanted to do was give him any reason to gloat or feel like he had any effect on her life whatsoever.

Jacob saw her as she approached the shop and put out his cigarette. He moved away from the wheels and stood directly in front of her. Maria stopped but ignored him and looked at something across the street.

"I know you're mad at me," he started, "and you have every right to be. I just want to apologize for yesterday. I didn't mean to scare you. And for all the whistling, I'm sorry. It won't happen again. I'll leave you alone."

Jacob tipped his cap toward her as he nodded his head. He smiled sombrely and backed away from her, turning into the shop when he reached the large open doorway. Maria watched him until he was out of sight. She thought she would be relieved to hear him surrender. This was what she had wanted to happen, wasn't it? Instead, she felt a loss. As if something had ended even though it hadn't yet begun.

—

"He did what?" Tina asked when Maria met her at their usual meeting place. As they walked the rest of the way to school, Maria recalled the events of the last few days to her friend, including the run-in after the baptism.

She elaborated the truth slightly, painting Jacob to be more of an imbecile than he actually was. She wasn't sure why she felt the need to make him sound terrible. Did she really think he was that bad? Was his incessant whistling as disrespectful as she made it out to be? Admittedly, she did enjoy the attention, to some degree. It boosted her confidence ever so minimally. Maybe it was the fact that she wasn't attracted to him. Had it been another boy she found especially handsome, perhaps it wouldn't bother her. Jacob was scrawny, with hardly any fat on him, but his eyes were gorgeous, she couldn't deny that.

"So, let me get this straight," Tina turned to her friend as they continued walking. "There's a man who is obviously attracted to you, who has the confidence to let you know he's interested in you, and has begged to get to know you. And you're upset about what?"

"Okay, it doesn't sound so bad when you put it that way."

"No, it doesn't. It sounds like every girl's dream come true." Tina nudged Maria with her elbow and laughed. "So, what's really the problem?"

Maria was silent for a minute. "I don't know. It just feels odd. I'm not used to getting attention from boys. I'd be lying if I said it didn't feel good. Of course it does! Besides, I don't know anything about him."

"So, get to know him! He's clearly interested in you or he would have given up long ago."

"I don't think he's a Christian, though. Aside from my baptism, I've never seen him at church."

"You don't have to marry the guy; you can just be friends, you know? Anyway, I've seen his family at church."

"You have?"

"Yeah. You've probably seen his sister, Marieche. I can't remember her last name. She helps with Sunday school. She's really nice. His parents are always there, too, and some younger siblings. At least, I think they're his siblings. They're really young, though. I wonder how many kids are in his family," she broke off, counting in her head how many children she had seen with his parents the previous Sunday. She shrugged her shoulders, losing count, and interest. "I think Marieche said they moved to Filadelfia a few months ago, but I can't remember from which village." She was quiet for a moment before blurting out, "Loewen! That's their last name." She smacked her knee in victory.

Loewen, Maria repeated in her head. *Jacob Loewen.*

"So, he can't be all that bad if his family goes to church, right?" Tina winked. "He obviously grew up going to church, if his parents still go. All I'm saying, Maria, is there's no harm in making a new friend, is there?"

Maria looked off into the distance. "No, I guess there isn't."

Jacob found it hard to concentrate on his work. He chided himself for his actions, for scaring the innocent girl. He knew that was the end of that. There was no chance for him now. Her eyes said it all – she despised him. He shook his head to erase the memory of her glare and turned his attention back on the aromatic Palo Santo wood in front of him.

"Maria."

He held his hammer in mid-air. The soft, angelic voice surprised him. He turned his head in the direction it came from. Maria stood in the giant doorway. She clutched a stack of books close to her chest, shifting her body uncomfortably, her cheeks flushed.

Jacob lowered his arm and turned the rest of his body. They stood a few feet apart but she refused to meet his eyes.

"Maria," she said again, awkwardly fingering the pages of one book. "My name. I'm Maria."

Jacob didn't say anything. He stared at her as the corners of his lips turned up. Finally, Maria looked at him, unsure of his silence. His eyes gleamed like sun dancing on the ocean. Awkward tension filled the space between them, and Maria nodded her head, as if to say goodbye, and turned to go.

"*Maria,*" Jacob whispered into the dusty air of the workshop. He punched the air with his fist in jubilation. Maybe it wasn't the end, after all.

13

January 1944

KAETHE SAT IN A SHADED CORNER BEHIND THE HOUSE. TEMPERATURES HAD reached a new high for that summer, and her clothes clung to her dampened skin. Their dog, Muppy, lay by her feet, tongue hanging out of her mouth. Kaethe poured cold water into the *Guampa*, a hollow bull's horn, filled with dry yerba leaves. She raised the horn to her mouth and closed her lips around the *Bombilla*, a metal straw with a sieve at on the bottom to separate the small tea leaf fragments from the water.

She took another sip of *Terere* as she read the articles in the *Mennoblatt*. It was filled with the usual articles about Fernheim and other colony-related news, but one article caught her attention. Lehrer Stahl, the teacher at the Zentralschule, would be leaving for Germany the following week to continue his studies. At least that was what he had told the newspaper. She wondered if he, too, was going to support Hitler's army. A number of men had returned to Germany over the last few years, hopeful that Hitler would restore Russia to what it once was, and they could all return home. She had initially felt hopeful, as well. The thought of returning home, to the way their lives had been before Stalin ruined everything, was enticing. They received little information about the war, but from what they did know, it didn't sound promising.

She brushed the thought aside and finished reading the article. Lehrer Stahl planned to return to Filadelfia after Christmas, which meant there would be no one to run the school in his absence.

Kaethe frowned as she lowered the paper. Maria would be crushed. Kaethe took a deep breath and called Maria to join her outside. Muppy raised her head at the sudden noise. Her tail wagged in the dirt when she saw Maria coming out of the house.

Maria sat in a vacant chair and Muppy lazily positioned herself by Maria's feet.

"What is it, Mama?"

Kaethe sighed before reading the article out loud. Maria listened attentively, the colour in her face paling. Kaethe hesitated to look up. Maria's cheeks were wet with tears and the dark depths of her eyes reflected her disappointment. Her lip quivered as she processed the weight of the news.

"I'm so sorry, Michi." Kaethe tried to reassure her daughter.

"What am I going to do if I'm not in school?" Maria leaned in closer to her mother, who had kneeled down in front of her and was stroking Maria's arms.

Kaethe placed her hand gently under Maria's chin and tilted her face upwards. Maria's skin was smooth, not even a slight crease could be found on her face, unlike the wrinkles that spread outward from the corners of her own eyes. Kaethe stared at Maria, and for a moment she was looking into the eyes of her one-year-old daughter, crying on her lap as they rocked back and forth in the rocking chair on the porch. She saw the whitewashed paint of the walls of their family estate, and the white pillars on either side of the stairs that led to the front door.

As happened every time she thought of Ebenfeld, her mind went to Nikolai's family, and she wondered again if they were still alive. Would she ever see them again? Aside from Maria, there were no relations or connections to Nikolai, and that knowledge overwhelmed her. She shook her head to clear her thoughts and once again saw the familiar deep brown eyes looking at her. Maria's brows nearly touch above the bridge of her nose, arched in concern.

"Are you all right, Mama?"

"Yes, Michi, I'm fine. What did you ask again?"

Maria tilted her head to the side and eyed her mother skeptically. "Were you thinking about Papa's family again?"

How does she always know? Kaethe wondered. Her face relaxed and her mouth curved into a soft smile.

"Yes, I was." She pushed herself up on the armrest of Maria's chair and pulled her chair closer to her daughter and sat down. "It's hard to believe we may really never see them again."

"But you don't know that for sure," Maria encouraged.

Kaethe smiled at her daughter's naivety. "No, I don't know that for sure, but it is very likely the truth, regardless."

"But you don't know, Mama, they might show up yet. Don't lose hope."

Kaethe patted Maria's leg and let her hand rest on her lap. "Okay. I won't." Kaethe sighed and reached for the Guampa. She took another sip. "Now, as for you," she turned to face Maria. "You'll need to find somewhere to work this year if you're not going to be in school."

Maria's head moved up and down slowly, reluctant to accept that she would not be starting school in a couple of months. Kaethe empathized with her, but there was nothing she could do to change the circumstances.

"I'll talk to Frü Neufeld and see if she could use another seamstress."

"But I can't sew," Maria reminded her.

"Not yet, no. But you're smart." Kaethe winked at Maria, who smiled back. Kaethe straightened herself in her chair, her eyes filled with mischievousness as she set down the Guampa and eagerly turned toward Maria. "Now, tell me about this Jacob boy."

—

Maria wandered through the Cooperative with an empty basket hanging from the crook of her elbow. Her mind was elsewhere that morning, and she found herself meandering slowly and mindlessly down each aisle. She held the yellowed paper marked with the few items she needed to purchase. Milk was at the top of the list, yet she walked right by the dairy section without grabbing a bottle.

She should have started school that day. She should be in class, learning, not picking up groceries. She had prayed relentlessly, begging God to send another teacher to step in so she could go to school. No one came to her rescue, her prayer going unanswered, and she was disappointed, as much as she tried not to be.

Maria stared at a pile of beans until she felt a gentle tap on her shoulder. She turned around, aroused from her mindless state, and saw Jacob standing before her.

"Oh. Hi." Maria blurted out, and instantly chastised herself for not being more calm and collected.

Jacob smiled endearingly, "*Goodendach*, good morning." Noticing her empty basket he added, "Just get here?"

Maria followed his gaze and suddenly flushed when she realized she hadn't yet grabbed any of the items on her list. She looked around, trying to find a clock. How long had she been in here already, and why was her basket still empty? And how long had Jacob been watching her? She was growing more embarrassed by the second.

"Uh, no, actually I've just been browsing mostly. You know, checking my options." She forced a weak smile.

Jacob moved his body to the side, looking past her at the beans. "Seems you only have two options here – garbanzo or black."

Maria looked at him quizzically. "What?" She turned around and saw the bins of dry beans behind her. "Oh, right. Yes. Black it is." She grabbed a bag and shoveled a small scoop of beans into it, even though beans weren't on the list. She felt foolish enough as it was, she didn't need to give him more reason to think her completely insane.

"I know we didn't get off to a very good start, Maria, but I would very much like to be friends. Would it be all right with you if I came by tonight? We could talk and get to know each other better."

The sound of her name as it rolled off his tongue made her unexpectedly giddy. Her heart softened as she looked into his eyes, and she smiled at the sheepish way he fidgeted with the hat he held in his hands. He was being genuine, she could tell.

She let out a long sigh. "Very well. You can come by my house tonight." She turned to walk away but paused for a moment. Without turning to face him again, she added, "But let me be clear – you're only coming as a friend."

—

Maria's stomach fluttered with anxiety as she smoothed out her hair, and buttoned up her blouse. She knew she wasn't attracted to Jacob as more than a friend, yet the thought of him sparked something inside her. This was a new feeling for her. Boys had always been just that – boys. When she was younger, they were her playmates, and as she got older, they were friends. But never had she felt any chemistry with any of them.

Perhaps it was because Jacob actually showed interest in her. The boys in her class never acted as if they saw her as anything other than a friend. She didn't mind, and she didn't blame them. She wasn't what she considered to be an attractive young woman. She was plain, simple. It had never bothered her, either, that she was never sought after like Tina or Helga often were. That was just the way it was, and had always been, and she was used to it.

But Jacob was different. As much as she despised his incessant whistles, she somehow liked his attention. Was it his age? At twenty years old, he had a maturity about him that the boys in her class lacked. He was the second oldest in a family of twelve children, as she had heard through the grapevine. Perhaps his older brother role added to his charm, especially since she came from a family with no siblings.

Maria was only fifteen, though her birthday was only a few months away. Being nearly five years younger than him, she couldn't help but wonder why he was so keen on her. She was still in high school. Surely there were other girls, older girls – women – who would better suit him.

There was a knock on the door. Her mother and grandparents were at the church for prayer meeting, leaving the house eerily quiet without them. Maria was suddenly keenly aware that she would be here, alone, with Jacob. She took a deep breath and smoothed one final hair back into place.

"Hi," she said nervously when she opened the door.

"Hi," his voice came out like a song, cracking slightly. She could tell he was nervous, too, but he seemed eager to be there.

She pointed at two chairs on the porch and they sat down. The light from the kitchen illuminated their faces on one side, the other sides darkened by shadows. There was an awkward, silent tension between them. They stayed quiet for some time, looking straight ahead, shifting their bodies every now and then.

"So—" they both began speaking simultaneously, followed by an awkward laugh.

"You go first," Jacob offered.

"I was going to ask, when did your family arrive in Paraguay?"

Jacob leaned back into his chair. "Since 1931. My dad wanted desperately to go to Canada, but Mother had trachoma so we weren't able to. We waited in Germany for another year, though most of the Mennonites had already left. Canada wasn't allowing any more refugees in, so eventually Father gave up and we came to Paraguay."

"And you settled in Kleefeld No. 2?"

"Yeah, for the first twelve years or so. And then we moved here. What about you? Where did your family originally settle?"

"Friedensruh No. 6."

"When did you move to Filadelfia?"

"In 1941. We moved just before I started Year Six."

"Were you excited to move?"

Maria laughed, "No, not at all. I didn't want to leave my friends. But I knew it was best for Mama, and Oma and Opa."

"Is that who you live with?"

"Yeah, it's just the four of us here."

"Where's your dad?"

"He died when I was two. A typhus epidemic went around shortly after we arrived."

"I'm so sorry. I heard about that. Lots of people died in a very short time."

"Yes, they did. But I don't remember anything about it, just stories that Mama has told me."

"So, aside from your friends, do you miss anything else from No. 6?"

Maria thought for a moment before answering. "Fresh sugar cane syrup! Mmm. Oma always boiled it to perfection. It tasted so good on freshly baked *tweeback*."

Maria smiled at the memory and turned to face Jacob. He was staring at her intently and she felt the familiar warmth move up her neck and cheeks, an occurrence that was happening all too often in his presence these days. She looked away and wondered again what it was about this boy that affected her so much.

Maria changed the subject and asked Jacob about his younger years growing up in Siberia. He was only eight when they left Russia, so his memories were vague. He told her things he had overheard his parents discussing when they thought they were alone, terrible things about the concentration camps Mennonite men had been sent to. Maria prayed her grandparents and uncles were not in those camps; the thought that they might have been made her stomach tighten. Jacob went on, repeating all the things his parents had said, and what he had since read about the corruptness of the nation as a whole since Stalin became the leader of Russia. At the mention of Stalin's name, Jacob's shoulders stiffened, and his jaw clenched. She had seen similar reactions from other Mennonites before, whenever *that* name came up.

The air was heavy around them as they reflected on the past. Eager to lighten the mood, Maria asked Jacob about his hobbies. From there, their conversations flowed from one topic to another, without divulging any deep, personal details of their lives. Maria was adamant that there be no reason for Jacob to think she had changed her mind about her stance on their friendship. She kept her questions neutral, and whenever she felt her guard coming down, she quickly changed the subject, bringing it back to something neutral.

By the end of the night, they had shared stories about their families, their likes and dislikes, and things they enjoyed doing in their free time. Maria found herself laughing often throughout the evening. Jacob had a witty sense of humour, and she enjoyed the way he told stories. She was even more drawn to his eyes in those moments, as he smiled with each memory, or made cheeky comments to her. The blues of his irises shone, like light catching the edges of a finely carved jewel. Maria was mesmerized.

As the evening went on, Maria felt more at ease in Jacob's presence. She relaxed and was able to be herself. He seemed to be enjoying himself, as well. She noted the way he leaned back in his chair, with his arms behind his head, and one leg resting on top of the other knee. Every now and then she caught his gaze, and he'd blush and turn to face the sky. She smiled, too, mildly entertained by the effect she apparently had on him.

All of a sudden, the light streaming through the open window vanished. They stopped talking for the first time that night, and looked toward the house. The village was nothing but darkness, save for the blanket of stars in the sky.

"I guess it's ten o'clock," Maria said, and they both laughed.

"Perhaps that's my cue to leave," Jacob said with a sigh and placed his hands on his thighs, making a clapping sound. He raised himself off his chair and Maria walked him to the gate, the moonlight lighting their path. She mindfully kept her body a few feet away from his but couldn't deny her desire to be closer to him.

"Thank you for having me," Jacob said when they reached the gate. "I had a really good time."

Maria felt the blood rushing through her veins, and into her cheeks yet again. "I had a good time, too. Maybe I'll see you at church tomorrow?"

"Maybe," he replied. He closed the gate, but didn't turn down the street right away. Instead, he looked Maria in the eyes. She felt her knees begin to shake and put a hand on the fence to support herself. "Goodbye, Maria." Jacob tipped his hat toward her and then he was off.

Maria watched him for a few minutes, gaining back her strength. In the stillness of the night, she whispered after him, "Goodbye, Jacob."

Jacob crouched in the tall grass. A military rifle balanced steadily in his hands. He eyed a deer in the distance and hardly breathed. Slowly, he moved the barrel of the gun, following the deer as it lowered its head to eat the leaves off a small bush. Jacob held his breath and pulled the trigger.

The deer instantly fell to the ground. He looked at his friend, Franz, before standing up and tromping through the tall grass toward his victim. As they walked, Jacob lit a cigarette and inhaled before exhaling a cloud of smoke.

"Nice shot," Franz admired.

"Thanks," Jacob slung the rifle over his shoulder.

"You've been seeing an awful lot of Maria lately. How are things going?" Franz inquired, hoping to get more details out of his friend.

"They're going," Jacob replied vaguely.

"That's it? That's all you're going to tell me?" Franz pestered him.

"What else do you want to know?"

"Anything! You've hardly said two words about her since you started going to her house, and that was months ago already! I thought I was your best friend. Can't you tell me anything else?"

"I've told you all there is to know, Franz. I'm sure she's aware that I like her, but she's made it very clear that she only wants to be friends. She'll be back in school next year and wants to focus on her studies. I can't blame her for that."

Franz surveyed Jacob with a doubtful eye. There was no use pushing him, though. Jacob never divulged any information that wasn't pertinent to the one receiving it.

When they got to the deer, Jacob crouched down beside it and inspected his aim – a clear shot straight through the neck. He smiled to himself, pleased, and placed the gun on the ground. Franz helped him pick up the animal and hung it from a tree by its hind legs.

While Franz was out looking for another deer, Jacob began the process of gutting and skinning the deer carcass. He grabbed the knife from his pack and slit the deer's throat. Blood streamed onto the ground, splattering bright red spots onto Jacob's shoes and pants. He moved through the next steps fluidly.

Hunting was his favourite pastime. Ever since he was old enough to hold and shoot a gun, he went hunting often. It became his way to unwind, when the noise and crowd of people in his home overwhelmed him. He preferred to be alone, but finding solitude in a small house with thirteen other people was a rarity.

As he waited for the blood to run dry, his thoughts went back to Maria, as they always seemed to do. He was smitten by her. He thought of her laugh and smiled. She laughed from her soul – wholeheartedly, unreserved and raw. He loved the subtle wrinkles that appeared at the corners of her eyes, nearly hidden by her glasses, when her smile stretched across her face.

She was beautiful, he thought. He was even more attracted to her by the fact that she didn't think she was attractive. She made comments now and then about other girls' hair or clothes, and how she wished she could look as lovely as them. He would assure her she looked even more beautiful than those girls, and she would blush and push him, accusing him of lying.

He meant it when he told Franz that he didn't blame Maria for wanting to focus on school. She was driven and couldn't be swayed from achieving her goals, which was another trait he found alluring. He admired her confidence and didn't mind that she often reiterated the boundaries of their relationship.

He took another drag of his cigarette before stubbing it on a nearby log. He obviously wanted more. He wanted to date her, to hold her hand, to be invited into the deepest parts of her heart and her mind. He was fascinated by her. But she had been clear and firm about her stance, and he knew that he would likely always stay her friend, and nothing more. Rather her friend than not have her in his life, at all, he reasoned.

—

By February, Maria, Tina, and another friend, Helga, were hired to sew pants and shirts for a local store, and were forced to learn the trade quickly. It took some time to learn, with many failed attempts along the way. Eventually, with lots of practice, they figured it out, drafting patterns and transferring them onto thin sheets of tracing paper before cutting the fabric and piecing it together. They each had their station. One would sit by the sewing machine, while another ironed, and the other drew out patterns and cut fabric. Soon enough, their work became effortless, but the strain on Maria's back from standing for hours on end kept her in constant pain.

Maria waited for the iron to heat on the fire. She laid the wide-legged trousers on the wooden board, flattening the seams. Helga and Tina hummed quietly to themselves while they worked. Maria was too absorbed in her own thoughts to join them. She thought about the only thing that seemed to occupy her mind these days – Jacob. She didn't want to like him, let alone fall in love with him. She had another year of school left, and wanted to focus on her studies, without the added distraction. Aside from that, she still felt she was too young – not just for Jacob, but for a relationship in general.

She knew the age difference was only an excuse. It was more than her age and schooling that deterred her from starting anything more serious with Jacob. It was the fact that Jacob didn't have a relationship with God. She knew he was a good man – loyal, honest, hardworking – and raised in a good, Christian home. He was kind and thoughtful toward Maria, and he made her feel valued and appreciated. But all those good qualities aside, he wasn't a Christian, and that had always been a priority for Maria.

Ever since she was a little girl, Maria assumed she would marry someone who shared the same faith as her. She wanted a husband who would encourage her in her walk with God, and be the spiritual leader in the home. It never occurred to her that she might one day have feelings for someone who not only didn't have a relationship with God, but who didn't want one, either. And now that she found herself thinking about him constantly, she felt conflicted. Was it even right for her, a Christian woman, to marry a man who was not?

Maria prayed for God to take Jacob's feelings for her away. She didn't know if that's what she really wanted or not, but she was scared, and having that burden off her shoulder would ease her heart. Then they could continue being friends, and he could meet and fall in love with someone else, though thinking of Jacob with someone else made her feel sad.

She brushed the thought aside and reached for the iron. The black metal was hot, and she felt its warmth through the towel wrapped around the handle to protect her skin. As she ironed the light brown pants, she whispered another silent prayer.

Jacob tried to fight the feelings, to convince himself that he merely revered Maria as a good person, but eventually he gave in to his heart. He couldn't deny it any longer – he was in love with Maria.

14

November 1944

DESPITE MARIA'S CONSTANT PLEAS WITH GOD TO SEND JACOB AWAY, AND TO stifle any feelings he had for her, their friendship continued. Jacob pursued her relentlessly, but patiently. Had she told him to stay away, he would have respected her wishes, but she hadn't uttered those words yet, and he hoped she never would.

They spent countless nights together, talking into the late hours of the night, long after her family had gone to sleep. They sat beside each other on the porch one evening, their skin damp from the humid air. She made sure there was lots of space between their chairs, despite both of them wanting to be closer.

Jacob had no intentions of acting on his feelings. At least not physically. He loved her, that much he knew, and he respected her too much to impose his feelings on her. Besides that, he was afraid of what she might do to him if he tried to kiss her. She wasn't one to sit idly when her rights were being threatened. He imagined she might punch him in the face, or at least slap him, if he made any advances.

He regarded Maria from the corner of his eye. Her legs were curled up beneath her on the chair, and a few strands of hair fell softly around the sides of her face. He envied the locks, caressing her cheeks lightly as they blew in the soft, summer breeze. She was looking up, lost in the grandeur of the endless stars gracing the heavens. The clouds from the rainstorm had receded, clearing the sky, which was illuminated by stars and the moon. He watched the moonlight dance in her eyes and his heart swelled with ardor as he stared at her.

"The stars remind me of the night I accepted Christ into my life."

Maria's voice was soft as she recollected the moment. She paused, and Jacob urged her to continue, sensing she wanted to share her story with him.

"When I was younger, Mama used to house students from other colonies for different reasons. At some point, when I was eleven years old, we had two girls stay with us. They were from Filadelfia, but they went to different colonies and made money picking cotton. She was paid to board them, and we needed any extra income we could get.

"One day, I was picking cotton in the same row as these girls. They talked the whole time about how happy and content they were with their lives. They seemed genuinely happy, and I marveled at them."

"Weren't you happy?" Jacob interjected.

"Of course, yes, I was very happy. But there was something different about these two girls." Maria looked up, as if looking beyond the stars. "I think it was joy. A sincere, inner joy. Whatever it was, I was attracted to it, to them.

"They went on to explain that they tried to live their lives like Jesus did – doing good for others and loving those around them. When they failed, as they often did, they prayed and asked God for forgiveness. And they knew that they were forgiven. They were confident about that. And they knew He loved them very much.

"For the rest of the day, I couldn't stop thinking about what they had said. I worked in silence after that, but my heart felt unsettled. I started crying nearing the end of the row of cotton. Mama was on the other side and heard me. She came around and asked me what was wrong, as she wiped the tears from my cheeks. I told her I didn't know what was wrong. I didn't know what was going on inside me. But she must have.

"She led me back to the house, and made some *Maté*. We sat at the table together, and Mama opened up her Bible. She read a verse from Proverbs, '*Ich liebe, die mich lieben; und die mich frühe suchen, finden mich.* I love them that love me; and those that seek me early shall find me.'

"Mama went on to explain God's love, and what His death on the cross means for us, today, and forgiveness and sins, and everything. We sat together for a long time, until the sun set, and the sky was dark and clear, just as it is tonight. The stars were twinkling so much, it looked like they were alive, dancing in the sky.

"It was hard to believe everything Mama was telling me, even though I'd heard it all before. But my heart started beating faster and the hair on my arms and the back of my neck stood on end. I knew I wanted to give my life to Christ, too. I prayed with Mama right there, and I was so excited. As soon as we were done praying, Mama gave me a big hug, and then I ran off to tell the two girls that I, too, was forgiven."

"And you still believe all that?"

"Oh, yes. I'm even more sure of it now than I was then. There's no doubt in my mind."

"Hm," Jacob sighed introspectively.

"You don't believe that, do you?" Maria asked hesitantly, reluctant to hear the words come out of his mouth.

Jacob exhaled slowly. He had been dreading this question and conversation. "No. I don't believe that," he said, almost apologetically. His heart sank as he watched Maria's reaction. She sat back in her chair and folded her hands in her lap. Jacob licked his lips and continued.

"I do believe in God. I believe there is someone, or some*thing*, out there that is far greater than us. Even if Jesus was, in fact, a real person, I don't believe that he was, or is, equal to God, or that you need to have Jesus in your heart in order to love others, or to be a good person.

"I like to think of myself as a good guy. Not perfect, by any means, but decent nonetheless. And I am that way because of me, not because some man lived a fairly perfect life thousands of years ago. I've seen many 'Christians' who go to church Sunday mornings, and wear their best suits, and point their fingers at the 'sins' of everyone else, yet Monday morning they're back to cheating in business, or smoking or lying, or whatever else. They're hypocrites. If being a Christian just means that I get to go to heaven, regardless of how I live my life, then I'd rather go to hell."

"You can't possibly mean that? What about grace and forgiveness?"

"I don't think I need forgiveness. And God is grace, is he not? It still has nothing to do with Jesus."

"But God sent Jesus to us as a human, God in the flesh, to die on the cross for us, for our sins, so that we don't have to suffer for our sins."

"I don't think I'm suffering. Besides, if Jesus was real, and he did die on the cross, that would be a horrible way to die. I would never sacrifice my own child for other people's lives, especially not if I was God himself, with all the power in the world. I do believe in God, but he certainly doesn't need to kill anyone to prove his love for me."

"Oh," was all Maria said in response. She sank further into her chair and stared at the ground for a long time.

That was the end of that conversation. Jacob felt unsettled and wished he hadn't said anything at all. The tension between them was thick. He wanted to change the topic, to wipe the frown from her face. She was upset because of him. He watched her twiddle her thumbs, moving them around each other in circles.

"I'm leaving next week, for work," Jacob attempted to break the silence. Maria looked up, slightly startled by the sudden interruption of her thoughts. "I don't know how long I'll be gone for. Probably a few weeks."

"Where are you going?" Maria asked.

"I'm not quite sure. Up north somewhere. We're building some houses for a man there. A few guys from work are going. We'll get paid really well, so I couldn't say no."

"Right, of course not. That should be nice though, to see a different part of Paraguay, at least."

"I don't know that it will look much different than here. Besides, we'll be working long days, I doubt we'll see much. There isn't anything near where we'll be working, either. My boss said we'll be sleeping in tents in the bush."

"Well, then I hope you don't encounter any wild cats while you're there."

Jacob laughed. "Me, too. I'll bring my gun just in case. Maybe I'll do some hunting if we end up having any spare time."

Jacob looked at Maria sitting beside him, illuminated only by the moonlight. Her skin, ethereal in the evening light, made her look angelic and otherworldly as she gazed into the distance. In the dim light, he thought he saw a trace of disappointment in her expression, but he didn't know if it was still lingering from their previous discussion, or if it was about him leaving. He hoped it was the latter – the thought of her missing him was oddly satisfying.

They sat in silence again, but Jacob couldn't keep his eyes off Maria. Blood coursed through his veins with great force as his affection for her intensified. He had never been in love before, but he knew his heart would burst if he didn't say something, and soon.

"Maria!" He didn't mean to speak so abruptly, and his tone obviously startled her.

"What is it, Jacob? What's wrong?" She leaned closer to make out the expression on his face.

"Um. Oh, nothing. I mean, er," he ran his hand through his hair, trying to compose himself. "*Ekj sie die goot*, Maria, I love you," the words finally came out.

She was taken aback by his declaration. Her cheeks flushed, partly from flattery, but mostly from embarrassment. Slowly, she leaned back into her chair. His words lingered in the air, pregnant with anticipation. Maria stared straight ahead, not willing to look him in the eyes. There was no response, and no indication that she was trying to formulate a response – just a blank stare. Jacob waited awkwardly until he felt too embarrassed to stay any longer. He stood, and looked toward the street.

"I should go," he said. He took a step, but stopped and turned back to Maria, this time looking her in the eyes. "I meant what I said, Maria." With that, and still no response from Maria, he headed for the gate. Maria didn't call out after him, and he didn't dare look back at her again.

———

Kaethe sat completely still at the table. She hadn't intended to overhear Jacob and Maria's conversation, but she just happened to be in the kitchen when he had awkwardly declared his love to her daughter, just outside the window. She froze when she stepped out of her room and heard Jacob's words, and then cringed at the deafening silence that followed. Her pulse raced as she imagined the thoughts running through Maria's head. *Poor Jacob*, she thought, as he waited, and waited, for Maria to respond. But she didn't. Instead, he bid her farewell and the sound of his footsteps faded as he walked away.

Kaethe let out her breath and found a match to light the candle. The electricity had turned off and the candle on the table flickered in the darkness. She carried it with her outside, and sat down in the chair Jacob had vacated. It was still warm. She set the candle on the windowsill behind them and crossed her legs.

"Is Jacob gone already?" Kaethe asked nonchalantly.

"Hm?" Maria looked up, noticing her mother for the first time. "Oh. Yes, he just left."

"Did you have a nice visit?"

"I guess you could say that."

"He wasn't here for very long, is everything all right?"

Maria exhaled slowly. "Mama, he told me he loves me."

"Is that right? Then why do you look like you've just been told that the world is going to end?"

Maria smiled faintly, only for a moment. "Mama, it's not funny. I don't want Jacob to love me."

"Why not?"

"Because," she sighed again and slouched back into her chair, massaging her temples with her fingers. "I've been praying for God to take Jacob's feelings for me away. I don't want to be with him, or anyone, for that matter. He's too old for me, and I'm still in school, and, most importantly, he's not a Christian." Kaethe could physically feel Maria's heart sink as she spoke the last words.

"But?"

"But what?" Maria looked Kaethe in the eyes.

"You've got a lot of excuses – reasons *not* to be with Jacob, *but* ... ?"

Maria crossed her arms and looked at her mother skeptically. She always seemed to know Maria's unspoken thoughts.

"But," Maria began, exasperated, "I find myself drawn to him, despite my protests."

Kaethe nodded her head in understanding.

"Mama? Do you think it's wrong for a Christian to be in a relationship with a non-Christian?"

Kaethe had wrestled with that very question many times over the course of the last few months, ever since Maria first mentioned Jacob. She prayed about it often, but she didn't have a clear answer for her daughter. Kaethe reached across and held Maria's hand in hers. It trembled slightly, and a tear slowly fell from Maria's eye.

"Michi, I don't have an answer for you. I don't think it would be easy to be married to someone who does not share your faith, but I would never tell God how to do His job. If it is His will that you should marry Jacob one day, then who are we to argue and disobey? God will reveal His plan for you. We'll keep praying for wisdom and guidance. But in the meantime, enjoy your friendship with Jacob, even if it doesn't turn into anything more."

Maria nodded and wiped her nose with a handkerchief.

"Do you love him, Michi?"

With those words, Maria's tears unleashed, and she dropped her head into her hands. "I don't know."

Kaethe moved closer to Maria and wrapped her arms around her shaking daughter, pulling her close to her body. "It's okay, Michi. You don't have to make any decisions just yet. Let God guide you. There's no rush, and there's no right or wrong decision."

Kaethe held Maria until her body stilled and her tears ceased, and then they continued sitting together in silence until the candlelight faded away and they were left in the darkness alone, holding hands. They walked to their bedroom together, neither saying another word.

—

Shades of pink and orange pastels brushed across the sky as Maria walked the perimeter of their yard. The last remnants of the sun's rays drew perspiration from her body and she wiped her brow with her sleeve. The air was thick, and heat rose from the hot dirt on the ground. She tucked into the shadows of the forest behind their house to find respite from the heat.

Jacob had been gone for over a month already, which left an unexpected void in Maria's life. She didn't realize how accustomed she had become to their evening chats, and his familiar wave, and tipping of his hat, as she passed the woodshop on her way to work with Tina. He didn't whistle at her anymore, in keeping with his promise, but she didn't mind. He still went out of his way to make sure she knew he saw her, whether with a wave of his hand, or a quick greeting.

She couldn't deny the fact that she missed his presence in her life since he'd left for his work trip. Even Christmas wasn't the same. It was one of the only days that Jacob could be found in the church, and every year, he and three of his siblings sang in a chorale ensemble together. His voice was deep, hitting the lowest bass notes that no one else could even attempt to reach. When they sang the *Friedensfürst* chorus, Maria felt Jacob's deep notes reverberate through her body. It was a highlight for her every Christmas.

But this year there was no deep bass voice resounding throughout the small church building. As much as Maria loved Christmas, she found it hard to be in the moment, when her thoughts kept reverting to Jacob. She found her thoughts centred around him, even now.

Hoping to distract herself, she moved further into the forest, stepping over cacti and thorn bushes. It was eerily quiet without the incessant singing of the cicadas, who had gone to sleep for the night. She forced herself to recite poems she could conjure up from her memory. It worked, at least for a few minutes. Her thoughts were on the words she memorized as a young girl, and not on Jacob.

Then she spotted something in the brush. A flower, white as milk, standing out in a sea of green foliage. She moved closer and knelt down beside it. It looked so regal, so elegant. She gently caressed the silky white petals, careful not to disrupt its poised stance. She had never seen anything like it, but she had read about it.

Die Königin der Nacht, The Queen of the Night, as it was so aptly named. The bud bloomed from the branch of a cactus. Thin green leaves curled out from the base of the flower, like a royal cape. Two layers of white petals circled around the long, green style in the centre of the flower, curving ever so slightly under the weight of the soft, yellow stigma. It was far more beautiful in person than in any photograph she had ever seen of it.

Maria inhaled the sweet, flavourful fragrance deep into her lungs. She closed her eyes to savour the scent, knowing that in a few hours, the flower would be gone. This rare species bloomed once every few years, and only in the evening, and withered away only a few hours after blooming. It was a shame such a beautiful gem was hidden in the confines of the forest.

Maria sat mesmerized as she stared at the rare beauty in front of her. *If only Jacob was here to see this,* she thought. She sat upright and looked past the flower, into the depths of the forest. In that moment, however irrelevant it seemed, she knew in her heart that she loved Jacob.

Her legs shook as she processed the gravity of her revelation. Despite her prayers asking God to take Jacob away, she realized she didn't want him out of her life, after all. In fact, the opposite was true – she wanted to be with Jacob. She wanted him home, now.

She felt a sudden urgency to tell Jacob how she felt, but it wasn't possible. He wasn't here. Her heart was pounding beneath her chest. The air grew thicker around her and she took a deep breath. There was no way to contact him. She would have to wait until he returned from his trip, however long that might be.

—

Every minute Jacob spent away from Maria felt like days. He hoped the long hours working would distract him enough to make time pass faster, but his efforts were futile. During the day, he could focus on the task at hand, but as soon as he laid down in the evening, his mind always went back to Maria. She was the last thing on his mind before he fell asleep, and the first thing he thought of when he woke.

He had been instantly attracted to her dark features – her chestnut brown hair and her rich, chocolatey brown eyes. Growing up in a family where every single one of his twelve siblings, both his parents, and himself, had the same blue eyes and blond hair, he welcomed the change in physical appearance. He had never been interested in a girl with light-coloured hair or eyes.

Though Maria's physical features initially lured him in, it was now her character that most attracted him. He admired her confidence, and her will. Even at such a young, fragile age, she was headstrong and could hold her own. He liked that.

Jacob missed her more than he thought he would. Their last meeting still plagued him, though. He chastised himself for telling Maria he loved her. It was true, no doubt about that, but he had clearly scared her. He feared he may have pushed her away. If he didn't see her again soon, to clear things up, she might be out of his life forever.

He couldn't wait to get home, and hoped she would agree to see him again, even if she set firmer boundaries with him. All he could do now was wait and see.

—

A few weeks into January, the sun was ripe with heat. Maria and Tina fanned themselves as they walked their usual route home after work, passing by the empty school. Only two more months and they would be back there, Maria thought. She couldn't wait. She waved to Tina as she turned into her yard. Maria continued walking the rest of the way home by herself.

A wagon passed in front of her at the end of the street. The Neufeld's waved to her as they drove by, and Maria waved back. When her path was clear, she took a step onto the street and looked up to see the familiar sight of the rickety old woodshop in front of her. Her breath caught in her throat when she saw a tall, thin body leaning against the door frame. She closed her eyes and took a deep breath. Jacob was still working up north, as far as she knew. Clearly she was thinking about him too often if she was imagining him there now.

When she opened her eyes again, Jacob was halfway across the street, a smile spread across his entire face. Realizing she wasn't dreaming after all, she ran toward him.

"Maria!" Jacob bent down and wrapped his arms around her petite figure. She returned the gesture, and they stood in the middle of the street, embracing each other. She felt the muscles in his back flex as he held her tightly. Her body pressed against his and she flushed. They had never hugged before, or touched the other's skin in any way. She had hugged boys before, but this felt different. Jacob's touch sent jolts of electricity through her body. Her heart beat a little faster as the warmth in her cheeks deepened.

Jacob loosened his grip on her, and she wished he hadn't. She wanted to be back in his firm arms. He stepped back, and crossed his arms over his chest, suddenly aware of his impertinence. She saw the shock in his face, mortified by his own behaviour. He rubbed the back of his neck in awkward embarrassment and Maria smiled at his boyish insecurity.

"How was your trip?" she asked. Her disregard for his actions caught him off guard, and he looked at her curiously. She smiled warmly at him, encouraging him to answer. He smiled back, relieved he hadn't done even more damage.

They walked together toward the woodshop, their bodies close, but not touching. He looked different to her somehow, and she forced herself to take her eyes off him. She couldn't believe there was a time, not long ago, when she didn't find him attractive. There was nothing visually unappealing about the statuesque man standing before her. His skin warm, darkened from hours spent in the sun. Even though he was thin, she could see the definition of the muscles through his shirt. His hair was pale, almost white, with a tinge of gold through-out. He combed his fingers through the blond strands, and Maria imagined running her own fingers through his hair and wondered what it would feel like.

He met her gaze and she looked intently into his eyes – those deep, blue, scintillating eyes. Though she had always been transfixed by Jacob's eyes, she had never seen them like this. It was as if she could see into his soul, and he into hers. She suddenly felt quite exposed and turned her head, clearing her throat in an attempt to regain her composure.

Jacob's smile grew wider. He lowered himself to the ground and reclined his back against the stack of wooden wagon wheels. Maria sat down right beside him, her knee lightly brushing against his. From the corner of her eye, she could see him eyeing the place where their knees were touching, and his cheeks reddened to match hers. Neither of them moved away. They sat close together and talked in the refuge of what little shade could be found at midday until Jacob needed to return to work.

15

July 1946

MARIA STOOD IN HER ROOM, WINCING AS SHE SLIPPED HER ARMS OUT OF HER dress. She put a hand to her lower back and rubbed it with her fingers. She stepped into an older dress and pulled the buttons on the front of the blouse through each corresponding buttonhole. When she finished changing, she slowly lowered herself onto her bed, keeping her back as straight as possible. The pain had worsened over the last two years. A rather large lump grew on her upper back, which was the source of most of her discomfort.

Maria never did return to school the previous March. Even though Lehrer Stahl had returned from Germany, and school resumed as per usual, Maria's family couldn't afford to send her. It was a devastating moment, for both Maria and her family. Kaethe apologized for months. Her guilt overwhelmed her, but Maria never blamed her. It wasn't her fault. Even with Maria working, they could still only just make ends meet.

"Jacob! Fine afternoon out there, isn't it? Not too hot, not too cold," Maria heard Johann greet Jacob in the other room. "How are you doing? How's work?"

Maria raised her body and leaned on one elbow. She clenched her teeth to keep from screaming as she lifted herself off the bed. The smell of chicken noodle soup wafted through the air. At least she would have a few minutes to sit and rest before starting her chores. She moved her hands down the skirt of her dress and straightened the buttons on her blouse before stepping out of her room.

Jacob stood to greet her. His face lit up at the mere sight of her. With lunch not quite ready yet, the two of them walked outside and sat on the porch. Maria's expression mirrored the pain she felt. Her eyes were closed but she sensed Jacob's worry.

"It's okay, Jasch, it's just my back. Again."

"It seems to be flaring up a lot lately," Jacob noted with sympathy.

"Yes, it is."

"Is there anything you can do? Any treatment you can undergo, or medication you can take, to make it better? Or at least ease the pain?" Jacob's forehead creased with worry. Maria found it rather endearing how much he cared.

"I did get treatment for it once, when I was nine," she began, looking out toward the street as she recollected the memory. "My back had formed a small lump, hardly anything noticeable, especially compared to now. It pained me only now and again, at first, but over time it became incessant. I wasn't able to lift anything, or to help with chores around the house without crying. It was the work – all those years of hard labour at such a young age that inevitably caused the lump, along with the pain. But the work was unavoidable. We all had to do our part around the farm, with chores and helping with the crops, as you know.

"News travelled to Friedensruh that a woman, a Mrs. Harder, was here from Germany. She had studied bones for many years and was offering treatments in Filadelfia. Mama talked to Oma and Opa about it, and they agreed that I should go see her.

"One day, Mama and I rode into town and found Mrs. Harder. I lifted my shirt over my head and she ran her cold hands up and down my spine, and around the small lump. It hurt when she pushed on it, but I kept my mouth shut and didn't scream, even though I wanted to. I remember that vividly.

"After assessing my back, and asking Mama a long list of questions about my health and everyday life, she told Mama that she was confident she could help me. I remember the look of relief on Mama's face, the sheen in her eyes, though I'm not sure if she was on the verge of tears, or if she was just really happy at the glimmer of hope Mrs. Harder had offered her.

"We began treatment that night. When we got home, Oma was preparing a chicken for supper, and Mama asked her to cut the fat off and put it aside for her. After supper, Mama boiled a large pot filled nearly to the brim with peanut oil. Once the oil was hot, she placed the pieces of chicken fat into it and fried it until the fat turned translucent in colour. She let the fat cool, and when I was ready for bed, I laid on my stomach on my bed, with my back exposed. She took the fried chicken fat and massaged it into my back, moving her fingers up and down my spine, and over and around the lump.

"Mrs. Harder said the fat would soften my bones. I was skeptical at first. It sounded a bit far-fetched. But after a week of applying the chicken fat to my back, we went back to Filadelfia for another appointment. Mrs. Harder felt my back again, and made sounds of affirmation as she moved her hands around. She massaged me some more, which hurt a bit, but not too bad.

"At the end of that appointment, she told us she was pleased with the way the fat was working and was sure she could have me lump-free and pain-free in no time. As I waited outside, Mama listened as Mrs. Harder explained the costs for the treatment and the time commitment it would involve.

"Mama discussed it with Oma and Opa that night when I was in bed. They thought I was asleep, but I heard their soft murmurs. Mama told them we would need to go into Filadelfia twice a week to begin with, and eventually only once a week, for at least a year. I wouldn't be allowed to do any work, not even pick up a broom, for the duration of the treatment. When I heard that, I got excited, which was selfish, I know. But I was nine and hated doing chores. My joy quickly faded, though. I heard the concern in their voices as they tried to assure themselves they could manage all the work without my contribution. Even though I was so little, my help was still needed, however limited it was.

"When Mama told them the cost of the treatment, the room was silent. I didn't hear how much it would cost, Mama said it too quietly. It was so silent, I thought I could hear Opa twisting the edge of his wiry moustache with his fingers. Then Opa said that if we sold all our animals, they could pay for it. They wouldn't let me become a cripple if they could avoid it. They would do whatever it took."

She paused for a second, once again feeling the burden she felt she had put on her family.

"Actually, Tina went to see Mrs. Harder for the same treatment around the same time that I was, though I didn't know her yet at the time. It came up once in our conversation, when we were walking home from school. She had to stop her treatment early, though, because her father couldn't afford it anymore.

"Anyway, after the year of treatment was over, the pain had lessened significantly. The lump was gone, but my back never fully gained back its strength. It never had the time to. As soon as that year was over, it was back to business as usual. I helped Opa with the harvest and whatever else Mama needed me to do around the house."

"Does Mrs. Harder still work here? Why don't we see if we can find her and you can do the treatment again?" Maria heard the hope in Jacob's tone, and her heart sank. She touched his arm softly with her hand. She needed to stop him before he got his hopes up any higher. She looked in his eyes solemnly and offered a sympathetic smile.

"It's not an option, Jacob. Even if we could afford it, I could never take another year off from doing any work, especially not now. Mama and I are the only ones that can go out of the home to work and make money for our family. Mama is worse off than I am, with her back and her stomach issues. I can't put that burden on her again. I won't."

They sat quietly, both reflecting on Maria's final words.

"You said Tina had to stop her treatments because her family couldn't afford it anymore. How did your family afford it?"

"At the time, I didn't realize how much it actually cost. It wasn't until I met Tina, and she told me about her experience, that I became curious. Tina's family was more or less on par with ours, as far as money was concerned. It was thanks to my dad that we could continue the treatment."

"Your dad? Didn't he pass away when you were two?"

"He did. Mrs. Harder knew some Penners from Crimea, and it turned out they were related to my dad. Those Penners clearly left a good impression, because once she made the connection, Mrs. Harder told us she would cut the cost of my treatments in half. In the end, we only had to pay a little bit of money, and the rest we compensated with butter and eggs from our farm.

"If it wasn't for that treatment, I would likely be a cripple today."

"But your back is still hurting you," Jacob frowned and held Maria's hand in his own.

"Yes, but I'm walking and I'm able to work, and help support my family. For that, I thank God every day."

—

After lunch, Kaethe, Oma and Opa retreated to their rooms for a *Meddachschlop*, nap. Jacob wasn't eager to leave just yet. He watched Maria tie a tattered apron around her waist. The pale blue flowers throughout the fabric barely visible after years of use. She saw his gaze linger on her hips, and blushed. With fisted hands, she kneaded the dough into a ball, while Jacob sat on the other side of the table.

"You're welcome to help, you know," she teased him.

Jacob stood from his chair and reached his arm across the table and wiped a patch of white flour from her cheek. "You're welcome," he sat back down, amused with himself. Maria laughed and continued kneading the dough.

"Did you ever have soldiers come through Kleefeld? During the Chaco war, I mean?" Maria asked Jacob. He leaned back in his chair and clasped his hands together behind his head. Maria loved the fact that she could bring up any topic of conversation with Jacob, no matter how lighthearted or serious it might be.

"I don't remember much from that time. I was only nine or ten when the war began. My parents tried to shelter us from anything to do with the war. But I remember that the doctor who travelled with the army would stop in Kleefeld every now and then, and check as many patients as he could before the army moved on to their next destination.

"He came to our home once. My brother, Hein, wasn't doing well. There wasn't much food for him, or anyone, for that matter. But Hein was only a baby, and he wasn't growing, and cried all the time. Mother didn't have enough of her own milk for him, given the little food that was available. Every morning she milked the cow, but even the cow had very little milk to offer. Mother would walk back inside with half a mug full of fresh milk. She gave half of it to Hein, and the other half she'd either use for cooking, or let the rest of us each have a sip."

Jacob's face took on a sombre expression as he sat quietly for a minute, deep in thought. "We almost lost Hein that summer. Thankfully the army had been in our village at the right time, and the doctor was able to bring some powdered milk for Hein to drink. Eventually he gained some weight and started to grow."

"That must have been awful for all of you, especially your mother," Maria consoled. "Imagine watching your child suffer so much, and become so ill that they were on the verge of death. And all because there wasn't enough food! That's not right. With all the land, animals, plants and crops that we have in this world, starvation should not be happening."

Jacob saw the passion rising in Maria. He loved how deeply, and genuinely, she empathized with others.

"What about you?" he asked her. "Any memories from the war?"

Maria spread the dough on the table and continued kneading as she spoke.

"I was too young to have many memories of my own, I think I was only four when it began. I remember the sound of the cannons in the distance, though – they always terrified me and gave me nightmares. I think that's the only memory

I have of my own. Most of the stories I heard about the war, and the soldiers, are what I heard from Mama.

"She told me the Paraguayan soldiers would often walk up and down our street, slowly scanning the yards, looking for young women to take advantage of. A few women had been victims of rape while out for their evening strolls through the colony. The sister of one of Mama's friends was raped, and got pregnant from that one encounter. It was awful, apparently. She was only fourteen years old. She had the baby and her family was grateful the little girl's skin was pale, like her mother's. Mama's friend's mum raised the baby as if it were her own daughter. The baby grew up thinking her actual mum was her sister, and her oma, her mother. I don't know if she knows the truth yet, but I imagine that would be a difficult conversation to have.

"I do remember one time, near the end of the war – I must have been almost seven – I was walking home from a friend's house with Mama one evening, when we saw a group of Paraguayan soldiers walking toward us. Mama grabbed my hand and held it so tight I began to protest in pain, but she didn't seem to notice, or didn't care in that moment. She moved along faster. We weren't far from our gate, but the soldiers started walking faster, too.

"When we got to the gate, Mama unlatched it with a shaky hand, but before she could open it all the way, a Paraguayan soldier reached for the swinging door and shut it again. He wasn't a pleasant man to look at. His dark skin was covered with scabs, and a cigarette hung lazily out of his mouth, like a dead limb. Mama didn't move, and I looked at her, and then at the soldier. He had a wry smile on his face that made my insides turn. It wasn't a kind smile, at all. There was an aura of evil around him, and his friends giggled like schoolgirls behind us as they watched.

"He spoke in Spanish, or Guaraní, I'm not sure. I didn't know what he was saying, but it sounded crude, nonetheless. He moved closer to Mama, who still hadn't moved her eyes from the gate. He reached his hand up and grazed her cheek with his fingers. Mama closed her eyes. I saw the fear tensing her body, which made me even more scared. The man's hand moved from her cheek, down to her arm, and Mama's neck grew red and hot with fury. Mama has never been one to hold her tongue, or to sit idly by when she, or someone she loved, was being treated wrongly, so it didn't surprise me when she slapped the man across the face.

"While he was distracted, Mama pulled me through the gate and we ran up to the house as fast as we could. She practically dragged me along in the dirt the whole way up the yard, but I didn't dare say anything. We could hear the soldier shouting at her, likely cursing her in his language, and the other soldiers laughed. I'm not sure if they were laughing at us, or at their friend, who had just been hit by a woman.

"You know," Maria stopped kneading and looked into Jacob's eyes, "Opa said Mr. Reimer, an elder at our church, once asked one of those Paraguayan soldiers, if the opportunity presented itself, would they sleep with their best friend's wife? Do you know what his answer was? 'If I could.' Isn't that terrible? Can you imagine, taking your best friend's wife into your bed? It's disgusting, and immoral."

Maria huffed and shook her head as she turned her attention back to the dough. She grabbed a large wooden dowel and rolled it back and forth over the dough until it spread across half of the table.

"Based on the stories my parents have told me, it seems that life here in the Chaco is pretty intense, compared to life in Russia," Jacob reflected. "It's probably a blessing that we moved here when we were still too young to remember life as it was before. I only have a few memories of our home in Siberia, but that's about it."

"You're right, it probably is a blessing. But I can't help but wish that I could go back to Ebenfeld and see the home where I was born, and the general store my grandparents loved so dearly."

She formed the dough into small balls and placed them on a pan. "Do you enjoy woodworking, Jacob?"

"I do. I really do. It's a rewarding job. I love working with my hands, too. I could never be a teacher, or anything else that didn't involve physical work. I love the challenge of taking a tree and creating something new, and useful. "

Maria smiled, "That's a beautiful image." Maria thought it made a great biblical metaphor, but kept that thought to herself, not wanting to start a theological debate.

The conversation ended naturally, and Jacob took the opportunity to excuse himself and went to the porch. Maria saw his profile out the kitchen window. He reached into his pocket and pulled out a cigarette and held it between his lips while he lit a match. She watched as he held the flame against the end of the unfiltered, white paper. The ends began to smoulder and turned red from the heat. He took a deep breath, and slowly exhaled a narrow stream of smoke.

—

Sunday evenings, the youth from church gathered outside the church and sang songs and visited. It was a highlight of Maria's week. She craved social interaction, and loved being with her friends, or more accurately, with people in general. Growing up as an only child, with only three other people in her family, she often felt lonely, something Jacob could never understand.

Jacob preferred to be alone, away from crowds. She didn't blame him, of course. With a family of thirteen, she could understand why he preferred time to himself, but it was a topic that often led to an argument between the two of them. Maria wanted him to come with her when she visited her friends, but Jacob always wanted to stay home with her.

She thought about Jacob now as she walked away from the church. The stars accompanied her down the quiet, darkened streets. It was a frigid evening in July and Maria rubbed her arms to warm her goose skin flesh. In the distance, she heard someone calling her name. She turned and strained her eyes to see in the dark. It wasn't until a tall slender figure appeared, silhouetted by the moonlight.

"Jacob!" Maria was excited to see him, and ran toward him.

"How was *Jügent Owent*?" he asked, as his steps fell in line with hers.

"Great! Though I would enjoy it more if you accompanied me." Maria knew she was treading thin ice with her comment. Aside from whether or not they would spend their time with other people, they often argued about church, and faith. Maria didn't need to look at him to know he was biting his lip.

"Maybe some other time," he replied, keeping his response neutral to avoid starting an argument.

"Yeah, maybe."

He reached for her hand and slipped it through his arm. She held on to the crook of his elbow as they walked the rest of the way to her house in silence, allowing the tension of their conversation to settle.

Jacob held the gate open for Maria and watched her body sway as she walked up to the house, the moonlight accentuating the curves of her hips. Their usual chairs on the porch were vacant, and Jacob sat down in one of them. Maria went inside to grab a blanket and wrapped it around her shoulders before sitting in the chair next to Jacob. It took a lot of effort for Jacob to keep himself from staring at her. He couldn't explain why, exactly, he was so mesmerized by this woman. The feelings she evoked in him were like nothing he'd ever experienced before. His body yearned for her, and his heart longed to be tied to hers.

"If you could be, or do, anything, what would it be?" Jacob asked her, needing to shift his attention.

"There aren't many options for me, aside from being a nurse or a teacher. I'm not sure I even want to be either of those things. Actually, if I could do anything, I would go back to school. Forever. I would take as many classes as I could, on as many different subjects as were available. Except mathematics. I hate mathematics. Or maybe I would move to Germany, but only if Mama and Oma and Opa came with me."

"What about me? I don't get to move to Germany with you?" He teased.

Maria gave him a sly smile, "I'm not sure yet."

He winked at her, enjoying her flirtatious mood, and prompted her to continue.

"But, all those things can't happen because we could never afford it."

"Does that upset you?" Jacob didn't make much more money than she did. He couldn't help but wonder if she would be happy with him. He rubbed his hands together as he waited anxiously for her to respond.

"No, it doesn't. As much as I would love to continue learning, I really would love nothing more than to get married and have a family of my own. A big family, too, not just one child. It's far too lonely growing up alone."

Jacob relaxed at her answer, and leaned back comfortably in his chair.

"How many children do you want?"

"I'm not sure, but definitely not just one."

"And not twelve. Then you'd never get any one-on-one time with your kids and they'd grow up being almost strangers to you."

Maria nodded sympathetically, and he couldn't help but stare at her. Why did she have this effect on him? *Pull yourself together, man,* he told himself, but he didn't know how. He had been waiting so long for the perfect moment to place his lips on hers, but never felt confident enough. He wasn't sure she would want him to, and he respected her too much to force her to do anything she wasn't ready to do.

But it was all he could think about now, in that moment. He thought of her body moving in the dark, her dark hair blowing in the wind, and her eyes – her deep, beautiful, soulful eyes – they were enough to paralyze him with just one glance. If he didn't kiss her soon, he feared he would regret it for the rest of his life.

"Is that how you feel about your family?" she asked. "Are your parents like strangers to you?"

Jacob cleared his throat and looked away from her soft pink lips. "Well, we certainly don't have a relationship like you and your mother, or your oma and opa, even. But I can't blame my parents. My mum had eleven kids, well, twelve actually, including Leni."

"Leni? Who's Leni? I've never met, or even heard of her before. Did she not come to Paraguay with you?"

"I never met her, either. She was the firstborn. She died when she was still a baby. I wasn't even born yet, I don't think. I'm not even sure, actually, my parents never talk about her. So there are eleven of us siblings, which meant that my mum was pretty much always pregnant or holding a baby in her arms. The amount of cooking and laundry she had to do, with at least one kid always in diapers over the course of twenty years, or so. She'd be up until dawn some days, sewing all through the night to mend all of our clothes. Between all my brothers and I, we wore through pants pretty quick.

"Father was never available – if he wasn't out in the fields, he'd be locked in his room writing another article for a newspaper, or working on a book. He probably couldn't tell you one thing about me, or about my childhood, that's how detached he was from us kids. Mother tried, I'll give her credit for that. She tried to make time to ask each of us a few questions every day, but usually the day would end before she had time to talk to all of us.

"It hasn't been the most functional home, but again, I don't blame them. Life got a lot harder when we moved here, and they did the best they could with what they had. But there are some things that I will do very differently when I'm married, and when I have children of my own."

"Like what?"

"My father seemed oblivious to the work my mother did – the chores around the house and garden, and with the children. He worked long hours in the fields, while my mum spent those same hours tirelessly bent over washboards, or milking cows, or sewing, and who knows what else that woman did. Every now and then she would have to help Father with the crops, too. He would plow the field, and Mother would be hanging laundry, waiting for his cue. She'd rush over and walk down the rows of tilled soil, dropping seeds as she went, and all of this with a baby on her hip or breast.

"Then my dad would come home for lunch, sit down at the table, and have the gall to complain about how tired he was. Meanwhile, Mother was still slaving away over a pot on the stove, and sloshing food onto the plates of her ungrateful children and husband." Jacob shook his head in astonishment.

"I don't know how they did it," Maria shook her head, as well. "All the women who left their homes and settled down here with young children in those early years. Whenever I bring this up with Mama, she always diverts the focus back to the blessing that it was that they were able to leave Russia and come to a place where they could freely worship God and everything. But still, it wasn't an easy time, for any of them. Those women, they are the real heroes."

Silence followed. He could tell Maria was deep in thought, but all Jacob could think about was kissing her. Before he realized what he was doing, he leaned out of his chair and pressed his lips against hers. She didn't pull away from him, she didn't move at all. With his eyes closed, his other senses heightened, accentuating the softness of her lips. They were smooth and silky, like how he imagined flower petals would feel against his lips, he thought.

He finally pulled himself away and bravely looked her in the eyes. They were wide – dazed and stunned at what had just transpired between them. Neither of them said anything. Jacob felt a strange knot in his chest that moved up into his neck. He assumed his first kiss with Maria would be unforgettable, but he didn't expect to feel such immense emotion. He tried to suppress the tears, but one made its way down the side of his cheek, and then another. Before he knew what was happening, he broke down in tears.

His body shook and he sobbed into his hands, embarrassed by his reaction. Then he felt a warm touch on his arm. He moved his hands from his face and looked at Maria's calloused fingers gently stroking him. She was looking at the stars, giving him the privacy he so desperately needed at the moment.

Jacob quickly composed himself and wiped his eyes. He put his hand on top of Maria's and leaned back in his chair. As mortified as he was, he was greatly satisfied with his decision. Clearly she wasn't mad at him, and she wasn't laughing at his emotional breakdown. They gazed at the stars in silence, holding hands, and Jacob dreamed about the next time he would be able to touch her sweet lips again.

Suds moved up Kaethe's arm as she moved a wet shirt forcefully over the washboard resting against the edge of the tin basin. Lise, the woman who hired Kaethe to clean her house and help with chores, came home from her outing, with a friend in tow.

Kaethe's fingers burned with pain. She rubbed her hands together as she moved toward the house and sat leaning against the wall, underneath the open kitchen window. She heard the soft murmurs of the two women as they walked into the house. Their voices grew louder as they entered the kitchen and sat at the table on the other side of the window. Their conversation clearly audible. Not wanting to risk being seen by the women, and accused of eavesdropping, Kaethe thought it best to go back to the basin and continue washing the laundry.

As she shifted her body to stand, her ears perked at the mention of Maria's name. She moved herself so her body was positioned right under the window, making their voices even clearer. Any doubt she had about hearing Maria's name was quickly put aside as the women continued talking about her daughter.

"I don't know what that young Penner girl is thinking, gallivanting around town with an *unbeliever*." The woman said the last word with emphasized contempt and horror. "Christians should not be tied to non-believers. It's not wise."

"Or biblical," the other woman chimed in with a disparaging tone in her voice. "Why does Kaethe allow her daughter to continue this ghastly behaviour? I would be disgraced to see my daughter in a relationship with a man who was not a Christian. Perhaps if Kaethe had a husband, he would have the boldness to put Maria in her place. Sheesh! If Maria and that boy end up married, I should hope they would not let her participate in the church plays anymore. It wouldn't look good to have a woman serving in the church who was married to an unbeliever."

"I agree. I'm even hesitant to have her participate in the plays now, being in a relationship with him."

"I would have never thought it would go on as long as it has. It's ridiculous, actually. She's setting a terrible example for the other girls at church."

Kaethe couldn't believe what she was hearing. Her heart was pounding in her chest, and her mind was going a mile a minute, thinking of all the things she wanted to say to these women. Without thinking it through, she stood up and looked through the window, startling the two women.

"Kaethe!" Lise gasped at Kaethe's sudden appearance.

"Such *godly* women you are, though," Kaethe's voice was firm but steady. "Without fault, or sin of your own. You hypocrites. Why don't you take the plank out of your own eye before judging someone else!"

Kaethe turned from the window and stormed off. In her haste, she tripped over the laundry basin, turning it on its side. Sudsy water spilled on her shoes. When Kaethe regained her balance, she walked vigilantly to the end of the yard without looking back toward the house, leaving a trail of wet footprints in the dirt.

She knew their comments were unjustified, and simply wrong, but she couldn't help feeling ashamed. She knew in her heart that there was nothing wrong with Maria and Jacob's relationship, yet she couldn't shake the feeling that maybe she shouldn't have let it get this far between them. Marrying someone who didn't share the same faith would inevitably yield a more difficult marriage, but did that make it wrong? She asked herself a million questions, again and again.

Kaethe went straight to her room when she got home and closed the door behind her. She leaned her back against the wood door and slowly lowered her body to the ground. Straw poked through the thin fabric of her skirt, tickling her skin. She brought her knees up to her chest and rested her forehead between them. Tears fell from her eyes into her skirt.

"Oh, Nikolai, I wish you were here," she whispered helplessly.

"Mama?" Maria's voice came from the other side of the door.

Kaethe wiped her face with her skirt and stood. She reached for the handle and pulled the door open. At the sight of Maria, she started crying again and wrapped her arms around her daughter.

"I love you, Michi. I know you've struggled with your feelings for Jacob, but I have trusted God throughout your entire relationship. I know you've been praying, too, and I believe you are meant to be with Jacob."

"Thanks, Mama. What happened to you?"

"Nothing, my dear. I just want you to know how happy I am for you, and I can't wait to see what God has in store for you."

Every year passed seemingly quicker than the year before. Maria was in the kitchen, preparing the hen they would eat after the Christmas Eve service. She sat at the table as plumage gathered around her feet. Outside the window, the cicadas sang their annual chorus – a continuous stream of chirping, the reason they were often referred to as *Wienachtscheepa*, Christmas chirpers.

From where she sat, Maria could see her new dress hanging on the door of the wardrobe. Her mother had insisted on sewing it for her, even though Maria was more than capable of sewing her own clothes now. Maria had obliged, knowing it meant a lot to Kaethe. The dress was azure blue, with black satin around the collar and sleeves. It was beautiful, but she had yet to make a dress that gave her the same satisfaction as the red silk dress from many Christmases ago.

Only a few feathers were left on the hen, exposing its pale pink, bumpy skin, and she plucked them mindlessly. Amongst the hum of cicadas, Maria thought she heard whispers and rustling outside. Before she had time to investigate, a melodious sound streamed through the window.

"*Stille Nacht! Heilige Nacht!* Silent night, holy night."

Four harmonious voices danced through the window. She recognized the bass voice instantly. Maria placed the featherless hen on the table and excitedly pushed her chair away from the table. She wiped her hands on her faded floral apron and looked out the window.

Jacob and three of his siblings, Marieche, Abram and David, were standing a few feet away, singing her favourite Christmas carol. Jacob smiled at her, pleased to have been able to surprise her. Maria was beaming. No one had ever surprised her like this before, and the thoughtfulness made her heart swell.

"*Alles schläft, einsam wacht, nur das traute heilige Paar; holder Knabe im lockigen Haar.* All is calm, all is bright. 'Round yon virgin mother and child. Holy infant so tender and mild."

She needed to get closer. She ran out the door and placed herself right in front of the quartet. The moment was so surreal, she closed her eyes to savour every note.

"*Schlaf in himmlischer Ruh, schlaf in himmlischer Ruh.* Sleep in heavenly peace, sleep in heavenly peace."

They sang all six verses of the familiar carol. By the final note, tears ran seamlessly down her cheeks, and her smile stretched across her face. She stood frozen in place, trancelike, even after the voices trailed off. No one dared speak, sensing a sacredness in the moment.

When Maria finally opened her eyes, she tried to utter the words to thank them, but couldn't. Understanding her intentions, the siblings nodded and smiled. Jacob moved closer to Maria and wrapped his arms around her. Marieche nudged her younger brothers and they left Jacob alone with Maria.

Maria stayed in Jacob's embrace for a long time. He inhaled the sweet fragrance of her hair – a mixture of flowers and honey. After some time, Maria slowly, and somewhat unwillingly, pulled herself away from him, just enough to see his face. Their eyes locked and Maria's heart stopped. Her chest tightened as she lost herself in Jacob's gaze. He moved a hand to her lower back, sending a wave of heat through her body. His other hand gently cupped her cheek and she thought she might faint.

His touch was magnetic. She put her hands around his neck and raised her body so she was standing on the tips of her toes. His eyes gave away his hopeful suspense. She pulled his head toward her and closed her eyes as her lips met his. With their bodies close, she felt the strong beat of his heart against her own.

When their lips parted, the ground beneath her felt like it might melt away, and Maria clung to Jacob's arms for support. Jacob rested his forehead against hers, and kept their bodies close, not ready to distance themselves from each other.

"*Ekj sie die goot,* Jacob," Maria broke the silence with a faint whisper.

Jacob let out a deep sigh. He had been waiting so long to hear those words and he let them sink in now. "Call me Jasch," he said, and leaned down and kissed her again.

16

March 1947

MARIA PULLED A BUCKET OF WATER FROM THE CISTERN AND POURED IT INTO the basin beside her until she could see her reflection in the shallow waters. Jacob helped her move it closer to the house before sitting down next to his friend, Bernhard. The two continued their conversation while Maria gathered the dirty laundry and set it on the table beside the basin.

Bernhard seemed to be doing most of the talking, while Jacob listened obligingly. Maria winked at him and smiled. She knew he would rather be alone with her. Bernhard walked up to them, unexpected, and Maria invited him to stay awhile. Jacob lit another cigarette and eyed his friend annoyingly.

Maria tied her apron around her neck and placed her glasses on the table before kneeling beside the basin. She had broken her glasses before, when they had slipped from her sweaty face while washing the laundry one day. It had cost her family a lot of time and money to replace them, and she wouldn't risk breaking them again. Since then, she washed the laundry with blurred vision.

Bernhard's voice trailed off. Maria looked in their direction, the sudden silence made her think she might have gone deaf. Not able to make out the expression on his face, she continued working the wet shirt over the washboard.

"Oh," Bernhard said with disgust, "you're not very attractive without your glasses on."

Maria froze. She kept her face turned down into the basin, wondering if she had heard him right, and if his comment was aimed at her. Then Jacob's voice boomed beside her.

"Bernhard, you will leave this place at once." Jacob was calm, yet firm in his instruction, but Bernhard laughed. Jacob was silent, and Bernhard stopped laughing abruptly.

"Oh, you're serious? I'm sorry, was it something I said?"

"Leave, Bernhard."

Maria stood and turned toward the fuzzy outlines of their bodies. "Jasch, why should he leave? He was only telling the truth." She moved closer to him so she could see his face. He turned toward her, his lips taut in a straight line.

"And you go with him," Jacob pointed toward the gate at the end of the yard. "No one speaks about my Mariechen like that. Not even you, Mariechen."

Bernhard excused himself and walked hurriedly toward the gate without looking back, and without apologizing. Jacob gently lifted a loose strand of Maria's hair and tucked it behind her ear.

"Mariechen, don't ever say that about yourself again. You are the most beautiful woman I have ever seen. I wish you could see yourself the way I do, then you would understand just how much beauty you possess, inside and out." He kissed the top of her head and Maria blushed at his compliment, even though she still doubted his words.

"I'm serious, Mariechen." His lips curled up on one side and Maria smiled sheepishly.

"Yes, sir."

Jacob kissed her and said goodbye, leaving her to finish the laundry in solitude while he went home to help his father with a task before returning to work.

—

Maria hummed to herself as she hung the freshly washed clothing and linen on a rope tied from a tree to the house. She thought about Bernhard's statement, and frowned. It was one thing to believe yourself to be unattractive, but to hear it from someone else – and a young man, to boot – had affected her more than she cared to admit.

"Hi, Maria."

With her back facing the gate, she didn't notice anyone enter the yard, and the sudden sound of a male voice frightened her. For a moment she feared it might be Bernhard, and she wondered what else he might possibly say to her. She turned on her heels and saw Franz standing in front of her. He was turning his hat agitatedly in his hands.

"Franz! You nearly gave me a heart attack!" Maria peered behind him, but didn't see Jacob anywhere. Franz never came to her house on his own. "Where's Jacob?"

Franz looked at her blankly, confused by her question. "Jacob? I don't know. Maria, I need to talk to you."

There was an urgency in his voice, and his words came out shaky, heightening Maria's concern. *Why is he here without Jacob?* she wondered, *and why is his voice quivering?* He struggled to compose himself, and she eyed him with consternation.

Then Franz began to cry. Maria feared something terrible had befallen Jacob. Franz's blubbering began to irritate her and she was losing patience.

"*Na oba Dietschlaunt, Mann,* for heaven's sake, what is going on? Where is Jacob? Is he all right?"

"Jacob is fine, Maria. This has nothing to do with him. Well, not exactly," he wiped his eyes. Maria let out a breath of relief.

"Then spit it out, already! What's going on?"

Franz cleared his throat. "Maria, I've been silent for too long, but I can only hope that I'm not too late." He looked down for a moment and took a deep breath. Maria's face mirrored the exasperation she felt. "Maria, I can't deny my feelings for you any longer. I love you. I have loved you for some time now. Is there any chance you might have feelings for me?"

Maria blinked twice, and then stared at him with her mouth agape. She tried to make sense of what just happened, and wondered if she had dreamt it all.

"Franz, you can't be serious."

"Oh, Maria, I'm very serious."

She eyed him again, one eyebrow arched high as she scrutinized him. "Franz, you've gone mad! Do you realize what you've just done? You come to my house, uninvited, crying like a baby, and tell me that you love me. Your *best friend's girlfriend*! Are you drunk?" She peered at him with narrow eyes, searching for any sign of overindulgence. Or heat stroke, for that matter.

"No, Maria, I'm not drunk, and I know how ridiculous this must sound, but it's the truth. I wouldn't forgive myself if I never told you how I felt."

"I wish you would have kept your mouth shut. You would have, if you had any respect for Jacob, or yourself." She tossed a wet rag from the line toward him and he caught it. "Clean yourself up, you look a mess. Now, listen to me carefully, you fool. I don't love you. I never have, and I never will. I'm in love with Jacob, and when he finds out what you've done, he's going to be very upset, and extremely hurt. You need to go tell him what you just did, or I will. And he won't be as forgiving if he hears it from me first."

"Are you sure there's no chance you mi—"

"Franz! Go!" Maria stopped him before he humiliated himself any further, and pointed toward the gate.

Jacob's tools lay sprawled out on the wooden bench. He held a wooden spoke with his right hand and marked the spot where he would nail it to the felloes. The shop was quiet – the others wouldn't arrive for another fifteen minutes, at least.

"There you are," Franz was breathless as he ran into the shop. Sweat dripped down his chin, onto the fallen wood chips scattered around the ground. "I've been looking everywhere for you."

Jacob's left arm was suspended in the air, gripping the handle of a hammer. Franz eyed the tool in Jacob's hand. He slowly moved toward him and reached for the hammer. "Maybe I'll just set that down over here." Franz stepped back slowly and placed the hammer on a bench beside him.

"Before I start, let me assure you that I have thought through my actions and I realize how very, *very* foolish I was. I regret it completely, and I hope that you will understand, and find it in your heart to forgive me for my folly and arrogance."

"Franz, what's going on? What did you do?"

Franz wiped his glistening brow before he began. "This afternoon, I went to Maria's house—"

"My Maria?" Jacob asked, confused. "Why did you go there? You knew I would only be there for lunch before going home to help my dad fix the cultivator."

"Yes, I know. I wasn't looking for you," he lowered his head and stared at the floor. "Listen, I told Maria that I loved her, but I regret it, and wish I could take it back."

"You did what?" Anger rose up from his chest into his neck, burning his cheeks. His muscles tightened and his eyes pierced Franz, who was avoiding eye contact with Jacob.

"I'm sorry, Jacob. I asked her if there was any chance she might have feelings for me, too, but she assured me she didn't, and never would. She loves you, Jacob." Franz looked up and saw the fury in Jacob's eyes. He backed away, raising his hands in defence. "I know it was foolish. I wasn't thinking straight. I know she doesn't love me; she's so obviously madly in love with you. I couldn't help myself, though. I see the way she looks at you and I instinctively picture myself in your position. I've never had that with a woman – to be so loved and revered by someone."

His voice softened, "I'm so sorry, Jacob. There is no excuse for what I did and I ask your forgiveness, but I understand if you choose not to. Again, I know how very wrong I was, and I am ashamed of myself."

Jacob didn't say anything. He stared at his so-called friend, his body revving with anger, hurt and disbelief.

"I can't believe you did that," his tone was even, but his words hung heavy in the air, and on Franz, who turned and walked out of the woodshop with hunched shoulders.

—

Maria wasn't surprised to see Jacob walking up the yard later that day. Franz had decided to tell him, she thought. That was the only explanation for his visit, they hadn't made plans to see each other that night. Maria placed the black metal iron back on the fire and wiped her hands on her apron. She folded the wrinkle-free pants and laid them on the wooden board as Jacob slowly drew nearer. She saw the swell-like creases on his forehead, deep and concerned.

She waited until his tall frame stood right in front of her and then raised her hands up to cup his face. She pulled his body lower, so her lips could touch his. His forehead eventually smoothed as he stood with his arms around her, clinging to her.

"Jasch, you're squeezing me too tight, I can't breathe," Maria spoke in jest, but it was clear he was in no mood for jokes. "Franz told you then, did he?"

"Yeah, he came by my work."

"You don't look well." Maria searched his expression. "You didn't hurt him, did you?"

"No, I didn't hurt him," Jacob dropped his arms and moved to the porch and sat in a chair. He pulled out a cigarette and lit a match. "I wanted to. Hurt him, that is. How could he do that to me? To you, Mariechen! I'm sorry he put you in that position."

"Jasch, it's not your fault," she sat close to him and brushed her fingers through his silky white hair. "Don't forget, I'm quite capable of defending myself. There was no harm done. Franz wasn't thinking clearly, either. He didn't mean it, I'm sure. He just wants to have a relationship of his own."

"That's what Franz said, too," he didn't look convinced though. Another cloud of smoke lingered in the space between them.

"Jasch, look at me. Look at me!" He turned to face her reluctantly. "I love *you*, and only you. So much. You have to trust that, and me. If I wanted to have Franz, I could've had him, but I don't. I'm in love with you and that's about as much as I can handle." Maria kissed him again, the taste of tobacco on his lips. "Sorry, Jasch, but you're stuck with me, whether you like it or not."

Jacob finally relaxed enough to smile.

"So, will you forgive him then?" Maria asked.

"If you insist."

Jacob pulled her to him and put one hand on the small of her back. With the other, he touched her cheek and locked his eyes on hers. She felt her stomach twist from the intensity of his gaze, the same soul-piercing gaze that had made her weak in the knees the time they had bumped into each other at her baptism. His effect on her hadn't lessened over time.

"I love you, Mariechen."

"I love you, too, Jasch."

She leaned back in her chair, but their hands stayed interlocked, resting on her thigh. He stroked her hand with his thumb as they sat in silence. Jacob snubbed the end of his cigarette on the ground and placed it on the table.

"Maybe it's time we set a date," Jacob broke the silence.

"Date for what?" Maria asked, not quite sure what he was referring to.

"For the wedding."

Maria sat straight and moved her body to the edge of her seat, her heart racing. "What wedding?"

"Our wedding," he smiled cunningly. "That *is* where our relationship is going, isn't it?"

"Of course it is! I just wasn't expecting this. Not yet, anyway."

Jacob moved to the end of his seat and leaned closer to Maria, taking hold of both her hands. "I love you, Mariechen, with my whole heart. I hate saying goodbye to you and going home alone, only to miss you for the rest of the night. I want your face to be the last thing I see when I go to bed, and the first thing I see when I wake. I know you're only eighteen, but I've waited long enough. If I could have married you three years ago when we first met, I would have. You are everything to me, Maria. There's no point delaying the wedding if it's what we both want. And I can't bear to see you suffer so much with your back. When we're married, you won't have to work as hard anymore – I'll take care of you."

Maria stared at him, motionless and without expression, as she pondered his words. She knew she loved Jacob, and would inevitably marry him one day, which she wanted very much, but she hadn't thought about it actually happening. She finally looked Jacob in the eyes and saw the small creases on his forehead return as he waited vulnerably for her response.

"So?" he whispered. "Do you want to marry me?"

"Yes! Of course I do!" She wrapped her arms around his neck and kissed him hard, not wanting the moment to end. "I can't wait to marry you, Jasch."

"The feeling is mutual."

—

The room was quiet, save for the whir of the sewing machine. Kaethe sat behind it, gently and meticulously moving the white silk under the presser foot. Anna sat at the table, moving a needle and thread in and out of a shirt seam. Maria sat across from her, staring at a list of names scribbled on a piece of paper. With the tip of her pencil, she counted each name.

"Two hundred fifty," she announced. "That's too many, isn't it?

Kaethe lifted her foot off the pedal but kept her hands securely on the fabric. "If we weren't in the middle of a revolution, it wouldn't be. Unfortunately, we can't feed that many people with the limited amount of flour we have coming into town right now. I'm sorry, Michi. I wish we could invite everyone, but it just isn't possible."

"I know. You're right. I just don't know who to eliminate. Most of the guests on here are from Jacob. I'll need to go through it with him."

"It'll all come together, my dear, just wait and see."

With that assurance, the sewing machine hummed back to life. Kaethe struggled to compose herself when it came to planning Maria's wedding. She knew the day would come, and had been dreaming about this day since Maria was born, but now that it was about to happen, she couldn't help but feel torn between joy and immense sadness.

Maria was her best friend. Quite often, it felt like she was her only friend. After Nikolai passed away, Kaethe clung to Maria, probably to a fault. She couldn't help herself, though. Maria was all she had left, and she became a part of Kaethe in so many ways. And now she had to let her go. In a few weeks, Maria would belong to Jacob, and Kaethe would feel like she was all alone, despite still living with her parents.

She took a deep breath to keep the tears behind her eyes at bay. Maria had enough worries of her own, she couldn't burden her with any more. Besides, it wasn't that Kaethe was unhappy about the arrangement, quite the contrary. Jacob was an exceptional young man, with manners that exceeded those of his peers. He made an effort to greet Kaethe and her parents any time he came to the house. Most importantly, though, was how much he adored Maria. There had been numerous occasions when Kaethe had watched the two from a distance, smiling as Jacob stole a side glance at Maria when she wasn't looking. Even from across the yard, Kaethe had been able to see his cheeks redden. It was beyond sweet.

Maria was clearly equally as infatuated with him as he was of her. She talked about him all the time, and confided in Kaethe when problems arose. They had their fair share of arguments, as any healthy relationship would. There were many times that Maria had run through the house, cheeks wet from tears, slamming the door to their bedroom. But she loved him beyond reason. As angry as she could be with him, she had never even mentioned the idea of ending their relationship.

Kaethe would miss their daily chats and prayers, and the duets they sang together as they whiled away the hours, working side by side. Or the evenings when neither could fall asleep, and they would lay in their beds, looking at the straw above them, whispering to each other.

Their relationship had grown and changed so much over the years, like the ebb and flow of the sea. She remembered the helplessness she felt when Maria was a baby – not knowing how to calm her fitful cries – to the fear she felt on the boat, sailing away from their homeland. Raising Maria alone had its challenges, but through it all, they had grown close, and Kaethe could not be more proud of who her daughter had become, and knew that Nikolai would agree.

It felt surreal to sew her daughter's wedding dress. Kaethe had sewn many dresses for Maria over the years, but her hand shook slightly as she cut the delicate fabric. They had gone to the Cooperative together to choose the fabric. The selection had increased significantly from when the store first opened nearly twenty years earlier. White rolls of fabric lined one wall at the back of the store. From cotton, to satin, and everything in between. Maria's eyes had locked instantly on the silk. Maria's face shined as she held the fabric against her body and Kaethe pictured Maria draped in the flowing silk on her wedding day, and her throat caught with emotion.

"Oma?" Maria's voice interrupted the silence. "Would you be willing to bake our wedding cake? I don't trust anyone else – your baking is by far the best in all the colonies combined. It would mean so much to us!"

With her hands clasped over her heart, Anna replied, "*Oba jo*, of course. It would be my pleasure." She touched Maria's hand and smiled endearingly.

—

The evening before the wedding, the Penner's backyard was littered with young folk for their *Polterabend* – a celebration of the bride and groom. Maria beamed with delight as she moved from one conversation to the next. Jacob sat near the house with his brother, Abram, and Franz. He looked content, though Maria knew he was only there because she wanted him there.

"Are you excited for tomorrow?" Helga asked as she hugged Maria.

"I am! I can't believe it's actually happening."

"I'm so happy for you, Maria. It's going to be a beautiful day! Oh, my mother wanted me to tell you that she can bake a loaf of bread for you tomorrow."

"Perfect! Thank you, Helga."

The two girls chatted for a while longer, and soon more girls joined them. She kept looking back at Jacob. He was leaning against the house, smoking a cigarette, while holding a glass of whiskey and water. He looked up and his eyes instantly met hers. Jacob smiled and Maria walked toward him, pulled by his alluring blue gaze. His arm found its place around the small of her back and he pulled her close to his body, kissing the top of her head.

"Should we officially start the program now?" she asked. "Tina said they're ready to start whenever we give the signal."

Jacob whistled loudly with his fingers in his mouth to get everyone's attention and they seated themselves in front of the makeshift stage. A curtain made of two bed sheets swayed calmly in the evening breeze, like ghosts dancing to the same tune. Jacob and Maria sat in the front row and waited eagerly for the show to begin.

The split in the curtain opened and Tina jumped out, dressed like a gypsy. For half an hour, Tina and the other actors entertained the crowd, bringing them to hysterics on more than one occasion. Maria held her abdomen, which ached from laughing so hard. Once the show finished, and the actors bowed to their audience, the guests arranged their chairs in a circle.

Gifts lay piled in front of Jacob and Maria. Everyone watched as Maria pulled the end of a string of twine. The bow unravelled and she slid it out and placed it on the pile of ribbons beside her. She opened the top of the box that she balanced on her lap, and peered inside, anxious to see what she would find. She reached in and grasped a handle and pulled out a very small pot. Her excitement quickly faded and diffused into confusion, mixed with disappointment. She couldn't think of any possible use for such a small pot. Perhaps she could use it to melt butter, she thought, as she turned the pot in her hands, observing its size. But even that seemed impractical – she would still need to pour the butter into another pot or bowl to accommodate the other ingredients, which meant having to wash extra dishes.

"Thank you, Friedrich," she feigned gratitude, smiling as she lifted her face, not wanting to hurt the boy's feelings. She passed the small, insignificant pot to Jacob. He seemed unphased by the miniature pot, and added it to the pile of opened gifts. Towels, dishes, a gravy boat, and baking pans were among the stack of newly-acquired items for the couple.

"This one's from Abram, David and I," Marieche explained as she handed their gift to Maria.

Maria passed it to Jacob. "You should open it, then."

Jacob balanced the box on his lap and tore the paper away, revealing a hand held coffee grinder. Maria grabbed it from his hands and thanked her soon-to-be in-laws. She didn't have a grinder of her own, and the thought of not being able to make her own coffee once Jacob and Maria were married terrified her. Her morning coffee had become as much a part of her life as it was for her grandparents.

After the last gift was opened and added to the pile of others, Jacob and Maria thanked everyone. Then the singing began. The sky darkened progressively throughout the rest of the evening, cueing Maria to end the festivities.

Jacob stood with his arm around Maria's waist as they watched their friends leave. They waved to Marieche, David and Abram, the final guests to leave.

Maria turned to face Jacob and wrapped her arms around his neck. His eyes shone despite the darkness surrounding them.

"I guess I'll see you tomorrow." Jacob stroked her cheek with his thumb.

"I'll be the one in white." Maria put her hand over his, and leaned into the warmth of his touch.

"Well, this will be the last time I say 'goodbye'. Starting tomorrow, it'll be 'goodenacht', good night."

He leaned down and kissed her. She kissed him back and pulled him closer, willing him not to leave. They kissed passionately in the darkness of the night, the stars their only witness. Maria's heart pounded against her chest, and blood rushed through her body, and into her cheeks. Eventually, she pried herself away from him and rested her forehead against his. She could hear him breathing, and felt the softness of his exhale against her skin.

"Goodbye, Jasch."

"*Schlop goot*, Mariechen, sleep well."

He pressed his lips against the top of her head and moved away from her, walking backwards, not wanting to take his eyes off her. Maria closed the gate, and the latch clicked into place. When Jacob was out of sight, she took a deep breath and walked toward the house, where the faint flicker of a candle danced through the small open window.

17

April 26, 1947

MARIA TURNED IN HER BED, WOKEN FROM THE SOFT RUSTLING OF HER mother's movements across the room. Dawn had not yet graced the sky, and the only light illuminating the small room came through the door that stood slightly ajar. Though she had slept soundly, her eyes stung with fatigue. Maria pulled the sheets over her face and turned to her side, not yet comprehending the significance of the day.

"Good morning, beautiful bride," Kaethe's soft, choral-like voice flowed gracefully through the stillness of the room.

Maria revealed her face and tried to focus on her mother's eyes in the darkness. Kaethe sat on the bed beside Maria and stroked her tousled hair, moving loose strands away from her face.

"*Morje*, Mama."

Kaethe smiled endearingly, and Maria knew she was struggling to compose herself.

"Coffee's ready."

She kissed the top of Maria's head and dabbed the corner of her eye with her finger. Maria sat on the edge of her bed and looked out the small window. The sky slowly diffused into a deep shade of indigo as the sun began its morning ritual.

A nearly-filled notebook lay open on the nightstand beside her bed. Maria reached for it, along with a pen, and looked at the black ink scrawling on the page. The word '*A'prell*, April,' was written at the top of the page, with the numbers one to twenty-six written vertically below it. Twenty-five numbers were crossed out with a bold line, leaving only one unmarked.

"It's my wedding day," Maria exhaled in disbelief.

Any slumber that still lingered in her body lifted instantly at the realization that she would be marrying Jacob that day. A smile spread across her face and she sprang up from the bed and slid out of her nightgown and into a brassiere and a blue-paisley cotton dress. She quickly pinned her hair on top of her head, not wasting time attempting to achieve any volume, knowing it would be beautified before the ceremony.

There was already lots of commotion in the kitchen when she emerged from her room. Johann mixed flour and water in a large bowl, preparing the dough for the bread that would need to be baked later that morning. Anna leaned over a decadent, three-tiered cake, concentrating as she outlined the edges with ribbons of frosting. She caught sight of Maria and smiled, her dust-covered cheeks rising as her mouth turned upwards.

"Good morning, Michi! You look rested. Here, try this." Anna held a spoon up to Maria's face. White, silky buttercream icing nearly dripped off the sides, ready to fall into Anna's waiting hand that hovered inches below the wooden spoon. Maria took a bite and licked her lips as she sighed her approval. It was the most delectable icing she had ever tasted – rich, creamy, and oh so smooth.

"It's amazing, Oma! I can't wait to eat it tonight, though I don't really want to share it with the guests now."

Maria sat down at the table where a mug of coffee had already been poured for her. Steam rose wistfully and filled her lungs with the rich aroma. Kaethe stood across from her, carving thin slices from the large slabs of boiled meat on the cutting board. She sipped her coffee quietly, regarding those she loved most doing whatever they could to make sure everything came together for the wedding.

She sat in awe. The four of them had been each other's everything for Maria's entire life. Despite her desire to have had siblings and a father, and a larger family in general, she would never trade these three people for anything. The thought of having to leave them weighed on her.

She wouldn't have to leave them right away, at least. Jacob and Maria planned to live with her family for some time so they could save some money, and Jacob's added income would help ease their financial burden during that time. Maria didn't mind, she wasn't ready to leave them. Jacob would prefer to be on their own straight away after the wedding, but he understood her reluctance and had no qualms about the decision. Kaethe found it harder and harder to work with her back, and Anna felt ill most days as she dealt with some intestinal health issues. However, beyond the physical and financial worries of leaving them, the truth was, Maria would simply miss them far too much.

—

Maria regarded Opa through the kitchen window as he arranged each bench under the tent in the backyard with precision, until two rows lined up evenly on either side of the centre aisle. She smiled fondly as she watched him bring two chairs to the front of the aisle for her and Jacob to sit on during the ceremony. She admired him so much. He was so genuine and loyal to his friends and family. He worked constantly and tirelessly, until his hands bled and his breathing became laboured, and never complained. In those ways, he reminded her of Jacob.

There was a knock on the door and Marieche and Lottie, Jacob's sisters, bounded through the door with smiles and excitement as they greeted everyone with hugs and kisses. Jacob was the first to marry in his family, and his sisters were thrilled. They gladly did anything Maria asked of them, grateful to be part of the wedding in any way they could.

Kaethe ushered the two girls to the table where the dough bubbled over the rim of the bowl, ready for kneading. While they worked on the bread, Kaethe resumed her place by the stove, chopping and adding vegetables to the large pot filled with boiling broth.

With a final tilt back of her head, the last drop of coffee ran into her mouth and she set the mug back on the table. The faded blue foliage on the now-yellowed apron hung from a nail beside the door and Maria tied it around her waist. She grabbed a bucket and iron shears from outside the house and walked toward Johann.

"It looks perfect, Opa, thank you so much."

Opa turned at the sound of her voice and smiled. "You're welcome, Michi."

"Join me?" she raised the bucket and pointed toward the garden where a sea of blooming flowers craned their necks to feel the warmth of the sun. Opa wiped the sweat from his brow and walked beside Maria. He was never one to refuse an opportunity to spend time with his only grandchild.

Maria cut stem after stem and placed them gently in the bucket, brightening the brushed metal with the luminous blooms. She worked in silence for some time as Opa watched her from where he sat on the ground beside the garden.

"Do you have any wisdom to impart on your *Grootdochta*, granddaughter, on her wedding day?"

He thought for a moment, adjusting his hat, "Don't ever be too proud to say 'I'm sorry.' And when he asks for forgiveness, forgive him, and then never mention it again." There was a long pause, and Maria sat still as she let his words sink in. "Oh, and always laugh at his jokes, even if they're not funny." Opa winked and Maria laughed.

"Is that the secret to a long lasting marriage like yours and Oma's?" She winked back before clipping another flower. Before long, white and pink flowers spilled from the top of the bucket. She stood and brushed the dust from her knees. With her arm weaved through her opa's, they walked back to the house and she began arranging her bouquet.

—

Jacob walked through Maria's gate with a few of his brothers in tow. He saw movement in the house through the open windows, and heard the din of numerous conversations throughout the yard. Anna walked out the door holding a bucket filled with food scraps.

"Oh, Jacob! *Wellkom*, welcome!" She shuffled toward him, jostling a potato peel and it fell to the ground in her wake.

"Good morning, Frü Warkentin," he bent to reach her extended arms and hugged her. "How are the preparations coming along?"

"Oh, shush, you can call me 'Oma' now," she patted his cheek and smiled. "Everything's coming together just wonderfully."

Anna continued on her way and Jacob walked into the house. He searched the room, looking for Kaethe, and spotted her in the backyard, struggling to move a table. He ran out and grabbed one end of the table, lightening the load for her.

"Let me help," he offered.

"Jacob! I didn't see you arrive. Thank you."

"My pleasure."

They set the table down in a shaded area beside the house and Kaethe leaned against it, catching her breath. "How are you doing this morning?" she inquired.

"Pretty good," he answered sincerely, though his cheeks blushed slightly. "I can't wait to marry your daughter."

"She shares your excitement," Kaethe grinned, noticing a gleam in his eye as he thought about her daughter.

"Speaking of Maria, I haven't seen her yet. Do you mind if I go back inside to find her?"

"Of course I don't mind!" She shooed him away with her hands and assured him she was all right.

Jacob peered into the house and scanned the small room. He spotted her almost immediately. He moved fluidly so as not to startle her. She was focused intently on the Borscht boiling in the pot in front of her and hadn't noticed him. Jacob wrapped his arms around Maria's waist and kissed the side of her neck. She raised her head and started slightly at his touch.

"Jacob, not now, everyone can see us!" Maria blushed as she tried to pull Jacob's hands away from her but he only moved closer. She didn't resist his advances and their lips touched. The chaos of the room faded until her lips left his. She was unaware of just how much power she possessed over him. One look in his direction, or the faintest touch of her skin against his, was enough to completely intoxicate him.

"Here, try this," Maria raised a ladle of Borscht. "Does it need more salt?"

Jacob took a bite and licked his lips to stop a drop of broth from running down his chin.

"It's perfect," he assured her, though he wasn't only referring to the soup, and her cheeks reddened further, into a deep maroon.

—

The house was empty, save for Maria and her family. They welcomed the calmness, a stark contrast to the rushing and clamour of the last few hours. Maria sat in the middle of the kitchen as her mother combed through her fine, limp hair. It reminded Maria of all the times her mother combed her hair when she was a little girl, untangling the knots that coiled together from playing without inhibition. But she wasn't a little girl anymore. In just over an hour, she would be a wife.

"Opa helped me move my bed into the other room today," Kaethe informed her, "and we've got a double bed in your room now, for you and Jacob." Kaethe clipped the last roller into place on Maria's head and wiped her hands on her apron.

Maria heard the heaviness Kaethe tried to dismiss as she spoke. She was trying to sound nonchalant about the fact, but it was obvious to Maria that her marriage to Jacob was proving to be a more difficult transition for her mother than she cared to admit. If she was honest, Maria was weary of the transition herself.

"Mama," she grabbed her mother's wrist gently. Kaethe turned slowly, and Maria gestured for her to sit in the chair across from her. Reluctantly, Kaethe sat down, avoiding eye contact. "Mama, look at me." With tear-brimmed eyes, Kaethe lifted her face to look at Maria. "I want you to know how grateful I am for all the work you've done – and are still doing – to help with the wedding, and for everything else. You've been an amazing mother, and I cherish you deeply."

Maria's tears flowed then, which instinctively led to Kaethe's undoing. The pair held each other and cried, until Kaethe composed herself enough to speak.

"This is silly. You're not even moving out of the house yet! I'm just going to sleep in another room. We'll see each other every day, and drink coffee together every morning, like we always do. Nothing is going to change."

"Then why does it feel like everything is changing?" Maria sobbed. Her shoulders rose and fell in a rhythmic motion.

"Oh, my darling Michi. Everything will be all right. Better than all right! Getting married is a big step, and lots does change, but it just as quickly becomes normal, and you won't be able to imagine your life any different. Even this moment will be forgotten. The blessings of marriage far outweigh the fear of change. You'll see. Oh, my Michi, come here."

Kaethe held Maria's quivering body in her arms and stroked her back. Without another thought, she began singing, comforting her daughter with the encouraging lyrics and tune of a familiar hymn. Kaethe wiped Maria's shimmering cheeks with the edge of her apron.

"There, there. Let's finish your hair now. We don't have long before the guests arrive."

—

The silky fabric felt smooth on her legs as she stepped into the gown, one leg at a time. She pulled the delicate dress up her legs, and over her hips, before it hung elegantly from her waist. She slid one arm into a long silk sleeve, and then the other, shifting her shoulders to align the dress perfectly. A row of hand sewn silk buttons lined the front of the gown, and Maria pulled each one through its corresponding buttonhole.

Her mother walked into the room and stood silently staring at Maria, the stem of a small garden flower held between her thumb and forefinger. Maria reached for the silk belt that lay on the bed and extended her arm toward Kaethe.

"Would you mind helping me with the belt?"

"I would love to."

Kaethe tied, and re-tied, the silk fabric until she tied a bow deemed worthy of a bride. The small flower she carried into the room was pinned to the collar of Maria's dress, right above the first button. Maria sat on the edge of the bed and slipped her small feet into the white leather sandals with a low, thick heel that sat on the floor. She wiped the dust from the front of one shoe, where her toes peeked out of the end.

After fastening the buckles, Maria stood and brushed the skirt of her gown and straightened the pleats. Kaethe held a small mirror across the room and Maria moved her body so she could see herself in the small looking glass. She saw herself from the neck down and her lungs stopped breathing for a moment as she took in the sight.

Her waist looked slim. *Jasch will like that,* she thought, and smiled as she pictured his eyes lingering on her accentuated curves, and the struggle he would inevitably feel as he was forced to keep his hands to himself during the ceremony. Her hair was pulled back and set in pins to give her as much volume as she could muster from her thin hair, and a crown of small, white flowers sat on the top of her head. From it, a long, white veil flowed to the ground and gathered around her feet.

"You look beautiful," Kaethe beamed, nearly breathless.

Maria looked in the mirror again. She was really a bride, she thought. With another deep breath she looked at her mother and smiled.

"I'm ready."

—

It was a balmy autumn day that brushed everyone's skin with a thin layer of dampness as they waited under the white tent. The sun was past its peak, casting a warm glow over the village. Maria peered discreetly out the bedroom window, nerves building with each tick of the clock on the nightstand.

"Hi, Frü Penner," Jacob's familiar voice greeted her mother in the next room. Maria's heart raced and she thought she might lose her stomach right then and there. Her palms felt damp and her head felt light. She leaned against the wardrobe and took a deep breath.

"Jacob! Don't you look dapper in your suit!" It was quiet for a moment and Maria pictured her mother looking Jacob up and down, smiling, though Jacob was likely blushing, not one to thrive on attention. "Oh, before I forget ..." It was silent again, save for the soft rustling of fabric. Maria moved closer to the door and listened. Her mother must have been pinning his boutonniere onto the lapel of his jacket.

"How's Maria?" he asked, a slight crack in his voice. Maria was glad she wasn't the only one feeling nervous.

"She's great. I'll let her know you're here and then I'll tell *Prediger* Klassen it's almost time to start."

The straw cracked under Kaethe's feet as she moved toward the bedroom. Maria quickly stepped back, away from the door, not wanting Jacob to catch sight of her a moment sooner than planned. Kaethe poked her head into the room, telling Maria the same thing she just told Jacob. She smiled and winked before closing the door behind her again.

Maria took a deep breath and looked at herself in the tiny mirror one last time. She realigned the buttons on the front of the gown and pulled her veil around her shoulders, blanketing her with hope and promise for a long and happy marriage with Jacob.

With her bouquet in hand, she turned the handle and opened the door.

—

Jacob tapped his thighs with his hands as he waited anxiously for Maria to appear. He watched Kaethe from the window as she tapped the pastor on the shoulders and pointed toward the house with a nod. Jacob's legs felt weak beneath him as the reality of what was about to ensue set in. Small drops of sweat clung to his temples and he wondered if he would get through the whole ordeal without fainting.

He shuddered at the thought of all those people watching him, but before he could work himself into more of a frenzy, he heard the door behind him as it moved over the straw. He stood taller and pulled on his navy suit jacket as he turned to face the bedroom. The world around him faded as he watched the figure in white move fluidly out of the bedroom, as if gliding toward him in slow motion. The afternoon light shone majestically through the window, making her angelic appearance look even more heavenly. His jaw dropped at the sight of her.

"Hi," Maria said shyly, her cheeks reddening from his intense stare. She shifted her weight, intimidated by his unmoving gaze. She felt vulnerable as she stood there, with Jacob not saying or doing anything for some time. When his eyes locked on hers, he snapped back to reality and closed his mouth.

"Hi," his voice cracked like a prepubescent schoolboy, and he cleared his throat instantly, clearly embarrassed. "Hi," he tried again, this time with a lower and even tone. Maria thought it adorable and took a few steps closer to him. "Mariechen, you look … I mean, your dress … What I mean to say is, you look stunning. Absolutely gorgeous. I'm the luckiest man alive."

Jacob moved intently toward her, his eyes fixed on hers. Her face flushed slightly at his compliments, which only made her more beautiful, in Jacob's opinion. He cupped her face in his strong hands and pressed his lips against hers. As he kissed her, he felt the pent up anxiety leave his body as he relaxed into hers. He licked his lips and wondered when he could kiss her again, and hoped he would never have to stop.

"*Najo*, well then?" he said, "Shall we get married?"

18

April 27, 1947

MARIA WOKE WITH THE SUN AND LIFTED HER ARM TO MOVE A STRAND OF hair from her face. She looked across the room, where her mother usually slept, but there was no bed there. Jacob stirred beside her and she jumped. She forgot she wasn't alone and was suddenly vividly aware of her bare skin – and his – under the sheets. She pulled the sheets up to her neck and Jacob looked at her through barely open eyes.

"Good morning," he whispered before pulling her body closer to his so she was nestled against him. His touch calmed her and she relaxed into his grip. Memories of the night before played through her mind and her heart slowed to a normal pace as everything began to make sense. She had spent the night with Jacob. She was married now.

She laid her head beside his and smiled as she fingered the gold band around the third finger of her left hand. He kissed her cheek and moved his hand over her abdomen, causing goosebumps to cover her skin. Euphoria rushed through her veins. Not only had they spent their first night together, but for the first time, they also didn't have to say goodbye. Despite the expected awkwardness of being naked in front of each other, she had fallen asleep entangled in her husband's arms, happy, content, safe, at peace.

"I don't know if I'll ever get used to calling you my *husband*."

"Well, you've got lots of time to practice, Frü Loewen," he said, emphasizing the 'Frü.' They laid silently for some time before Jacob spoke again, his voice soft, with a touch of emotion. "I'll never forget the moment you walked out of this room. I swore I had died and gone to heaven and was standing in the presence of an angel."

"You didn't look so bad yourself, *Herr* Loewen. I think navy was the perfect colour for your suit. And it fit you so nicely, unlike your usual oversized work clothes. I had to look twice to make sure it was actually you and that I wasn't walking down the aisle with some other man."

Jacob pinched her sides, tickling her. She laughed, the way she always did when she felt safe and genuinely happy. She squirmed at his touch and pleaded with him to stop. He eventually obliged and turned her body to face his. His smile faded as he looked honestly into her eyes, causing her to shy away from his intensity.

"I love you, Mariechen, and I will spend the rest of my life making sure you know just how much you mean to me."

Maria combed his hair with her fingers and met his gaze, her eyes equally as honest and transparent as his. Maria kissed Jacob and they showed with their actions what they could not adequately say with their words.

Maria (15) getting baptized.

The woodshop in Filadelfia where Jacob worked. Jacob is in the doorway, second from the left.
Franz is sitting on the wagon wheels, far right.

Jacob and three of his siblings, early to mid 1940s.
From left to right: Jacob, Marieche, David and Abram.

Maria (16), standing behind the ironing board.
Taken in 1944, the year she didn't go to school and learned to sew.

Jacob and Maria on their wedding day, April 26, 1947. Maria (18), Jacob (23).

Family photo from Jacob and Maria's wedding. Sitting, left to right: Maria and Johann Warkentin, Johann's widowed sister-in-law, Johann's sister-in-law and brother, Heinrich Warkentin. Standing, starting fourth from left: Marieche, David, Abram, Kaethe, Maria and Jacob. Far right: Jacob's parents, Abram and Helena Loewen. Unnamed on left are cousins of Kaethe Penner. Unnamed on right are cousins of Helena Loewen.

PART FOUR

19

November 1947

DUST LINGERED IN THE AIR, SUSPENDED, LIKE DENSE FOG. MARIA COVERED her nose and mouth with a handkerchief as she held on to Jacob's arm to keep steady. She wore her wedding dress, though it looked nothing like it did on their wedding day. The hem had been taken up to her knees, and the long sleeves cut short to make it more suitable for hot weather. The dress was reserved for Sunday mornings and special occasions, for the time being. Eventually, when it became too tattered and stained, it would be demoted once again.

Maria wiped the dust from her skirt, marking the white silk with brown streaks. She frowned, tired of the endless dust and dirt that loomed everywhere. She looked at Jacob, his face and arms covered in a fine layer of dust. A few drops of sweat trickled down his arm, leaving wet marks on his skin like the trail of a snake slithering through a desert.

"It's so nice of the colony to throw a big party for me on my birthday every year," Jacob said.

"And it's so nice of you to make the same comment every year, as well," she mocked.

"Now, now, there's no need for such sarcasm," he moved his body into hers and bumped her with his hip. She lost her footing and clung to his arm. Jacob pulled her to her feet and laughed. Maria hit him on the arm, but continued holding on to the crook of his elbow.

"Seriously, Jasch, how many more years am I going to have to hear you make the same comment as we walk to the November 25th celebration?"

"That depends," he raised his chin to make him look more scholarly, "how many more years do you plan to walk with me to the November 25th celebration?"

Maria rolled her eyes and said nothing in response. Jacob squeezed her hand with his elbow and smiled; he loved teasing her. He knew she was fond of his wit, or at least he liked to believe she found it endearing.

The crowd in the distance marked their destination. The church yard was filled with nearly everyone in the surrounding colonies as they celebrated another year since they escaped Russia. Jacob inhaled deeply as they approached the sea of people, steadying his frustration. He quite despised large group settings. Not only did the musings over minute details of farming and weather bore him, but the conversation usually turned to church, and his lack of attendance Sunday mornings.

He only wished the colony's holiday didn't have to be on his birthday, of all days. He knew no one was forcing him to go to the celebration, yet he felt obligated to attend. If it were up to Jacob, he would spend his birthday at home, with Maria, but he knew that wasn't an option. Maria was a social butterfly and thrived on social gatherings. If he wanted to be with Maria, he had to accept that he would need to make an appearance to more outings than he preferred, or she would go without him.

A hand rose above the crowd and waved furiously in the air like a flag. Franz moved toward them with Leni, his girlfriend, following behind. The couple hadn't been together for long, but it was obvious that they were very much smitten with each other. Leni was good for him, and Jacob made sure Franz knew that. He teased him often, telling Franz that if he didn't marry her soon, someone else might come along and she'd realize she could do better. Jacob's comments didn't amuse Franz very much.

While the four friends chatted, a little boy ran up to them and wrapped his arms around Jacob's waist. Jacob's body swayed from the impact, and the shock, and he looked down to find a blond-haired boy clinging to his leg.

"Wilmar!" Jacob's face beamed. He reached down and picked up the five-year-old, resting him on his hip. Wilmar smiled at his brother, and then quickly straightened his lips and scowled at Jacob. The others tried not to laugh, not wanting to offend the boy's efforts to look truly upset. "What's the matter, boy? Aren't you happy to see me?"

"*Oba nä*, no," Wilmar blurted out.

"Why not?"

"Because. I'm mad at you."

"You are, hey? What for?" Jacob played along.

"Because you don't come home anymore," he turned his face away from Jacob, toward the sky. "Every time I ask Mother where you are, she says you're at the *Penners.*" He spoke Maria's maiden name as if it were two words, Pen and Ners, and glared at Maria as he said it. "You spend too much time at the *Penners.*" He crossed his arms to emphasize his point.

"Ah," Jacob nodded. "I see. Well, I'm sorry you're upset, but you do remember that I married Maria, right?" He paused and Wilmar nodded slowly, still avoiding eye contact with Jacob. "And you know that I live with Maria now, right?" Wilmar glared at Maria through small slits in his eyes and she covered her mouth to hide the smile she couldn't avoid.

"Oh, yes," Wilmar spoke slowly, "I remember."

Jacob burst out laughing and lowered Wilmar back to the ground. Crouching, he looked Wilmar in the eyes. "How about we make a deal? I'll come by once a week and you and I can play Tip-Tip together. How's that sound?"

Wilmar pinched his chin with thumb and forefinger as he contemplated Jacob's proposal.

"Deal!" Wilmar's smile returned and he extended his hand to Jacob. They shook hands and the boy ran off.

They continued making their rounds, and Jacob grew more annoyed by the minute. Maria stopped to greet anyone that crossed their path. He was tired of the judgemental glances from the older women as they asked Maria how she was doing. He knew they were referring to him, her *ungodly* husband. She smiled politely as she responded to their impertinent prying into their marriage and personal lives.

The heat only intensified his resentment. His shirt clung to his body, and where his skin was bare, perspiration sparkled in the sunlight. He bit his tongue to keep from yelling at everyone to mind their own business, and to beg Maria to leave with him. He wondered if he should just go, Maria clearly didn't need him to be present to enjoy herself. She stood in a circle with her friends and he could see her mouth move, but he was too far away to hear what she was saying. Every now and then he heard her laugh rise through the crowd. It caught his attention like a beacon, and he'd search for her, drawn to the melodious sound. She never met his gaze, though, immersed in conversation with her friends.

With the sun at its peak, the crowds slowly dispersed, making their way home for lunch and their afternoon *Meddachschlop*. Maria held Jacob's hand as they walked toward the house, and noticed the tightness in his muscles, and the straight line of his lips. Not wanting to have the same argument, again, about their differing social needs, she began sharing tidbits from all the conversations she had had.

"Leni said that Franz told her he loved her last night! Isn't that something? She obviously loves him, too, and told him so. I suppose we'll have a wedding to attend in a few weeks. Although, Leni did say she would prefer to wait until after the summer." Maria paused for a moment, and Jacob moved his jaw side to side, gritting his teeth together. He wasn't interested in hearing about all her conversations just then. He needed silence, and solitude.

"I like Leni," Maria continued. "We've gotten to know each other quite well since they started dating. She's good for Franz, and I'm happy for him. He's a good guy.

"Prediger Klassen stopped me earlier," she added, without taking a breath. Jacob wiped his brow, but one drop of sweat escaped down his temple and fell off his jaw onto the fine powder of dust on the ground. "He asked if I would be willing to sing in a small ensemble for the Christmas Eve program. The first practice is on Sunday. You don't mind, do you? I assumed it would be fine. And the choir will be practicing again for the usual Sunday mornings after New Years. I'd love to join them again, as well. Maybe you could come listen to us sing every now and—"

"Maria!" Jacob interrupted her with a harshness in his voice. She quieted instantly and stopped in her tracks. He wiped his eyes, instantly regretting his tone, but he couldn't help it. She kept talking and talking with hardly a breath between each thought. Maria dropped her arms to her sides and walked past him hurriedly. "Maria, I'm sorry!" Jacob called after her, and picked up his pace to catch up. "I didn't mean to yell."

He placed his hand on her shoulder, a small puff of dust rose from the impact and lingered in her wake. She shrugged her shoulder, forcing him to remove his hand. Jacob put his hands in his pockets and walked beside her. A tear crawled down her sun-kissed cheek and the pit in his stomach grew.

He knew from the very beginning of their relationship that her faith was an important part of Maria's life, if not *the* most important. Although he respected her choices and beliefs, he always found himself trying to defend his own beliefs – or lack thereof. He didn't believe that having Jesus in your heart, or life, or even acknowledging his existence, was the answer to all of life's problems. There was no amount of evidence that could convince him to believe that accepting the whole Jesus thing would improve the quality of his life. But somehow Maria didn't see that, or at least couldn't understand.

While dating, Jacob and Maria talked about their upbringings and beliefs, but somehow their differing perspectives caused constant strife and dissension between them once they'd married. He never forbade her to attend church, and he never would, that was a fact. He did honestly respect her beliefs and he wouldn't stop her from going to church, but he refused to attend with her, aside from Christmas, and occasionally Easter. He would not, and physically could not, pretend to be something he wasn't. He vowed never to be a hypocrite, choosing instead to live a life with morals, values, love, and good ethics. Apparently that wasn't a good enough life according to the so-called 'Christians' in town. He wasn't immune to their judgement – the hushed whispers as he passed a group of women on the street, or the not-so-subtle glances over shoulders as men rode past him on carriages.

Even Maria experienced her fair share of judgement from the church for marrying Jacob. People gossiped endlessly about her, and she was no longer allowed to recite poems at church, because she chose to be 'yoked to an unbeliever.' That, in itself, was enough to send Jacob into a raging fit, and he couldn't understand why she still believed in God if that was how His followers treated her. It hurt her, which hurt him, but her faith in God never wavered. She had experienced God personally in too many ways, she could never deny his existence, or love, despite others' misinterpretations of that love.

That was what baffled Jacob. Even after all the exclusions and judgement she endured, she still wanted to sing in the choir with the very people that were judging her? Jacob couldn't fathom it.

He didn't want Maria to sing in the choir. The thought of it aroused something in him that he tried to rationalize. He couldn't tell if he was concerned about his own ego, and what others would think of him if his wife was so actively involved in church, with a husband who stayed at home and wanted nothing to do with it. It was true, but there was something else yet. Guilt? Jacob had an amazing voice. Together, Jacob's bass and Maria's soprano formed quite the duet. If Maria sang in the choir, and he didn't, it would make him look bad, or so he reasoned.

Singing on Christmas Eve, like he had for many years, seemed somehow different than singing Sunday mornings. Christmas was celebrated worldwide, by people of all different religions, and, in his opinion, was more of a cultural tradition. It didn't feel like a spiritual occasion to him.

If Jacob wouldn't sing in the choir, then he didn't want Maria to, either. Was that so wrong?

Jacob cleared his throat.

"Actually, I do mind," his voice was steady yet firm. "I don't want you to sing in the choir. Not for Christmas Eve, or any other day." Jacob took a few more steps before he realized Maria wasn't beside him anymore. He stopped and turned around to find her standing with her arms crossed, her neck and cheeks blazing red. She stared at him with fiery eyes, burning him on the inside as he looked back, forcing himself not to look away.

"Excuse me?" She said the first word as if it were two words, emphasizing her fury. Jacob had never seen her this angry before. The muscles in his face softened and he raised his brows, wondering if he was wrong to say what he had.

"I don't want you to sing in the choir," he said again, this time with more gentleness in his tone. "I'm sorry, Mariechen, I'm not comfortable with it."

"It's your decision not to accompany me Sunday mornings, but you have no right to tell me what I can and can't be a part of when it comes to church. You've known from the beginning that my faith is the most important thing in my life, and I'm sorry if you're jealous or feel inferior by that somehow, but that's how it is, and it's never going to change."

Tears fell freely and her chest moved visibly in and out as she breathed heavily. "I get enough judgement from the women at church as is, just because I'm married to a non-Christian. If I don't join the choir because you forbade me to, it would only perch them higher on their pedestals, proving that this will never work." She moved her finger back and forth between them.

"This is what I don't understand!" Jacob spread his arms out, exasperated. "Don't you see the hypocrisy? You claim to love a God who cares for and loves others, and you hear the pastor preach about loving your neighbour and not judging others and all that, and yet you are being judged and treated unfairly because you've chosen to marry me! How does that not bother you? Maybe God isn't who you think He is."

Maria scowled at Jacob, "I'll start taking biblical advice from you when you start attending church with me."

She stormed off, bumping Jacob with her shoulder as she moved past him. He touched the spot where her shoulder had impacted him and watched as her body jolted side to side as she ran the rest of the way home.

—

Maria was fuming by the time she got home. She had never felt so much rage toward someone before. Her blood rushed forcefully through her body, and she lost herself momentarily in the rhythmic sensation, her hand resting on the gate. She walked through and slammed it behind her. With her head down, she tramped toward the house. She didn't notice her grandparents sitting on the porch until she reached them.

"Michi? What's wrong?" Johann's brows arched in concern. Ralph, their replacement for Muppy after she died earlier that year, lifted his groggy face, and lowered it again when he saw it was only Maria.

Maria's arm was already extended toward the door, and she rested her hand on the handle. Her shoulders slumped and her rage turned to overwhelming sorrow. The weight of her future hung on her shoulders. She turned toward her grandparents and fell to the floor beside Anna. With her head resting on Anna's frail lap, she cried, while Anna's stiff, calloused fingers stroked her hair.

Maria lifted her head to remove her glasses and wiped her eyes on the handkerchief Johann offered in his outstretched hand. She looked at her grandparents with envy. They never argued about faith because they both believed the same things. Another round of tears fell from Maria's eyes.

"This is how it will be for the rest of my life, isn't it?" she asked.

"What happened, my dear?" Anna's voice was raspy and barely audible. Her stomach pains had worsened over the last year, and she was never without pain, though the only proof of that was the subtle wince on her face.

Maria told them everything that had transpired between her and Jacob. She stopped a few times to blow her nose into the handkerchief before lamenting further. "He claims to respect my beliefs, but he will never fully support them, will he?" She looked into their eyes for reassurance, but saw only empathy. "How do I do this? How do I live through the rest of my life constantly fighting with my husband about church and faith? Why won't he just see that he needs Jesus?"

Anna leaned forward slowly. She shut her eyes tightly against the pain, a multitude of creases appearing at the corners of her eyes. She held on to the armrest of the chair with one hand to keep herself upright, and placed her other hand delicately on Maria's cheek.

"Michi, you have to take one day at a time. Every marriage has its struggles, but you know you were meant to love Jacob. So trust God with His perfect timing. Every morning when you wake up, you have to choose to love Jacob, and when arguments arise, which they will, then you choose love. God is using you in Jacob's life, even if you don't think anything is changing." Maria slumped to the ground, unimpressed with Anna's response. "And Michi, be careful. Don't push Jacob too hard, or you might push him further than he already is."

Anna coughed until she was in a fit and could hardly breathe. Johann came to her aid, and with Maria's help they lifted her off the chair and brought her to bed. Maria stood outside the door, listening to the wheezing on the other side of the door, and prayed her oma would be all right.

She went back to the porch and sat on the now vacant chair. The wood beneath her was still warm, which oddly comforted her. Anna always knew what to say to Maria, no matter what the circumstance. She knew Anna's time on earth was running out, but Maria wouldn't let her mind go there. She felt a glimpse of the void she would experience when that day came, and brushed the thought aside.

Maria shook her head to clear it and went back to her conversation with Jacob. Her chest rose as she took a deep breath and her nerves settled ever so slightly as she exhaled. Life would not be easy, she realized that, but she wondered how long she could hold on to any hope of Jacob ever coming to accept Christ for himself.

The thought of raising children without a husband who would encourage them to go to church and to seek God's will paralyzed her. Since it was just the two of them, it didn't seem as big of an issue, but she did want to have a family. Maria closed her eyes and prayed for patience and forgiveness. When she opened her eyes, Jacob was walking through the gate.

—

In the months that followed, Anna's health continued to deteriorate. Without proper equipment to run tests, they had no confirmed diagnosis, but based on her symptoms, the doctors were confident she had cancer in her liver. In April, Anna passed away peacefully in her bed, with Johann clutching her hand in his. Kaethe sat on the other side of her, stroking the top of her head, feeling the coarse strands between her fingers, watching the colour in her cheeks fade to a soft grey. Maria sat beside Kaethe, holding Anna's other hand up to her cheek. Her tears moved down Anna's arm, curving around the bones, and soaked into the sheets where her elbow rested.

She was buried later that day in the cemetery on the outskirts of Filadelfia. Kaethe and Maria had stood on either side of Johann. He watched with silent trepidation as his wife of forty years was lowered into the ground. His eyes were glassy with emotion, but his dark, leathered cheeks remained dry. Kaethe knew he was trying to be strong for her and Maria.

It wasn't until that evening, in the confines of his room, that Johann allowed himself the freedom to grieve his wife. Kaethe and Maria stood outside his bedroom door, clinging to each other. He was never the same after that. A part of Johann died with his wife that day.

He rarely left his bedroom, aside from joining the others for meals. Not even a pot of coffee could coax him to join them. Every now and then they would catch a glimpse of his jovial personality, but it was quickly replaced with the usual frown he had worn in the months that followed.

One Sunday afternoon, while sitting on the porch with Jacob, Maria looked at the closed door of her grandparents' bedroom and sighed. "Opa hasn't been the same since Oma died. He looks so sad and lonely."

Jacob stubbed out his cigarette. "That's because he *is* sad and lonely."

"But he has Mama, and us." She turned back to face Jacob and crossed her legs, intertwining her fingers, and placed her hands on her lap.

"You know that's not the same. And I don't blame him, either. If anything happened to you, I'd be just as depressed as he is."

"I know. I realize that," she turned her thumbs in circles around each other. "It just breaks my heart to see him like this. He's not the same man he was before."

"Do you love him any less because of it?"

"Of course not!"

"Exactly."

Jacob leaned back in his chair and slowly dozed off, softly snoring beside her as memories of Opa and Oma played through her mind.

"Oh, I like this one!" Leni placed a roll of white lace on the pile of other fabrics sprawled out on the counter. "Yes, I think this is the one!"

Leni asked Maria to join her at the Cooperative to select the fabric for her wedding gown. Maria was honoured at the request. Her friendship with Leni had grown since she had started dating Franz, and Maria viewed her more as a sister than a friend by this point. When Franz asked Leni to marry him at the end of August, Leni was giddy with excitement and constantly asked Maria questions about her wedding, and about marriage, in general.

After purchasing the lace, buttons, and thread, the two women walked toward Maria's house. The sun warmed their skin, and by the time they arrived, their blouses were damp from perspiration. Maria's glasses slipped down her nose and she pushed them back up with one finger. In the kitchen, she filled two glasses with cold coffee. They moved two chairs into the shade of the passageway and settled into their seats, dabbing their faces and necks with handkerchiefs.

"Franz told me what he said to you, before you and Jacob were engaged," Leni said sheepishly.

Maria knew what her friend was referring to, though she couldn't make out whether she was apologizing or looking for Maria to give her an explanation of some sort.

"Oh, yeah?" Maria offered, still not sure what kind of response Leni was hoping to get from her.

"I know I'm probably being ridiculous – actually, I *know* I'm being ridiculous. He explained it all and assured me you had been very clear about your feelings for Jacob and that you were in no way interested in Franz, and never had been." She leaned back into her seat and crossed her feet. Her eyes met Maria's for the first time since they stopped walking. "I just need to hear it from you, and then I can put the whole thing to rest and not have to think about it anymore."

Maria forced herself not to laugh, but smiled at her friend. "Leni, if I wanted to have Franz, I could have. But I didn't – not then, and not ever. You have nothing to worry about. It was a silly thing for him to do, and he regretted it instantly. Like I told Jacob that day, it wasn't that Franz loved me, it was that he wanted to have someone love him the way I love Jacob. And now he does! Look, if Jacob can move past it, so can you. I promise you I never had feelings for

Franz. That boy is so madly and hopelessly in love with you." Maria squeezed her friend's shoulder and tilted her head and smiled again.

"Okay, thanks," Leni grinned, somewhat embarrassed for harbouring such insecurities. They sipped their beverages in silence, enjoying the cool sensation moving down their throats. "How many children do you and Jacob want?" Leni asked after a few minutes.

Maria took another sip and licked a drop of coffee from her lips. "We're not sure. We haven't said a final number yet. We've agreed that we won't have just one. I didn't like growing up alone, but we also don't want eleven, like Jacob's family, because, well, that's just far too many children!"

They both laughed and took another sip of their drinks.

"Franz and I would like five or six. At least that's what we've said." Leni moved her hand that held her coffee in small circles, making the contents swirl like an eddy. "Maria, can I ask you a question?" Her face scrunched up, and a soft shade of pink brushed across her cheeks. "If it's too personal, you don't have to answer." Maria eyed her friend, intrigued.

"All right. What do you want to know?" Maria leaned back into her chair, eager to hear what Leni would ask her.

Leni shifted in her seat, the redness in her cheeks deepening in colour. "I don't talk to my mother about, well, you know, marriage related things. And you're the only close friend I have that's married, and, quite frankly, you're the only one I feel like I could ask about this," she fingered a loose thread on her skirt as she formulated her next sentence. "How do you … I mean, what do you do … that is, how are you not yet, you know …"

"You mean, how do we keep from getting pregnant?" Maria said matter-of-factly.

"Yes!" Leni sighed in relief.

Maria smiled at her friend's shy naivety, though she could fully relate. She had asked her mother the same question before she married Jacob. Then, after the wedding, Maria and Jacob discussed it somewhat awkwardly, as well. They knew they wanted to have kids, but they weren't in any rush to start their family. They wanted to live on their own before they had children, and enjoy time together just the two of them.

"Well, hm, how can I say this without making you feel even more uncomfortable?" Maria thought for a second. "Jacob had a saying: 'The man has to leave the church before the closing song is sung.'" She winked at her friend.

Leni squealed and covered her mouth with her free hand and Maria laughed as Leni squirmed in her seat.

"That's it?" Leni asked when she had recovered.

"That's it." Maria assured her. "I mean, if God wants you to have a baby, you'll have a baby regardless, but that's the best way to delay it from happening, as far as we can control. It's either that or not be intimate at all until you actually want to have a baby. But I don't think that's a viable option for most couples." Maria laughed. Leni smiled back, cheeks still flushed.

That was all that was said about the matter, and they quickly moved on to less intimate topics. It was late into the afternoon when Leni finally stood to leave. She picked up her bag of white cotton and lace fabrics and walked to the gate with Maria. Ralph followed a few paces behind. His tongue hung out the side of his mouth, dropping thick saliva onto the parched dirt. He sat on his hind legs beside Maria as they watched Leni walk down the street. Maria stroked the top of his head and his tail wagged, forming a cloud of dust behind him.

"Well, Ralph. Shall we prepare leftovers for supper? Jasch will be home soon."

At the mention of food, Ralph got up and ran toward the house barking. His ears flapped as his body bounded up the yard. Maria smiled as she watched him, until her gaze landed on the room across the passageway where her opa was likely sleeping.

Her heart sank every time she thought of him. She couldn't imagine what it must feel like for him to have lost his wife. Maria couldn't even begin to think of anything happening to Jacob, and she'd only known him a few years. Oma and Opa had been together for decades. As much as she missed Oma, she missed Opa just as much.

Maria walked into the kitchen and grabbed a pot of leftover *Cotletten*, deep fried hamburger patties, and placed them on a plate. She thought of Oma and missed her radiant smile, her wisdom, her delicious cakes. She missed hearing her stories most of all, even though she had heard them all a thousand times over and knew them all from memory herself. It was Oma's demeanor while telling the stories that she longed to witness again. Her whole face lit up when she recalled moments from her past, and every time she told a familiar story, she always added or changed one minor detail or another. Maria was especially fond of Oma's memories from Ebenfeld – their house, the general store, the goods Opa would find on his journeys to Moscow. But nothing delighted Anna more than to reminisce on her courtship with Johann.

Maria thought about the stories she would one day tell her own children and grandchildren about these early years in her relationship with Jacob. She wondered if she, too, would repeat her favourite memories over and over, and if her grandchildren would think of her as often as she thought of her oma, after she passed away.

In the pantry, she scoured the shelves for a bottle of vinegar and brought it to the counter. She unscrewed the lid and inhaled its tangy scent. A wave of nausea rushed through her and she turned her face, covering her mouth with her hand. She replaced the lid and moved away from the counter. With a nearby towel she covered her nose to keep the smell away. Ralph looked up at her, his head cocked to one side, regarding her quizzically.

"I'm okay, Ralph," she mumbled through the towel. "I'm not sure what happened there."

—

Maria groaned as she lay in bed the next morning, clutching her stomach, her eyes still closed. She sat up slowly, focusing on her breathing instead of the nausea rising in her throat. When she had tied her housecoat securely around her waist, she opened the door, her hand still resting on her stomach.

"*Waut es los met die,* what's wrong with you?" Kaethe looked up from the magazine she was reading.

"I don't feel well."

"Is it the flu?"

"I think so," she assumed it was, at least. Suddenly her eyes bulged and she walked frantically to the pantry, "I need a bucket!"

Pots and pans clanked from behind the wall, followed by the sound of Maria vomiting. Kaethe walked into the pantry and found Maria kneeling on the floor, wiping her mouth with the back of her hand. Kaethe grabbed the little pot and offered to clean it, and instructed Maria to go back to bed.

Maria walked back to her room with a clean pot cradled in her arms. She laid down in bed, pulled the covers up to her neck and hugged her knees against her chest. Jacob, still in bed, turned toward her and wrapped his arm around her body.

"What time is it?" he asked, his voice deep and hoarse with sleep. "Why are you wearing your housecoat in bed? Is everything all right?"

"No," the strain in her voice affirmed her answer. She closed her eyes, and again focused her attention on her breathing so she wouldn't think about the nausea.

The next time Maria opened her eyes, the clock on the nightstand beside her showed that it was just past eleven o'clock. She sat up and another wave of nausea rolled through her. She clung to her pot, holding it just under her chin. The nausea was relentless, refusing to pass and give her a moment's comfort. Frustrated, she got up and walked into the kitchen.

The house was empty, and there was no food on the table yet. Her mother must be working, or at the Cooperative, she assumed. Jacob would be home in half an hour and would need to eat, so she walked into the pantry and lifted the lid off a large pot filled with salt. She reached into the course white grains with both hands and pulled out a large slab of pork. Bile crept up her throat and she instinctively turned her face away from the meat. She had never been repulsed by the smell of pork before.

While a large pot of peanut oil slowly heated on the stove, Maria carved a few slices of meat on a wooden board and placed the rest back in the pot of salt. The smell of the meat and the peanut oil suddenly overwhelmed her, and it was all she could do to stay upright. She leaned against the counter, steadying herself.

The oil bubbled to life and Maria slowly placed the pork slices into the pot. Another wave of nausea overcame her and she grabbed the empty pot and retched uncontrollably until her forehead dripped with sweat. The whistle blew in the distance. She wiped her face with a towel and went outside to clean her pot.

—

The nausea stayed with Maria for the next two weeks, with no sign of relief. She sat on her bed one afternoon, and opened her diary, counting back the days. She didn't need a calendar to tell her what she already knew – she was pregnant.

Jacob walked into the room and Maria looked up from the black scribbles on the ivory paper. A gentle smile caressed her lips and her eyes glistened as she thought of the baby growing inside her.

"What's wrong, Mariechen? You weren't in the kitchen to greet me like you usually do, and I was worried. Is everything all right? What happened?"

He sat beside her on the bed and wrapped his arm around her shoulders. Maria nuzzled her forehead into his neck.

"Nothing's wrong, Jasch," her voice sounded far off, as if she were speaking in a dream. "We're going to have a baby, is all."

His arm stopped stroking hers and he froze, staring at a clump of dirt on the floor. His expression was even, and Maria grew slightly more nervous with each second that passed while Jacob sat silently.

"A baby?"

"Yes, Jasch, you're going to be a papa."

Finally a smile broke across his face and Maria exhaled. He turned to face her, his eyes dancing with joy. He hugged her as he repeated the words, "a baby," over and over until he could believe it.

"Let's go tell your mother and Opa."

Maria nodded as euphoria rushed through her veins, intoxicating her. *A baby*, she thought again, not quite sure she could believe it to be true herself. Before she had any more time to doubt, Jacob pulled her to her feet and she reached back to grab the silver pot as they left the room.

20

June 1949

THE LAST RAINFALL OF THE SEASON CAME DOWN ONE SATURDAY MORNING the following June. Water flooded the city in a span of an hour, leaving nothing untouched, filling cisterns and replenishing gardens one last time before they sat dry for months on end.

Later that day, the sun chased the clouds away, and the ground resumed its usual dusty form. Jacob laid a blanket in the front yard of their new house. With the upcoming arrival of their baby, Jacob and Maria moved into their own house, knowing the time had come to live on their own.

It wasn't an easy decision for Maria, or her mother, even though Jacob and Maria only moved a few blocks away. Maria visited Kaethe and Johann many times a week. Johann was weak, and Kaethe spent most of her time caring for him, while also sewing for stores to bring in what little income she could for the two of them. Maria felt guilty for placing the burden on her mother, but everyone knew it was the right decision, and Kaethe never complained about it.

Maria wobbled out of the house carrying a bowl of freshly picked and peeled mandarin oranges in one hand, and a pitcher of cold coffee in the other. Jacob watched as she moved toward him, her belly protruding out of her small body. There was evidence of discomfort in her face as she strained to lower herself beside Jacob. He held her arm as she sat and smiled at her. Growing a child looked beautiful on her, he thought.

The pregnancy had not been easy for Maria. For six months she lay bedridden, dehydrated from constant nausea, which still plagued her, even near the end. She was grateful to be having a baby, so she kept her discomfort to herself, at least the majority of the time.

Jacob's cigarette hung from his mouth, held loosely in place with his lips. He laid down on his back, crossed his arms behind his head and closed his eyes. The sky was clear and bright, and the slightest breeze moved through the yard, cooling their skin just enough to sit comfortably in the shade. Maria shimmied herself close to Jacob and laid on her side with her head on his chest. She placed both hands on her belly, moving them wherever she felt the jabs of the baby kicking.

"Are you hoping for a son or daughter?" Maria asked him as the baby kicked again. Jacob exhaled another stream of smoke into the air before answering.

"I'd love to have a son, that's for sure. But I'd rather have a daughter with dark hair, than a son with blond hair."

Maria hit his stomach in jest. "Oh Jasch. You can't put that pressure on a baby! We have no more control over the colour of its hair than he or she does!"

"I know, I know," he lifted his head and kissed the top of Maria's. "I'm just saying, it would be nice." He inhaled and exhaled another drag of his cigarette. "Do you think you'll want to have more children after this pregnancy?"

"Oh, yes. There's no question about that." Jacob was mildly surprised by her response. Seeing the question in his eyes, she elaborated. "Pregnancy is nine months of physical discomfort, but then it's over. A family is forever. I want a family, and I'll go through all of this again, and then some, if that's what it takes to have a family of my own. It's raising the children that worries me."

"What do you mean?"

"Well, being pregnant is physically difficult, but only for a short time, whereas raising a child goes on for a lifetime, nearly. That's the hardest part, I imagine. It's daunting to think about raising a child to grow up to be honest, loyal and hopefully, God willing, grow to love the Lord. Parenting is what scares me."

"You're going to be a great mother, Mariechen. I don't doubt it for a second."

"And you're going to be an amazing father."

"I hope so." Jacob extinguished the end of his cigarette on the ground.

"You will be, Jasch," Maria pushed herself off of Jacob so she could face him. Jacob shielded his eyes with his hand so he could meet Maria's gaze.

"I still worry that I'll have a relationship with my kids like my father had with us. I don't want that." He closed his eyes again and laid back on his hands.

"That's why you won't. You know you want to have a good relationship with your kids, so you'll make it happen. Besides, your father isn't normal, sorry for saying. I'm not trying to be mean, I'm just being honest. I don't know many fathers that don't ever want to spend time with their kids. Your dad doesn't even know who Franz is, or any of your siblings' friends. Heck, I reckon he hardly knows you're married. If I had a relationship with my children like you have with your father, I would cry myself to death."

Jacob didn't respond. He knew what Maria was saying, and figured she was right, about all of it, but he still worried. After a few minutes of silent reflection, Maria ventured to change to the subject.

"We haven't settled on any names yet. We only have another week or so before baby arrives, so I would feel better knowing we had a name for it before then. Why don't we narrow down our options? I like Peter, for a boy. What do you think?"

"Peter's all right," Jacob sat up and ate a slice of orange. "I'm just not sure I want it for my own son."

"Why not? That was my grandfather's name on my dad's side. I like it."

"I know, but I just don't particularly like the name, is all. It needs to be a common name, but not too overused. And nothing too 'out there,' either."

Maria sighed, "What about Sylvia, for a girl?"

"Sylvia? Where did you hear a name like Sylvia?" He scrunched his nose. Maria smacked his arm, and clicked her tongue in disapproval.

"Don't say that! It's a lovely name, and you know it! Mama mentioned it to me the other day. She went to see a play and one of the main characters was named Sylvia. Tina played that role, actually. Mama said she did a great job."

"Sylvia," he let the name hang in the air for a few seconds. "It's all right. What are our other options?"

They spouted off names for some time, though Maria did most of the suggesting and Jacob did most of the protesting. Defeated, they laid in silence beside each other again.

"Are we going to your mother's house on Wednesday to celebrate your birthday?"

"Yes and no. She's invited us over for dinner tomorrow night, instead. I told her to come to our house on Wednesday night with Opa for coffee. Is that all right?"

"Sure. But only if she brings her chocolates. And maybe some *Trubochki*."

Jacob's lips turned up on one side and Maria jabbed him in the side. They laughed and stayed beside each other for the rest of the evening.

—

"See you after *Meddachschlop*, then. Bye."

Maria kissed her mother and Opa on the cheek before she turned down the street toward her house, and they, toward theirs. They met every Sunday morning at the corner where Jacob's woodshop was, and walked the rest of the way to church together, and back again.

Maria walked slowly, her swollen body weighing her down. She saw Jacob as she approached the gate. He was sitting in the shade outside the house reading the latest *Mennoblatt*. A cloud of smoke gathered around him, and for a moment she could barely make out his face in the haze. When she reached him, she kissed his inviting lips. The taste of burnt tobacco lingered as she walked into the house. She undressed in her bedroom and slipped into something more casual.

She sat on the edge of the bed to buckle her shoes. When she finished, she couldn't help but lie down to catch her breath and rest her weary feet for a moment. She hadn't planned on sleeping, but her eyes closed as soon as her head rested on the pillow, and she didn't stir when Jacob came looking for her and fell asleep beside her.

Maria woke suddenly, startled. It felt like she had been asleep for hours, and feared they were late for supper at her mother's. She reached for the clock on the nightstand and brought it close to her face so she could make out the time. They weren't late at all, which relieved her, but she was shocked that she had only been asleep for twenty minutes.

Her heart was still racing and she wondered why she had woken in such a fit when she had been sleeping so soundly. Still tired, she lowered her head onto the pillow again and shifted her body until she found a comfortable position. She had nearly drifted off again when a stabbing pain shot across her lower abdomen and around to her lower back. She gasped and turned her body to the other side, assuming she had pinched a nerve. The pain slowly subsided and she relaxed into her bed once more.

Mere minutes passed before another shooting pain coursed through mid-section, and this time she felt her stomach tighten. She placed her hand on it and it felt stiff as a board beneath her fingers. The pain moved all around her middle, and she tried to sit up, but her stomach was too taut, making it impossible to move. She writhed in pain until her stomach relaxed again, allowing her freedom to move.

She sat up and moved her legs off the side of the bed, breathing heavily and embracing the moment without pain. Maria sat breathless and worried as she waited to see what would happen next. A few more minutes passed and the pain had not returned. Hopeful that it was behind her now, she started to lower herself back into bed when it hit her again, this time with more force.

Maria moaned out loud, clutching her stomach. Jacob woke and looked around the room in a daze. When he saw Maria rocking at the end of the bed, he threw the sheets off his body and flew across the bed. He sat behind her and put his hands on her shoulders.

"What's wrong, Mariechen?"

Maria was still moaning and unable to respond until the pain lessened and she felt her body relax. She leaned back into Jacob's firm body, her face damp with sweat.

"I think the baby's coming," she whispered breathlessly.

—

Jacob's eyes were heavy and he succumbed to the desire to close them. The relief he felt when everything went black felt almost euphoric at that point, having been awake all through the night. The sound of other men snoring, and pencils scratching paper, and screams from the delivery rooms faded into nothingness along with his vision. Thoughts of sleep consumed him, until he heard another cry, or the din of a tool dropping, and his eyes opened, his pulse quickening, and then he remembered Maria, still labouring in one of the delivery rooms.

He was so tired, and unable to think clearly. For hours – or had it been days already, he couldn't say – he paced back and forth in the small waiting room of the hospital. He watched the sunset the night before, and watched it appear again hours later, and now it was beginning its descent yet again. Through the same small window he watched people walk up and down the street, clueless as to the agony he was experiencing inside that building.

Jacob thought about those people, going about their business as usual, just as they had the day before, and would the day after. Yet for Jacob and Maria, their lives would never be the same after that day, if the baby would actually ever come out. He was starting to lose faith in the whole birthing process.

When he wasn't forcing himself to stay awake, or catching glimpses into Maria's room when a nurse walked in or out, he was waiting for the nurses to update him. They didn't come often, and when they did, they always said the same thing – *she's moving along nicely*. What did that even mean?

Jacob rested his forehead against the window. The cool glass felt refreshing against his clammy skin. The sound of Maria's painful moaning grew louder as the door to her room opened and a nurse walked out. Jacob turned his head sharply and craned his neck to look inside. He saw her lying on the bed, on her side. Her back was to him, but the thin gown she wore was wet and clung to her back.

The door closed with a loud thud and Maria was out of sight once again. Jacob slumped into a chair, frustrated with the lack of help he could be to his wife. Maria's nurse was leaning over the counter, talking with another nurse in uniform seated behind it. Her stance, and the tone of her voice, sounded irritated somehow. He strained to hear their hushed voices. He could make out enough to know that she was annoyed with Maria's slow progress. Anger swelled in Jacob's chest, his neck and cheeks quickly turned red.

He stood, ready to confront the rude nurse, but she turned to leave, removing the cap from her head as she walked through another door and out of sight. Another nurse simultaneously walked into the room from the same door. She looked refreshed and happy, donning a huge smile on her face that showed all her teeth. Her hair was dark, and tied up neatly against her head, under a small white cap. Near her left shoulder was a nametag that read "Margaret." She grabbed a folder from the nurse behind the counter and read the notes intently before walking into Maria's room.

Again, Jacob watched his wife through the open door for all of three seconds before it came closing with a resounding thud, and then she was gone. The intermittent sounds of her moans were the only connection to his wife and he longed for more.

—

"Hi Maria, my name is Margaret, I'll be taking over as your nurse now." The door closed behind her as she made her way toward the bed. She held the yellow folder open with one hand and quickly read the notes scrawled across the pages. "I see you've been here for some time already. You must be exhausted."

Maria leaned back into the bed, her eyes closed. She savoured the moment of peace, knowing it wouldn't last long. She knew Margaret was talking to her, but she couldn't find the strength to open her eyes to look at her, or to respond.

Instead, she listened to the melody of the nurse's soothing voice as she encouraged her, until another contraction began.

Maria screamed and writhed in the bed, clutching the hand Margaret offered her. "That's a good one, Maria. Keep breathing, you're doing great." As the rush subsided, Maria began to cry. Margaret sat beside her on the bed and held her. Maria smelled the faint aroma of Palo Santo on the nurse's uniform, mixed with the scent of yerba on her breath. Both scents brought a soothing sensation, mixed with nostalgia and familiarity.

"Is it normal for labour to go on for so long?" Maria asked wearily, her eyes still closed.

"Yes, love. This is completely normal, especially for your first birth. You're on your way, though, and your contractions are moving along nicely. You're doing great."

"I don't feel great." Maria sunk back into the bed, both hands pushing on either side of her belly, as another contraction rolled through her. "Please, there must be something you can give me to ease the pain. I don't know how much more of this I can handle."

"I'm sorry, love, there's nothing I can give you. The pain is part of the process if you want to have children." Margaret smiled empathetically, but Maria, too tired for niceties, didn't smile back.

"Have you got any whiskey? Surely I could at least have something stiff to drink."

For the next many hours, Margaret stayed by Maria's side, encouraging her and guiding her with instructions on how to work through every contraction. Finally, Maria was fully dilated, and Margaret beamed as she exclaimed the news to Maria.

"You're ready to push now, love!"

"Really?" Maria lifted her head and wiped the wet hair off her glistening face.

"Yes, really. Now, when you feel the next contraction, bear down. Can you do that for me?"

Maria nodded, though she doubted she'd be able to. Her eyelids felt heavy over her eyes, and her body was sore and exhausted. The next contraction came, and Maria pushed. Hours passed, and still Maria pushed. Despite the nurse's assurance that the baby was almost out, the baby was, in fact, still very much inside of her.

She was mentally and physically done. During her next contraction, Maria gave in to her frustration and screamed. The sound rolled softly inside her chest to start, and grew into a gut-wrenching roar as it came out of her mouth. The sound reverberated around the room, and everyone in the small chamber stood motionless, but only for a moment.

At the peak of her outburst, Maria felt an overwhelming release as the baby's body left her own. Maria gasped at the sudden relief. The faintest cries filled the cramped space. She lifted her head and saw Margaret holding a tiny babe wrapped in a flannel blanket. She moved toward Maria and placed the baby in her arms, smiling.

"It's a girl."

Maria looked down at the tiny human crying in her arms. The little girl's head was covered with the darkest, curliest locks, and her small hands flailed as she worked her lungs for the first time. Surely she must be dreaming, Maria thought. One tear followed another, until she could hardly see anymore. She wrapped the blanket tighter around the little girl and kissed her perfectly round cheeks.

"Don't worry, little one, I've got you. You're safe."

A rustling sound came from the corner of the room. Jacob stood by the door, one hand still on the handle. He didn't move from his spot, and Maria smiled at him, endeared by his hesitance to move closer.

"Come meet your daughter, Jasch."

As if waiting for permission to approach her and the child, he slowly walked toward the bed. "It's a girl?"

"Yes, she is."

Jacob sat on the bed beside Maria and peeked at the face nestled close to Maria's chest. "She's beautiful."

"Because she has dark hair?" Maria teased.

Maria placed the baby in Jacob's arms and watched as her husband transformed into a father in that very moment. She saw the wonder and awe in his eyes as he stared down at his daughter. Jacob turned to face Maria and locked his eyes on hers. She saw the thoughts he longed to verbalize, but words failed him. Instead, he kissed the top of her head.

"And what shall we call our little princess?" he asked her as he placed the babe's small hand in his. Her tiny fingers spread open and closed around his thumb. Maria turned away from Jacob and looked at their daughter. She gently cupped the baby's head in her hand and emotion welled up in her throat.

"How about Gredel?"

"Gredel? Where did that come from? You've never mentioned it before."

"It's a form of Margaret."

Jacob looked toward the door. "As in, Margaret, your nurse?"

"Mm-hmm." Her eyes stayed fixed on their daughter.

Jacob was quiet for a moment as he repeated the name in his head. He looked down at the baby, now asleep, cradled in his arms. "Gredel," he whispered, "it's beautiful."

21

March 1953

THE YEARS PASSED EFFORTLESSLY, ONE DAY AFTER ANOTHER, AFTER another. In the same way, Maria rose to her title of Mother with comparable ease. Gredel grew and thrived, becoming independent and determined from a very young age. She never shied away from adventures or new experiences, and kept Maria busy. Life fell into rhythm. Gredel became part of their lives, and daily tasks and chores went on as per usual, with the added chores that came with raising a child.

Jacob walked into the house one morning, earlier than he would normally arrive home from work. His brow was creased with worry, relaxing slightly as he looked around the small kitchen. The room was empty, but he heard Gredel's voice through the window and caught sight of her in the back yard, playing with Ralph. He couldn't see Maria, but knew she was around, somewhere, though he was grateful she wasn't in the house at that moment. He wasn't ready to face her yet.

In the pantry, he grabbed a bottle of whiskey off the top shelf and poured a fair amount into a glass and topped it off with water. He took his drink outside and sat on a chair on the porch in front of the house, lighting a cigarette before leaning back and closing his eyes. He inhaled the cigarette slowly and held his breath for some time before slowly exhaling, forming a cloud of smoke around him. He brought the glass of whiskey to his mouth and drank half the contents in one sip.

The sound of footsteps grew louder as they neared. Ralph came up beside him and laid down by Jacob's feet. Faster footsteps followed, and Gredel appeared shortly after.

"Papa!" She climbed onto his lap and wrapped her arms around his neck. Her curly hair tickled his nose and he brushed it aside before hugging her back.

"Oh, hi," Maria turned the corner, carrying a basket of eggs. She looked surprised to see him, which Jacob expected. "You're home early." She peered through the window into the kitchen, straining her eyes to see the black numbers on the clock. "It's not even ten o'clock yet. What are you doing here? What's wrong?" Jacob watched as her face changed from surprise to worry. She was staring at him, her nose scrunched and the distance between her eyebrows lessening as she scrutinized him, searching his eyes for an explanation.

He feigned a smile, knowing what she was doing, and amazed, once again, at her ability to read him so well. "Gredel, why don't you take Ralph to the back and see if *Mutti*, Mama, missed any eggs."

The little girl sprang from his lap and called Ralph as she ran to the back. Ralph obliged, and plodded along slowly behind her. When she was out of sight, Maria pulled a chair beside Jacob.

"What's wrong?" she asked again.

Jacob looked away from her and took another long drag of his cigarette. "Herb closed the shop. Says he's too old to deal with the business." He took another sip of his drink, emptying the glass. Herb had run the woodshop where Jacob worked for nearly twenty years. Jacob still couldn't make himself look Maria in the eyes. She sat in silence for a long time, watching a large black beetle move across the dust in front of her feet.

"All right. God will have something else for you to do then. It will all work out. Do you have any ideas already?"

Jacob scoffed at the mention of God. As if God could get him a job, he thought. It was a pleasant thought, though – Jacob sitting around at home until God magically placed a new job in his lap. How convenient. No, God wasn't going to have something else for him to do, Jacob would find a job on his own, of his own will and effort, not God's. He knew better than to verbalize his thoughts to Maria, though. If he did, another argument about religion would surely ensue, and he was in no mood for that.

"Actually, I've been thinking," Jacob paused and turned to Maria. Intrigued, she turned toward him and waited for him to continue. "Well, it's been on my mind for a while now. I've already discussed it with Gerd."

"Discussed what? And with Gerd? You discussed something to do with a job with your brother before you discussed it with your wife?" Her face hung, weighted with hurt.

"It's not like that," he tried to reassure her, "I didn't want to concern you with it if there wasn't anything to be concerned about. I didn't know Herb was thinking about closing the shop, and I had no intention of leaving him to work for someone else. It was just an idea I had, so I shared it with Gerd one day, more so to just put the idea out there and see what he thought, with no intention of actually making any plans to pursue it."

"Well, what *is* your idea?" Maria was growing impatient.

"There's a shop on Hindenburgstrasse that's available for rent. I thought maybe Gerd would be interested in starting a business with me, doing the same kind of woodwork that I've been doing for Herb. The shop comes with tools and everything included in the rent. We could even potentially have a bit of a storefront where we could stock and sell hardware supplies. Or something like that. I haven't thought through all the details because I wasn't expecting to lose my job. Anyway, Gerd is interested. I just came from his work. We talked some more and decided we would discuss it with our wives and meet again tomorrow after he's done work to go over more details, if we're actually going to go through with it. We could even possibly meet with the owner of the shop tomorrow."

Maria looked out across the yard, rubbing one hand with the other. "It sounds like a good plan. I'll pray that the right decision will be made for both of you, and your families." She stood and kissed the top of Jacob's head. "Are you hungry? I was going to fry some eggs for Gredel and myself."

Jacob nodded and Maria brought the eggs into the kitchen. He could hear the clanking of pots inside as he took another drag of his cigarette. He looked across the yard and saw their elderly neighbour, Herr Rempel, walk up to the fence that separated their two properties, a yellowed paper clutched in one hand. Jacob got up and walked toward Herr Rempel, smiling. He nodded his head in greeting as he approached the fence.

"*Goodendach,*" Herr Rempel said without any emotion or warmth. He offered a forced smile, but his face was otherwise stoic.

"Good day," Jacob said slowly, trying to read his expression.

Herr Rempel extended his arm that held the paper toward Jacob. "From the Colony House. The news came over the radio this morning. They'll add more details in the next *Mennoblatt.*"

Confused, Jacob took the paper from him, "*Danksheen.*"

The men turned back to their homes. Jacob looked at the paper as he walked. Thin, black letters were scrawled across the page, the edges wrinkled or torn from having been passed on to many people before him. In some places, ink seeped into the page, blotting out certain letters, making it hard to read, but he could make out the gist of it.

"Yesterday, March 5, 1953, Joseph Stalin died in Moscow, Russia from a stroke."

Jacob reread the words. His insides churned as a multitude of thoughts ran through his mind. He felt relieved, and glad that Stalin was dead, but hatred overpowered him. He couldn't find even a trace of remorse for the man's passing. The man had made their lives miserable, and was responsible for the deaths of twenty million people, many of which were Mennonites – friends and family members of so many people he knew, including Maria.

Jacob looked toward the house at the thought of her. She was standing outside the kitchen, drying her hands on the same faded apron she had worn ever since he had known her.

"Your eggs are ready, Jasch," she informed him, but he didn't move or react in any way. Maria walked toward him and searched his face. The blues of his eyes were brightened by the sun, but there was a sombreness to them that unsettled her. "What is it, Jasch?"

"Stalin. He's dead." He raised his hand and she took the paper from him. Her eyes moved quickly over the words.

"Oh my," she stared at the paper for some time. Suddenly her arms fell and her chest began to heave. Her breathing quickened and her face contorted as she processed all the same emotions that Jacob was feeling. Despite the relief she felt knowing he was no longer alive, she knew nothing could change the course of events that had led them to where they were, all because of that man.

He took a step closer to Maria and pulled her into his body. She shook beneath his touch and he felt his guard go down. A tear slid out from the corner of his eye and moved slowly down the side of his nose, but he didn't brush it away. Another tear fell, following the same path as the one before. He longed to change the past, to bring families together again, including Maria's father's. The weight of the fact that he could not change the fate of the tens of thousands of Mennonites, and other innocent lives that were ended because of Stalin, felt too heavy, and he broke. Tears fell onto Maria's loosely pinned hair, and he cried for those that didn't make it out alive.

That night, Jacob lowered Gredel onto a bed that sat outside their bedroom. He brought the wrought iron bed frame home with him one afternoon and set it up outside. On hot nights, Jacob slept outside, claiming it was cooler to sleep in the openness of the yard, than the confines of their bedroom.

Jacob laid down next to Gredel's small body and folded his arms over his stomach and closed his eyes. Maria stood in the shadows of an overhang off the kitchen and watched the two of them with fondness.

"Papa, tell me about the stars again."

Jacob peered at Gredel with one eye open and shifted his body so he could wrap an arm around her. He laid his head back on the pillow and looked up at the plethora of celestial stars looking down at them.

He extended his long arm straight up, a pointed finger showing Gredel where he was looking. "Do you see that big, bright star twinkling way up there?" Gredel nodded. "That one's called Starlight." He moved his finger a few inches to the right. "And that one over there? That's Twinkleton."

Gredel giggled, "No, it's not!"

"Oh, yes it is," his voice was even and serious and Maria covered her mouth to muffle her laughter so she wouldn't disrupt them. "And that one way over there, that's my favourite one."

"What's it called?" Gredel sat and squinted, eager to see the flashing star in the distance.

"It's called Little Gredelein." His lips turned up on one side, and even in the dim light, Maria saw the playfulness in his eyes. Gredel squealed with glee, thrilled to share her name with a star.

Maria turned away and walked into the kitchen and sat at the table. A pit formed in her chest. As much as her heart filled with joy to watch Jacob with their daughter, she couldn't help the unwanted feeling of jealousy that arose every now and then when she saw them together. She envied their relationship, a closeness that Maria yearned to have with a father of her own.

Not wanting to linger over her disappointment, she found a magazine she had borrowed from her mother. She placed it on the table and stretched her sore back before taking a seat. She turned the cover, moving her hand up and down the fold in the centre, flattening the pages across the table. She began reading, but was interrupted at ten o'clock when the electricity turned off.

She rose from the table to find a candle, and gasped audibly at the sight of a dark shadow in the doorway.

"Jasch? Is that you?" She asked, her heart beating intensely inside her chest.

"I'm sorry I scared you," he said as he walked into the room. He moved fluidly toward her, keenly aware of where she was despite the darkness. He put one arm around her waist and slowly moved it lower down her back.

"Jasch," she flirted, trying to pry herself from his grasp, but he wouldn't oblige.

Jacob raised his other hand to Maria's cheek and looked earnestly down into her eyes. The trace of moonlight coming through the window made only the whites of his eyes visible, but she could picture the expression on his face, and felt the yearning desire in his eyes. It was silent in the house, aside from Maria's pounding heart, though its cause had shifted from fear to anticipation. Jacob tilted her chin upwards, and she felt the warmth of his lips against hers. They kissed in the kitchen until their bodies were eager for more of each other. Jacob took Maria's hand in his and quietly led her to their bedroom.

—

Kaethe sat at Maria's kitchen table as Maria poured steaming coffee into two mugs. The August air was frigid, and the coolness seeped deep into their bones. They took turns pouring a little bit of cream into their cups, the metal spoons clinking against the ceramic. With their mugs held under their noses, they inhaled the deep, sweet aroma and sighed. The first sip was always magical – sacred, even – and they sat silently until their next sip.

Maria's face suddenly went sour, and Kaethe noticed the change in her expression. "What happened?"

Maria closed her eyes and took a deep breath, waiting for the dizzy feeling to pass. When it did, she opened her eyes again.

"Just dizzy all of a sudden. I'm okay now." She cautiously took another sip of coffee and waited to see if the feeling would occur again. It didn't. "How's Opa doing?" Maria asked.

"About the same as usual," Kaethe pressed her lips together in an effort to smile. "I actually wanted to show you something."

Kaethe set her mug on the table and twisted her body in her chair to dig through the purse that hung on the seatback of her chair. She pulled out an envelope and put it on the table in front of Maria. Her mother's name and address were written on the front. The postage stamp indicated it had come from Brazil. Maria stared at it.

"Who's it from?"

"Read it," Kaethe permitted.

Maria picked up the envelope and turned it over. It had already been opened. She lifted the brown flap and pulled out a white piece of paper, folded in half. Maria eyed her mother as she unfolded the paper. Her lips moved as read the letter quietly to herself. When she finished, she lowered her hands onto the table and looked astonishingly at her mother.

"A brother?" Maria asked, stunned.

"Yes," Kaethe replied. "Kornelius. He's a year older than your father, the second oldest in the family."

"He's alive? I mean, Papa has family that made it out of Russia?"

Kaethe's eyes lit up with what Maria could only assume was a mixture of hope and relief. "Apparently, yes."

"How did you not know about this earlier?"

"He didn't know Nikolai and I made it out of Russia, either. There was no way to communicate with anyone. It was by God's grace that we were able to find Oma, Opa and Uncle Paul and go on the journey together. And that we actually made it. So many came as a family as far as Moscow, but not all of them made it out."

"And he's in Brazil now? With his family? Our family?" Maria tried to make sense of what it all meant.

"Yes, that's what he says in the letter. Kornelius, Elizabeth and their four children are moving to Canada soon. Ontario, I think." She pronounced it 'ohn-tahr-e-oh.'

"And the rest of Papa's family?"

Kaethe shook her head.

Kornelius explained that he and his family had escaped Russia safely. They immigrated to Brazil, but he, too, had never heard from his parents or siblings, but never gave up hope that he would see them again. He returned to Germany during World War II and enlisted as a soldier. They were stationed in Crimea at one point, and he went back to Ebenfeld – or what used to be Ebenfeld. There was no evidence of a village ever having been there. Not one house or structure stood erect, nor any remains left lying around anywhere. It had been completely destroyed. He stood on the land where his childhood home had been and looked out into nothingness. There was no house, no field – nothing.

While in Russia, he realized the extent of the horror that occurred after he had fled. After Stalin's announcement of *Dekulakization* – to abolish the *kulaks*, or peasants, which included Mennonites – mass terror and suffering befell those left behind. Village soviets, executive committees and activists could rid an area of peasants by expelling them off their property and to execute, imprison, or banish them when necessary. Those that were sent to concentration camps didn't survive.

Kaethe's shoulders fell at the knowledge that Nikolai's parents and his other eleven siblings died in Russia. Maria sat frozen as images of men, women and children tortured in camps flashed through her mind. Her stomach twisted and her head spun as she physically felt the fear those people must have experienced. Despite having never met any of her father's family, and with very few, vague memories of her father himself, she felt overwhelming sadness and grief for them.

Maria could feel all the hope Kaethe had held on to for all those years wash away with her tears. There was nothing, absolutely nothing Maria could say to encourage her mother. Instead, she held her the way Kaethe had always held Maria when she was upset. She silently prayed for those lives that were lost, and that God would forgive her for hating a man as much as she hated Stalin, and to give her the strength to forgive him – eventually.

—

Jacob sat motionless as Maria recounted her morning with Kaethe, and the contents of the letter. When she had finished, they both sat in silence.

Maria stared out toward the street, moving her eyes to follow the occasional horse and buggy that passed. She waved at them, and Jacob offered the obligatory nod of his head. A wave of nausea caught Maria by surprise and she leaned forward and vomited on the ground in front of her feet. A few drops landed on her white sandals, and were running between her toes that peeked through the edge.

"Are you all right, Mariechen?" Jacob passed her his handkerchief, and kicked some dust over the vomit to subdue the smell, and her obvious embarrassment.

Maria wiped her mouth and dabbed her toes with the handkerchief. She leaned back into the chair with her eyes closed until the nausea ebbed. She took a deep breath, and opened her mouth to respond, but before any words came out, another bout of nausea came over her and she leaned forward again. This time she thought to move her feet apart to avoid getting any more vomit on her feet.

After wiping her mouth off again, she looked at Jacob and laughed. He was trying hard to mask his disgust and at the same time, was clearly concerned by her sudden illness. She sympathetically patted his leg.

"*Nuscht no die bedauren*, nothing to worry yourself about. Well, maybe you should be a little worried." She winked at him and it took only a moment for him to register her meaning. His face turned to shock before his lips slipped into a smile, spread wide across this face.

"A baby?" He asked hesitantly.

"I guess we'll find out soon enough." She winked at him as he slowly reclined back into his chair, still smiling.

—

Jacob hammered another nail into two pieces of wood to hold them together. Only one more board along the bottom, and the coffin would be finished. After opening the woodshop with Gerd, they became the sole coffin constructors in the village. Jacob's impeccable attention to detail made him the obvious choice when it came to deciding who would build the coffins.

He didn't mind, he felt it an honour to help his friends in that way. The only drawback was being the only one in the village who could make them. He was called on at any time of day with news of another death, and had to work on the coffin immediately, regardless of the hour. Living in a small village also meant that everyone knew everyone. Every person who died was either a friend, colleague, neighbour, or classmate of yours. Fortunately, up until that day, he had never had to build a coffin for a family member.

Johann passed away earlier that afternoon from a hernia while helping Kaethe move a basin full of water. The doctors had operated but the damage to his intestines was too severe, and irreparable. Jacob had been working when Maria ran into the shop, eyes red and swollen, and told him that Johann had died.

Jacob smoothed all the edges of the wood panels and stood back to survey his work. He was proud of the coffin. He respected Johann far too much to let his final resting place be anything less than perfection. He ran across the street and asked his brother, Hans, to help move the coffin from the shop to the hospital, where Johann's body waited, and from there, to the cemetery at the outskirts of town.

By the time they arrived at the cemetery, a crowd of people had already gathered around the grave. It seemed the entire village had come to show their support and pay their respects to the family. Jacob saw Maria, arms wrapped around her mother. Kaethe held her handkerchief over her mouth, but it didn't stop the tears from falling off her chin. His heart ached for Kaethe – she had buried far too many loved ones in her lifetime. He didn't think it was fair for one person to have to suffer so much grief in such a short time.

With the help of a few other men, Jacob carried the coffin to the grave. During the service, he stood on the other side of Kaethe and put his arm around her waist so the majority of her weight rested on him, not Maria, who could barely stand herself from the added weight of the baby growing inside her. They stayed that way until the coffin was no longer visible. Only a pile of loose dirt marked the place where Johann's body lay.

—

Two-and-a-half months later, Maria gave birth to a son, Erwin. Near the end of her pregnancy, she asked Jacob one night if he was hoping for a boy, or another girl. He said he would ideally love to have a boy, but would rather have another dark-haired daughter than a blond son. Maria knew he was only teasing, at least for the most part. Gredel's hair had changed to blonde within the first year after she was born, and Jacob's love for her had not subsided in the slightest.

When their second baby was born with a full head of dark hair, and a boy to boot, Jacob was elated. He had never looked prouder than the moment he held Erwin for the very first time. Gredel had requested a sister, but despite her initial disapproval, she instantly fell in love with her little brother, and by the end of the year, they had adjusted to life with two children, busy as it was.

One hot November afternoon, after lunch, Erwin sat on a thin blanket between Jacob and Maria. He held a small branch in his hand and was contentedly hitting the blanket with it, drool hanging from his chin. Cicadas serenaded the country with their incessant choruses. The air was thick with heat, and even in the shade, they couldn't wipe away the drops of sweat falling down their skin fast enough.

Gredel ran around the yard with Ralph at her heels, her hair bouncing wildly with each step. Every now and then Erwin would catch sight of them and slowly move his body forward as he attempted to crawl, but he would inevitably fall on his face, not having perfected the motions yet. It was a comical sight, with his chubby legs kicking behind him as he tried to shuffle his body. Jacob and Maria laughed, enjoying the entertainment and the joy of watching their children learn new skills.

He had only been part of their lives for six months, yet Maria had a hard time remembering life without him. He was born at the end of May, after a long, and equally strenuous labour as it was with Gredel. They named him Erwin, a name Maria had come across in one of her novels. Jacob was indifferent to the name, neither loving nor hating it, so that was settled pretty quickly.

A shrill scream rang through the yard. Gredel ran toward the gate, arms and hair flailing. Kaethe walked through it and lowered herself to embrace Gredel. Hand in hand, they walked up to the house together. When they reached the porch, Ralph dropped his tired body beside Jacob's chair and closed his eyes. Maria pulled a chair closer to them and Kaethe lowered herself into it, pulling Gredel onto her lap.

"Hi, Mama," Maria welcomed her, "how are you? We weren't expecting you."

"Have you not heard?" Kaethe sounded surprised.

"Heard what?" Maria looked at Jacob who shook his head. If she was referring to a death, Jacob would likely have heard the news already. He was always one of the first to know so he could start working on the coffin straight away.

"About the accident?" Kaethe looked from Maria to Jacob and back to Maria, clearly bewildered by their unknowing.

"What accident?" Maria asked as she sat up straighter in her chair.

"The car accident. With David and Tina Thielmann, and a few others from Filadelfia." Tears began to form in the corners of Kaethe's eyes as she relayed the news to them.

Tina was a good friend of Kaethe's. They had met at church many years ago. David and Tina had been married for nearly twenty years, and had six children, their eldest a few years younger than Maria. David, Tina and Kaethe sang in the choir together and had grown quite close over the years. Tina had shown Kaethe much kindness and hospitality in recent years, bringing her meals after Oma and Opa passed away, and inviting her over for coffee and visits so she wouldn't feel too alone.

"They were on their way to Kleefeld, for a wedding," Kaethe continued, solemnly. "Alfred borrowed a truck from a friend and a whole group of them were driving there together. They came to a corner and Alfred turned, taking the corner a little too sharp, and probably a little too fast. The truck flipped—" She stopped, unable to speak through the onset of tears. She sniffled and blew her nose into the handkerchief she pulled out from her pocket. "Most of them were sitting in the bed of the truck. Tina was sitting in the passenger seat. She hit the corner of the truck, or the windshield, or something, and died instantly." Her words staggered again, making her words difficult to understand. "David is alive, but he hit his head and was bleeding profusely. He was apparently quite out of sorts, not knowing where he was or what was going on. He's still in the hospital, they're running some tests. They'll wait to bury Tina in the morning so that hopefully David can attend."

Tears fell softly down Kaethe's cheeks, but she kept herself composed around the children. Maria looked at Jacob and they nodded to each other. He stood and placed a hand on Kaethe's shoulders. Then he bent down to kiss Gredel on the top of the head and tousled Erwin's fine hair – which had also turned blond in recent months – before he left, heading in the direction of his shop.

22

January 1958

"YOU CAN'T TELL ME THAT I CAN'T GO TO *FRAUENVEREIN!*"

Maria tried to keep herself calm, but her hands began to shake. She was in their bedroom, about to leave for the church's ladies meeting, when Jacob confronted her. She finished buttoning up her dress and reached inside her purse for her lipstick, her mind racing with words she wanted to say to him. She applied a thin layer of red tint to her lips and pressed them together, making a smacking sound as her lips parted.

"You might be my husband, but you are not my dictator." She glared at him and closed her purse without taking her eyes off his. "I don't know why you're acting like this. You know I go to Frauenverein every month. I'm going, whether you approve of it or not."

She moved past him, leaving a rush of wind in her wake. He didn't say anything, or make any facial expressions while she was ranting. She felt his eyes burning into her back as she stormed out of the room, but she refused to look back at him. The door slammed closed behind her and she hurried down the yard and out the gate, fuming. Her heart pounded in her chest and she could hear, and feel, her blood as it coursed through her body.

The lights inside the church were on, and she knew they had already started their meeting. She stopped when she reached the door and exhaled. Her eyes closed and she let herself cry. Burdened, she lowered herself to the ground and leaned her back against the door.

She thought of her oma, and the wisdom she so often shared with Maria. Oh, how she longed to be able to visit with Oma now, to be encouraged and reminded that God had a plan, and she was part of that plan for Jacob's life. More tears flowed, and she berated herself for her next thought – why did she have to be the one for the job? Why did it have to be so difficult?

She loved Jacob, and wanted – needed – to be with him. For the majority of the time, Maria trusted that everything was as it was meant to be, that God knew what He was doing. It was days like these though, that made her doubt even God's supreme wisdom.

Instead of going into the church that night, Maria walked around the village, praying for Jacob. By the time she found herself in front of their house, her heart had softened, and she wasn't angry anymore. She slowly lifted the metal latch and walked through the gate. She knew it was late – the lights had turned off long ago – but she didn't know how late.

Inside their room, she found Gredel fast asleep, and Jacob lay quietly on their bed, facing the other way. After changing into her nightgown, she gently crawled into bed and pulled the covers up to her neck. She felt Jacob's warmth without even touching him. He turned then, and she strained her eyes in the darkness to see his face.

The moonlight streaming through the open window highlighted the curve of his cheek and jaw, and glimmered on the corner of his eye. The blue iris looked transparent in the light, like a frozen lake.

"I'm sorry," she whispered.

"I'm sorry, too." The softness in his voice broke down any remaining walls she might have had, and she turned to him, crying into his chest. He held her and stroked her back until she calmed. Turning her body, she nestled in close to his. He wrapped his arm around her waist and kissed her neck. The soft velvet touch of his lips sent a spark through her body, which grew as he continued to caress her. They moved silently under the sheets, not wanting to wake Gredel.

Despite their reconciliation, Maria still felt unsettled. Something akin to anxiety moved through her like the rise and fall of an ocean wave. She hated when they fought, but mostly, she hated doubting God. She laid in bed, listening to Jacob's deep breathing, until she fell asleep.

—

Maria knelt beside a basin in the shade of a Flaschenbaum, moving a wet shirt over a washboard. Suds multiplied and climbed up her arms. It had been a quiet morning. Gredel was at school, along with Ralph, and Erwin was running around the yard, kicking a fallen grapefruit. From the corner of her eye, she could see his blond hair moving rapidly from side to side as he passed the grapefruit from one foot to the other. The sun exaggerated the light colour of each white strand on his head.

When she lifted her face in his direction, his eyes met hers and he smiled. Unlike his extroverted, sociable sister, Erwin preferred to stay close to Maria. There was no fear of him ever wandering off on his own, and Maria was grateful for that. He was a relatively easy child, and Maria enjoyed his company, even at such a young age.

A sudden wave of nausea came over Maria and she leaned back on her heels to catch her breath. Her forehead glistened with perspiration. She rubbed her already protruding belly, and focused on inhaling and exhaling. Her attempts to breathe away the nausea failed, and she turned and vomited beside the basin.

Erwin stopped running, the grapefruit rolling ahead of him. He looked at her inquisitively, concern arching his brows, despite having witnessed her vomit numerous times over the last few months. Maria wiped her mouth and smiled reassuringly at him, and pointed to her belly, indicating it was just from the baby. Satisfied, he turned his attention back to the grapefruit.

Maria pulled herself to her feet with a groan and carried the basket of wet clothes to the side of the house. On a table pushed against the wall sat a mangle. One by one, Maria moved each piece of clothing through the rollers. The water squeezed from the clothes fell to the ground, forming a dark puddle. As she hung the laundry on the line to dry, she saw her mother walk into the yard.

Erwin ran to Kaethe, arms flailing about wildly at his sides. Hand in hand, they walked toward the house.

"Hi, Mama," Maria greeted her as she clipped the shoulder of one of Jacob's shirts to the line with a wooden peg.

"Hi, Michi." Kaethe pulled a chair into the shade and sat down. Erwin crawled onto her lap and leaned his head back against her chest.

"I've got Borscht simmering on the stove. You're welcome to stay for lunch. The whistle should blow shortly, I imagine."

"David asked me to marry him," she blurted out. Maria lowered her arms, along with the wet towel she was about to hang, and stared at her mother. She searched Kaethe's expression for any clue as to what her response had been, but found only a blank face looking back at her.

"And?" Maria asked. "Is that a good thing? Did you accept his proposal?"

Kaethe stroked Erwin's hair. "I haven't given him an answer yet. I wanted to speak with you first."

Maria raised her arms and hung the towel. "You don't need my permission to marry him. You're a grown woman."

"I realize that, Maria. I'm not asking for your permission. I just ... I don't know if getting married is what I really want."

"Is that really the reason for your hesitation?"

Kaethe sighed. "Yes, and no. I'm also not sure if it's more so David that I'm uncertain of."

After Tina's death, Kaethe and David had continued their friendship with each other. They often walked to choir practice together, and visited each other on the occasional weekend. Kaethe considered him a good friend, but had never quite fancied him in a romantic way. It wasn't that she wasn't attracted to him. She admired his dark and mysterious eyes set behind a pair of thick spectacles. Although, he wasn't the classic tall, dark and handsome man she'd read about in her romance novels. David stood merely an inch or two taller than Kaethe, and his hair, though dark, had receded significantly in recent years.

Kaethe had been on her own since Nikolai died, and even more so after her parents passed away. She was a year shy of turning fifty and didn't know if she had the energy to start a new relationship. She was set in her ways, and she knew she was stubborn at the best of times. Was it worth changing her life now, to accommodate for someone else to be part of it?

"I just came from Prediger Klassen's house," Kaethe continued. "I asked him his opinion, as well."

Maria processed her mother's words, along with the lack of enthusiasm in her tone as she spoke. "And, what did he say?"

"He thinks I should marry him, if only to bring a motherly figure into their lives again. David could use the help around the house."

"Mama, don't marry him out of pity for his children." Maria sat down in a chair beside her mother.

"No, I know that. I do love him, truly, but I'm not sure I love him the way he loves me." Her face went downcast and she fixed her gaze on Erwin's small hand, resting in hers. "Honestly, I don't think I'll ever love another man the way I loved your father." Her voice shook slightly, and her eyes brimmed with tears.

"Mama, it's okay if you never love someone like you loved Papa, but it doesn't mean you have to be alone for the rest of your life. You have my blessing and support to marry David, if that's what you want."

The whistle blew. Maria promised her mother she would pray for her, and kissed the top of her head.

"Are you staying for Borscht?"

Kaethe nodded and Maria went inside to set the table for the five of them.

—

Jacob reclined his body on his bed under the stars, clasping his hands beneath his head. He closed his eyes and his body relaxed into the mattress. As he began to slowly drift away, the bed shook, rousing him from his near-sleep state. A small body pressed against Jacob's, fine, wispy hair tickling his neck.

"Tell me a story, Papa!" Erwin's eyes gleamed under the moonlight, and Jacob couldn't refuse his son's request, regardless how tired he might be.

"Hm, what story shall I tell you tonight, my boy?"

"Hmmmmm," Erwin pinched his chin with thumb and forefinger as he thought earnestly about his answer. "Oh! Tell me the story about the jaguar! That's a funny one."

"Ah, a classic," Jacob moved his arm around Erwin's body and together they looked up at the star-filled sky. "Once, a long, long, looooooong time ago, when I was only just a boy, my brothers and a few friends of mine were out in the forest. The trees were dense and the brush was thick, making it hard to run through. We were playing hide-and-seek, and Onkel Abram was *it*. I was so far out into the forest that I couldn't hear anyone anymore. I knew I would win that round, for sure.

"All of a sudden, my stomach rumbled, and I knew I needed to go to the bathroom, right away. I was too far from home to run back and use the outhouse, and I obviously didn't want to give up my amazing hiding spot, so I did what I had to do. I looked around," he turned his head emphatically from left to right, and Erwin giggled.

"There was no one in sight, and nothing to be heard. Not a soul was around as far as the eye could see, and the ear could hear, and the nose could smell, and the—"

"Papaaa," Erwin said, growing impatient.

"Anyway, I did the only logical thing in such a situation. I unbuttoned my trousers and looked around one more time, just to be extra sure I was all alone. Then I dropped my pants, and my *unjabetze*, underwear, to my ankles. I squatted, hovering over thorn bushes and cacti, and as I was about to, you know, do my business, I heard deep breathing coming from behind me. I thought someone found me, and I was mortified." Erwin giggled again, covering his mouth with his hands.

"I cringed with embarrassment and slowly turned to face whoever it was that found me. But it wasn't another boy who was standing in front of me. I would have preferred if it had been. But no, instead, I found myself looking into the eyes of a large, giant toothed jaguar. He was crouched low to the ground, but his eyes were fixed on mine. His long tail moved in slow motion behind him – back and forth, back and forth. He was clearly ready to pounce on my arse.

"And, wouldn't you know it? I suddenly didn't need to go to the bathroom anymore! I stood up and ran, pulling my pants up as I stumbled through the brush. I didn't stop running until I was out of that forest and back at home, with the gate shut securely behind me.

"My clothes were torn to shreds from snagging on thorns, but I didn't even notice, or care. Oma and Opa cared, though. They weren't very sympathetic of my near-death experience. I had to wash dishes by myself for the rest of the week because I ruined my pants. The end."

Silence. Erwin was fast asleep. Jacob kissed the golden hair and looked toward the house. Maria and Gredel sat on the porch. Gredel watched Jacob and Erwin with envy. Ever since Erwin was old enough to appreciate Jacob's stories, he took the spot beside Jacob, and Gredel was left to watch from the porch.

Maria looked up from the magazine she was reading and met Jacob's gaze. She smiled and he winked at her before laying his head back down on the pillow.

—

Kaethe married David in May and moved into his house. Jacob and Maria moved into Kaethe's vacated house, back to the home where Maria had grown up. Despite the familiarity of the home, it took Maria some time to adjust to their new living quarters. She and Jacob slept in the room across the passage-way, where Oma and Opa had slept, and Gredel and Erwin shared the room off the kitchen in the main house.

There was a coop in the back yard that housed their chickens, and a small fenced off area in the front for their cow, and her calf, if it was still drinking its mother's milk. It was all very much the way it had been when Maria lived there as a little girl, up until a year after her and Jacob's wedding. And though it still felt new and strange to be living there again, it really did feel like she was hüss, home.

23

February 1965

THE SILVER NEEDLE MOVED IN AND OUT OF THE FADED WHITE FABRIC WITH ease, dodging Maria's fingers with each stitch. The shadows under the overhang at the back of the house provided enough respite from the summer heat so she could work somewhat more comfortably. Every few stitches, Maria wiped her brow with the sleeve of her dress and pushed her glasses further up the bridge of her nose.

Across the yard, Erwin balanced a wooden crate on an angle with a small branch, while Sylvia lay sprawled on her stomach on the dusty ground, arms folded under her chin. Sylvia watched Erwin intently, noting each careful step he took. After the crate was sufficiently propped up, he gently pulled the string tied to the branch and moved further away from the crate. Sylvia followed suit, dust rising around her feet as she ran after him.

From the corner of her eye, Maria spotted movement and looked in that direction. Angelika, their youngest, crawled toward her brother and sister with as much speed as a nine-month-old could muster. She stopped to inspect an object along her path that caught her attention. Maria squinted, but couldn't decipher if her findings were of the bug, rock or stick variety. Bored with the object, Angelika continued her pursuit and moved toward her siblings once again.

Maria looked toward Erwin and Sylvia; both were lying on the ground. Erwin pulled on the rope until it was taut, without pulling the branch away from the crate. Sylvia covered her mouth with both her hands, giddy with excitement and anticipation of what would ensue.

Above them, red-crested cardinals flew across the sky, blurred dots of red, white and grey darting from one tree to the next. A few of the birds spotted the peanuts piled under the crate and they circled above it. Erwin licked his lips as one eager cardinal pointed his beak toward the ground and dove. Erwin lifted the string, ready to pull the branch as soon as the cardinal landed inside. The cardinal changed directions suddenly and retreated to a nearby tree. The rope in Erwin's hand slackened and he looked toward the crate.

"*Geli!*" he groaned. His lips turned downward into a frown. Angelika sat beside the overturned crate, and waved the branch in her hand. Annoyed, Erwin stood and walked toward his little sister, his shirt and pants browned with dust. He picked her up around the waist and carried her to Maria, placing her on her lap. "Can you please keep her out of the way, *Mutti*? I'm trying to run a business here."

Maria tried to stifle her unavoidable smile, waiting until Erwin turned and walked back to the crate before letting out a soft chuckle. She would hate for him to think she was undermining his current business endeavour. He was making money, so she supposed he was accurate in calling it a business. There was a market for pet cardinals, and Erwin gladly took the opportunity to trap the birds and sell them to a family friend, who then sold them to his customers.

Maria kissed the top of Angelika's head and wrapped her arms around her, savouring the smallness of her body. She inhaled the sweet, honey smell of the little girl, knowing it would be the last time she would have a child this young. As much as Maria wanted to have more children, she and Jacob agreed that Angelika would be their last.

While pregnant with their fourth child, Maria had developed a heart condition, and the strenuous and intense labour made her heart nearly stop from overexertion. It wasn't until after Angelika was born that they were told how severe the situation had been, and that it had nearly killed Maria. The doctor had advised them not to have any more children. He feared that if she struggled through another labour, it could quite possibly end her life.

It wasn't until months later that Maria finally grieved over the news. As Angelika weaned from the breast, Maria was filled with a heaviness, and felt the weight of the doctor's word – she would never birth or hold another baby of her own. Angelika would be the last child she would watch take their first steps, say their first words, and leave for their first day of school.

Jacob thought it might be good news for Maria, that she wouldn't have to endure another nine months of nausea and discomfort, but Maria had assured him it would have been worth it. She would go through any amount of discomfort, and plaguing nausea, and even the pain of childbirth twice over if it meant she would have a child in return. She couldn't complain though, she had been blessed with four healthy children.

Erwin and Sylvia were lying flat on the ground by the fence again. The crate was balancing on the stick, and Erwin held the string taut in his hands. One curious cardinal flew overhead, assessing the scene beneath him. It flew to the ground and hopped cautiously toward the crate. The aroma of nuts intoxicated the small bird and it hopped underneath the opening, and without hesitation, Erwin tugged the string and the branch flew back. The crate wobbled as it landed on the ground. The bird squawked and flapped its wings frantically inside the cage. Black and red feathers floated out of the small gaps between the wooden boards.

Erwin and Sylvia ran toward the crate, their eyes mirroring the triumph they felt. Erwin slid the last few feet on his hip, and observed his catch. Sylvia squealed with equal parts excitement and heartache at the trapped bird. Erwin's face beamed as he raised one fisted hand in the air – victory.

Maria draped the unfinished shirt over the back of her chair and went into the kitchen, carrying Angelika on her hip. Inside, she placed Angelika on the floor, who immediately began scouring the room for anything she could possibly use as a toy. Maria set a large heavy pot on the counter and wiped the dust off the lid with her hand before removing it. The familiar smell of peanut oil and meat wafted from the pot. She placed the large slab of tender meat on the cutting board and sliced enough meat to feed everyone for supper.

She looked at the clock as she walked past it, placing the pot of meat and oil back in the pantry. It wasn't long before Jacob would be done working for the day. Next, she put one *tweeback* for each person on a plate, and then set the table. As she counted the utensils, she thought of Jacob. He had changed over the last few years. There was an air of depression about him. She didn't blame him, though. The last few years had been taxing on all of them, but especially for Jacob.

An accident at work left Jacob unable to sing. A piece of wood ricocheted off a nail that Jacob was hammering and hit him in the throat. Had it gone any deeper, the damage would have left him speechless for the rest of his life, but that was a silver lining he could not easily accept. His beautiful, soul-shaking bass voice was never heard again. Maria missed his singing immensely. Christmas carols hadn't been the same since then.

There was another event, though, that Jacob had not been able to move past. The previous year, Jacob and Gerd's shop had been broken into. Jacob had arrived at work that morning and found a window broken, the shattered glass piled on the ground beneath it. Shelves had been rummaged through, and a few items had gone missing. At the end of the day, a man came in and explained that he had needed some hardware for the project he had been working on at home the previous night, but they were already closed. He spoke smugly, as if his actions were justified. He apologized, though his words were empty, forced and inauthentic. He then paid for the items he had stolen, and left.

Maria cringed as Jacob recounted the situation to her after work that day, and her heart sunk when Jacob told her the name of the man – he was a deacon of their church. She could tell Jacob was not only hurt by the intrusion and deceit of the matter, but the fact that it had been a 'Christian' made Jacob even angrier. It was one more reason for Jacob to despise the church, and he told Maria that if becoming a Christian meant he was in the same league as men like that, then he wanted nothing to do with it.

Maria sighed at the memory of their conversation that night. At the same time, Gredel walked into the kitchen and Angelika crawled toward her. Gredel placed her little sister on her lap as Maria slid the pan of meat into the oven.

"Back already? I didn't hear the whistle. How was work today?" Maria asked her.

"It was all right," Gredel began, "until Frü Kliewer showed up." She rolled her eyes and moaned with irritation. "That woman is impossible! She can never make up her mind! Everyone else saw her coming and conveniently went on their breaks at the same time, but I was restocking a shelf, with my back facing the door, and didn't see her. So I was the only one around when she came in and I was stuck with her for at least an hour." Gredel pried Angelika's small, chubby fingers off her necklace. "Oh, I got paid today," she said as she reached into her purse and pulled some change out. She placed it on the table and Maria slid the coins off the edge, into her palm, and put them in a jar with the rest of their money.

They continued talking about Gredel's day while they set the table, until Ernst came in. Gredel stood to greet him with a hug. The two had been officially dating for a few weeks, though he and Gredel had been close for some time already. Being nearly seven years her senior, it took some time for Jacob and

Maria to trust him, but it didn't take long for them to accept his frequent visits to their home.

Erwin and Sylvia were called into the house and instructed to wash their hands before taking their usual seats at the table. Maria looked at the clock and wondered where Jacob was. His shop was only a few blocks away, further than the Cooperative where Gredel worked, and yet he still wasn't home.

They all sat waiting, and the younger children grew more impatient with every minute that passed. Maria eyed the meat sitting on the table, cooling off significantly. She felt the warmth of anger rising in her chest. She looked at the clock again – they had been waiting for half an hour. The children whined and complained they were dying of hunger. Hungry herself, she eventually served the meat and ate with the children.

Another twenty minutes passed before the door opened and Jacob stepped into the kitchen. He swayed slightly as he stood in the doorway, one hand still on the handle. Maria was fuming. She didn't dare take her eyes off her food, fearing she would start yelling if she focused on Jacob, and bit her tongue to keep her words at bay.

Jacob didn't say anything as he surveyed the room. Everyone sat quietly, the younger ones fidgeting with their forks, unsure of what to do or say, but very aware of the tension that entered the room with Jacob's arrival. Jacob made his way unsteadily to the empty chair at one end of the table and nodded his head to Ernst, who nodded back without saying anything.

Maria looked up and glared at Jacob across the table. The fact that he didn't seem to notice her only fueled her rage. The stench of cigarettes and alcohol lingered in the air. Erwin covered his nose, trying to be subtle, but Sylvia pinched her nose and let out a loud, "Ew."

Jacob began to cough, and continued coughing. The thick mucus in the back of his throat gurgled and sputtered, and everyone winced disgustingly at the sound. Angelika began to cry. When his fit passed, he looked at everyone's plates, with only a few remnants of food left, and then looked at his own plate. It was empty, save for a thin layer of dust that had accumulated since they'd set the table.

"Where's my food?" he barked rudely at Maria.

"It's on the stove," she answered, making sure to keep her voice steady and sure. "We were tired of waiting, and the children were hungry, so we started without you." She took another bite without looking at him.

Jacob pounded his fists against the table and Angelika cried louder. He stood and took his plate to the stove. "It's cold!"

"Yes, I suppose it would be," Maria said, her voice still even. "That's what happens when food is left sitting out for too long."

"Why didn't you keep it in the oven?" She knew he was glaring at her, but she refused to give him the satisfaction of meeting his gaze. One look at him and she was sure to break and cause an even bigger scene.

"Because then it would have overcooked, and you don't like your meat over-cooked. Isn't that right?" She bit her tongue to restrain herself from saying more.

The atmosphere was tense and uncomfortable for everyone. Angelika was still crying, and the others stared at their plates, moving food around with their forks, afraid to make any large movements that might draw their father's attention on them. Jacob filled his plate forcefully with meat, clanking the metal spoon against the plate.

No one spoke for the remainder of the meal. Erwin was the first to finish, having shoveled his food into his mouth so he could be excused, preferring to avoid conflict as much as possible. Ernst and Gredel stacked their plates and went outside to sit on the porch. Sylvia wiped her mouth on the sleeve of her dress and followed them. Maria carried Angelika outside to the new addition they had built beside the house where Jacob and Maria slept. A crib stood against a wall and Maria placed Angelika in it, covering it with her wedding veil to keep the bugs away.

When Maria went back into the kitchen, Jacob was reclining in his chair, smoking a cigarette. Maria's anger grew even more – he knew she hated smoke in the house.

"Where were you? After work, where were you?" She demanded.

He inhaled his cigarette, his gaze fixed on the open window in front of him. "With the guys."

"With the guys? Doing what?"

"Nothing. We had a few drinks."

Maria shifted her weight onto her other leg and crossed her arms. "Let me get this straight. Even though you know we eat supper every day at the same time, and even though you hate eating cold or overcooked food, you still chose to go out after work and hang out with the guys and drink, coming home almost an hour late? Without even telling me?" Her voice rose with each word. "And *then* you have the audacity to get mad at *me* because your supper was cold?"

"You know I don't like it when my food goes cold," he said coolly, taking another drag of his cigarette.

"Then *don't* come home late!" Maria lost it. She yelled at him for a while longer, and Jacob yelled back.

They argued not only about Jacob coming home late, but of any other grievance they had against the other. Among other things, Maria brought up Jacob's smoking, and the need for God in his life. The last attack struck a chord with Jacob and he yelled even louder. Despite the damage to his vocal chords, his voice still boomed throughout the small house, but Maria refused to back down.

The door flung open and Gredel matched their tone and volume as she yelled, "That's enough! Stop arguing right now!" Her pointed finger moved from one parent to the other.

"Gredel," Jacob stood straighter and puffed out his chest, "you mind your own business."

"This *is* my business," she retorted. "Sylvia is in her room crying because she's terrified. I'm sure Erwin is hiding under his covers, as well. The whole town is probably talking about you two by now, since they've likely been able to hear everything, too."

Maria rushed past Gredel. As soon as she was in the passageway, she heard Sylvia's sobs. Maria forced back her own tears, the thought of having upset her children pained her. She opened the door and saw Sylvia on the bed, hugging her knees, her cheeks wet from tears. Maria sat on the bed next to her and wrapped her arms around her daughter. "I'm so sorry, Sylvia," she knew the words couldn't turn back time, though she wished desperately that they could. Maria stayed with Sylvia, rocking her and singing softly, until she fell asleep in her arms.

—

Jacob sat on the porch, one leg crossed over the other, listening to the hum of Maria's voice as she calmed Sylvia. He wiped his face with both hands and exhaled deeply. He hadn't meant to cause an argument with Maria, let alone frighten the children. What had possessed him to yell like that, he wondered. It wasn't Maria's fault that he decided to hang out with his friends after work.

He was still berating himself when he heard the soft clicking sound of a door closing in the passageway behind him. He peered around the corner and saw Maria standing outside the girls' bedroom, rubbing her arms as if she were chilled, despite the hot evening air. She turned and walked toward the kitchen in the dark.

"I'm sorry," Jacob's deep voice pierced the darkness of the evening, startling Maria.

She looked in his direction, but his body wasn't visible from where she stood. Jacob couldn't see her, either, and wondered if she'd heard him, or if she had and decided to go into the kitchen anyway. He wouldn't blame her if that were the case. There was a rustling sound and her small figure appeared. The moon illuminated the yard and caressed Maria's skin, highlighting the paths her tears had left down her cheeks.

Maria sat down in a vacant chair and looked out past the yard, into nothingness. The expression on her face was soft, youth-like, and Jacob felt his arm rise involuntarily to touch her cheek, but he pulled it back, not sure she would want him to touch her.

Eventually, Jacob shifted his body, wracking his brain to find the words to say. He cleared his throat before he spoke. "I shouldn't have been late for supper. It was my fault that my food was cold. I'm sorry for yelling at you."

"I forgive you," Maria assured him. "And I'm sorry for yelling, too, and for saying more than I should have."

Jacob reached his arm toward her and placed it on her thigh, squeezing gently. Maria rested a hand on top of his, stroking his weathered skin with her thumb. They sat quietly, mesmerized by the symphony of stars above them, each one twinkling in turn, lighting up the black sky.

"I placed our meat order today," Maria said after some time. "Our supply of deer meat from your last hunting trip is running low. I also ordered some more wood."

"I suppose it's time I go hunting again. Maybe I should ask Hans to join me."

"I doubt Gerlinda would like that very much. Roswitha only just turned one, I don't know that she'd want to be alone for an entire week."

"Maybe we could just go for a weekend then. I enjoy spending time with him."

"I hear the sentiment is mutual. Gerlinda told me last week how much Hans looks up to you."

"Yeah?"

"Yes," Maria squeezed his hand, "he really admires you. As do I."

Jacob looked at her, her eyes brilliant with the moonlight shining on her. The skin around her eyes creased in an array of fine lines as she smiled at him. He smiled back, thinking how beautiful she was, even more so now than the day he first saw her from the woodshop. How long had it been now, he wondered. He counted backward in his head – twenty-three years.

Physically, her body had inevitably changed over the course of their years together, but she was still the same girl he had fallen in love with. Her passion and drive were as potent and rampant today, as a woman in her thirties, as they were when she was a teenager. She was never without an opinion, and never shied away from sharing that opinion with anyone, regardless if they wanted to hear it or not. He ardently admired her for standing firm in what she believed in, no matter what others might think of her.

He supposed that was why she was so fierce about her faith, and wanting Jacob to believe the same things she believed. He revered her dedication – every Sunday she got the children out the door and to the church, and she always prayed with them before meals and at bedtimes. If he was being honest, there was something that inspired him about the peace she exuded after her grand-parents passed away. She had mourned their loss, but she knew, with certainty, that she would see them again one day. She was so unshakably sure about her faith. He envied that steadiness.

"Jasch? Are you awake? Did you hear me?" Maria's voice jarred him back into the moment. He opened his eyes – when had he closed them? Clouds started to move across the sky in dark patches, making her face less visible.

"Yes, I'm awake."

"I'm going to bed now. Are you coming?"

They rose and walked to their bedroom together, arms wrapped around each other's waists. Before they parted to fit through the door, Jacob leaned down and kissed Maria.

"I love you, Mariechen."

"I know. I love you, too."

The cheeks lifted as she smiled flirtatiously. Jacob grinned and pulled her toward him. He lifted her off the ground and carried her into the room, kicking the door closed behind them.

—

The next morning, Jacob woke before the alarm went off. He sat on the edge of the bed and pulled up his socks as the shrill ring of the small bell resounded through the room. Maria groaned and rolled to the other side, pulling the sheet over her face to block the light streaming through the window. A warm hand touched the small of her back under the covers, followed by a graceful kiss on her neck.

"*Morje.*"

"What time is it?" Maria unveiled her face and squinted at Jacob.

"The same time it always is when the alarm goes off. Six o'clock."

Maria groaned again and slid her legs out from under the covers and let them hang off the side of the bed, feet not quite touching the ground. She grabbed her glasses from the nightstand and placed the thin metal wires securely around her ears. Jacob tucked his shirt into his trousers and walked out of the room.

When Maria had changed, she carried a handful of wood pieces from the pile in the front yard and brought them to the kitchen. Jacob was already seated at the table, reading the *Mennoblatt*. Maria unlatched the metal door of the stove and arranged the wood inside and lit the kindling with a match. The same white apron with light blue flowers hung on a crooked nail beside the stove. She grabbed it and tied it around her waist. The thin fabric faded almost to the point where the flowers were barely noticeable, and mismatched fabrics were sewn on in random places, patched over holes. Despite its shabby state, Maria couldn't bear the thought of throwing the apron away – it held far too many memories.

With her apron in place, and a bucket in hand, Maria made her daily visit with the family's cow. The cow and her calf stood by the fence at the front of the yard. Long strings of thick saliva hung from their mouths as their jaws moved in circular motions, chewing their breakfast. Maria positioned the stool near the hind legs of the cow and lowered herself onto it.

When the last drop of milk fell into the bucket, Maria brought a fresh bucket of sorghum and corn for the calf to eat. With the calf preoccupied, she opened the gate and ushered the cow through it. Its swollen body moved laboriously side to side as it walked down the street. Other cows roamed the streets, as well, and Maria's cow fell in line with a few others before turning down a street, out of sight. She closed the gate and walked back up to the house, milk sloshing around in the bucket.

Coffee was made and poured into mugs for herself and Jacob. Maria sat across from him and opened her Bible. She heard movement in the bedroom and the door opened. Erwin appeared, already dressed for school. Sleep still lingered in his eyes, and his cheeks were creased from the folds in his pillow. He yawned as he sat beside Maria.

"Nah, Erwin. *Goot je'schlop*, sleep good?" Jacob asked, without taking his eyes off the text in front of him.

"I did once you two stopped fighting."

Maria and Jacob looked at each other – regret seeped in once again. They had forgotten about the previous night's ordeal. "We're so sorry about that, Erwin." Maria rubbed his back.

Jacob changed the subject, "I was going to ask Onkel Hans if he'd want to come hunting with us this weekend. What would you think of that?" Jacob's eyes were focused on the paper again, but he smiled as he watched Erwin's reaction from his peripheral.

Erwin's face lit up. "Really, Papa? I can go hunting, too?" The boy was on the edge of his seat.

"Sure, I think it's time you learned how to shoot a gun. In any case, you might enjoy being away from your sisters for a day or two, no?" Jacob folded the newspaper and laid it on the table.

"Oh, yes!" His smile covered his face, but quickly faded as he turned to Maria, with a mixture of fear and hope in his eyes. "Am I allowed to go, Mutti?"

Maria laughed. "Of course you can go! Papa wouldn't ask you if he hadn't discussed it with me first."

"Oh, thank you, Mutti!" He got up and wrapped his arms around her neck.

"You're welcome. But, you can only go if you've finished all your schoolwork beforehand."

"When do I ever have schoolwork?"

He was right. The boy was too smart for his own good. They were only four days into the new school year and his teacher had already commented on his aptitude for learning, and the drawbacks of such a gift. Erwin caught on to new concepts quickly, and never had to be taught something twice. While his classmates worked on their exercises, or asked the teacher to repeat himself, Erwin would get impatient and restless and eventually distract the other students by starting up conversations. She reminded Erwin often to keep silent, but figured if that was his greatest fault, she could live with it, and so she never reprimanded him for it.

"I'm just saying," Maria reiterated, "*if* you have schoolwork that needs to be done, you have to finish it before you go. And," she turned to Jacob, looking at him intently, "only for one night. You can leave Saturday after school, but you have to be back by Sunday evening. I don't want him missing any school."

24

March 1965

MARIA STOOD BY THE GATE, WITH ANGELIKA BALANCED ON HER HIP, AS SHE waved her hand. Erwin and Sylvia ran in one direction toward school, and Gredel walked the other way toward the Cooperative.

"Well, Geli, I guess it's just you and me again," Maria kissed her daughter's blonde hair and walked back to the house.

Thursdays were typically the day she set aside to sew. The sewing machine was already set up in the kitchen, along with various piles – clothes that needed mending and fabric that needed to be cut and sewn into something practical. Today, she planned to make a new dress for Gredel to wear on Sundays and to special occasions. Maria opened the magazine Gredel had dog-eared the night before, and surveyed the dress the model was wearing, trying to decide how best to draft the pattern onto tissue paper.

Angelika walked to the backyard, her body swaying with each step as she tried to balance herself. She sat down near a family of bunnies, grabbing the closest one to her and forcing them onto her lap. She either didn't notice their struggle to escape, or simply didn't care – her love of all things furry trumped their desire for freedom.

Looking at the measurements scrawled on a paper beside her, she sketched a few lines into a notebook with a pencil, forming the A-line skirt. She looked at the sketch and back to the dress in the magazine, and back to her sketch, chewing the end of the pencil as she studied the design. Her thoughts were interrupted by a knock at the door.

"Come in!" she said, placing the pencil on the table.

The door opened and Gerlinda appeared with Roswitha in her arms.

"Gerlinda! So nice to see you! What brings you here so early this morning?"

Gerlinda lowered her daughter to the ground and pulled a chair out from the table and sat down. "Hans went to work early today. They're fixing some power lines on Hindenburgstrasse, and it needs to get done as soon as possible or the shops can't work properly. Or something like that."

"Is everything all right?" Maria asked, noticing the sombre expression she wore on her face.

"Oh, yes, everything's fine. Roswitha hardly slept last night. Teething, I suppose. Then she was up before the whistle. I needed to stop at the Cooperative today anyway, so I figured there was no sense waiting around at home with a cranky child."

"Right. I'm sorry to hear about your night. Are you all right otherwise? You look a bit pale."

Gerlinda touched her cheek, "I think I'm coming down with a cold. I've been feeling out of sorts for the last few days."

"Ah. No rest for a mother."

"No, indeed. Anyway, I thought since I was walking by your place, I would stop in and see if I might be able to borrow a book. I finished the last one you lent me." She reached into her bag and pulled out a tattered book, the pages worn from all the times Maria had read it.

"Yes, of course," Maria reached for the basket of books and placed it on the table for Gerlinda to sift through. While Gerlinda fingered through the books, reading the titles of each one, Maria bent down and lifted Roswitha into her arms. "My, she sure has grown since I last saw her, and that was only a few weeks ago!" Maria made grand facial expressions that made her niece giggle.

"I know, she's growing so fast. It's hard to believe she's already one. Ah, this one looks interesting," Gerlinda pulled a book out of the basket and read the synopsis on the back. "I think I'll borrow this one, if you don't mind."

"Not at all. Enjoy! You might want to grab another one while you're here – Jacob is planning on asking Hans to go hunting with him and Erwin this weekend. Just for one night."

"Oh, Hans will love that. He's been craving some male interaction. Not sure how much reading I'll be able to do, though, if the nights are anything like they were yesterday." Gerlinda sighed. "Erwin's going, too, is he? Will this be his first time?"

"Yes. Well, his first time shooting a gun, that is. He's been on many trips with Jacob before."

"He must be excited."

Maria laughed, "That would be an understatement."

"Hans still remembers his first time hunting. Actually, I think it was with Jacob, too. Were Abram and David there, as well? I can't remember. Hans tells a lot of stories."

"Why don't you come by with Roswitha on Sunday after *Meddachschlop*? Sylvia has been asking when she'll be able to see Roswitha again."

"That sounds great, thank you. You know, Sylvia and all your kids are welcome to come over any time. We love having them. Watching your kids play with Roswitha makes us excited to have more children. Hans would love to have a big family. Not quite as big as his own, mind you, if I have any say in the matter."

Maria raised her eyebrows in agreement. "Children really are a blessing."

"Actually," Gerlinda's voice quieted, "that might be the reason why I've been feeling a little off these days. My stomach is feeling queasy, and there have been a few other ... *symptoms* ... that are leading me to believe I might be pregnant."

"Oh, Gerlinda! How wonderful!" Maria clapped her hands together.

"Hushhh," Gerlinda cautioned with a smile on her lips. "I haven't even told Hans about my suspicions. There's no need getting his hopes up until I know for sure. Another week or so and I'll be more certain, one way or another. Until then, not a word to anyone! Not even Jacob. Please."

"Of course, you have my word."

Gerlinda tucked the novel into her bag and slung the bag over her shoulder as she stood. Roswitha climbed into her outstretched arms and they moved toward the door.

"*Danksheen*, for everything." Gerlinda said.

"You're welcome."

"Not just for the book."

"I know." Maria hugged her and kissed her cheek, and Roswitha's, before they walked out. Roswitha waved her arms wildly behind her mother's back until they were out of sight.

—

The morning hours whiled away as Maria sat for hours at the sewing machine. The pile of clothes that needed mending dwindled significantly, but not entirely.

She looked at the clock, it was just after eleven. The rest of the mending would have to wait until she had time to work on them again.

Jacob came home from work and greeted Maria with a kiss as she arranged a plate of deli meat. He rubbed the small of her back before sitting down beside Angelika's highchair. She offered him a piece of squished guava, which he kindly refused.

The metal clang of the gate signalled someone else's arrival. They heard Sylvia's voice greeting the neighbour. "Hi, *Onkel* Rempel!" Maria looked out the window and saw Sylvia running toward the house. Erwin raised a hand to their elderly neighbour. The man stood with his broom in hand and nodded his head toward the young boy.

Sylvia entered the kitchen first, breathless. She kissed Angelika on the cheek and set her backpack on the floor before sitting down next to her sister. Without another breath, she began divulging every detail of her day at record speed, though most of what she said was inaudible from the lack of air in her lungs.

"Uh, uh, uh," Maria interjected, pointing to the backpack and giving Sylvia a look that needed no explanation. The girl sighed and rolled her eyes, but knew better than to protest. She slid off her chair and picked up her backpack and started for the door. Erwin approached the door as she rushed past him and he pressed his body against the doorframe to avoid being hit. After she passed, he walked to his room and set his backpack on his bed before joining his dad and Angelika at the table.

"How was your day?" Maria asked him as she set the large pot of soup on the table and began spooning it into everyone's bowls.

"Good," he responded nonchalantly. It was his usual answer, and Maria knew there was no point prodding him for more details – he was a boy of few words.

Sylvia joined them shortly after and continued relaying her day from where she had left off. Maria smiled and tried to keep up with everything she was saying. Gredel arrived a few minutes later and the family ate their meal.

—

Sylvia was still sobbing uncontrollably by the time Maria finished wrapping Erwin's toe with gauze, even though Erwin hardly seemed phased by the amount of blood flowing from it. The culprit, a metal spade, lay on the ground by Sylvia's feet. She hadn't moved since the moment the tip of the spade went into Erwin's big toe.

With the toe relatively cleaned and dressed, Maria urged Sylvia to calm down and delegated their afternoon chores. Still sniffling, Sylvia trudged to the back of the house with Erwin and they each grabbed a broom. Neither one was thrilled with the futile task of sweeping the loose dirt off the packed dirt around the outside of the house.

"Why do I always get the bigger half of the house?" Sylvia grumbled.

"You don't," Maria assured her as she walked into the kitchen. "I make you switch sides every week to keep it fair."

Maria looked out the kitchen window to see where Angelika had wandered off to. She spotted her by the bunnies, until a cat walked by, catching the little girl's attention. Angelika crawled toward the cat, who had stopped and was now hunched in the dirt, motionless. Angelika didn't stop when she reached the cat, and continued crawling. The cat's ears stood straight up, and its eyes were locked on something in front of him.

Maria looked from the cat to Angelika, who was making her way toward the chickens. From the corner of her eye, she saw a flash of light as the sun reflected off something shiny moving behind the coop. She watched the figure move smoothly in the dirt, like a wave, slithering toward the hens and their nests.

"*En schlange,*" she exhaled the words in a whisper of disbelief as she watched Angelika move closer to the coop. "A SNAKE!" she yelled as she ran out of the house. All three children stopped and looked at her. Maria looked at the snake again when she came around the house. Erwin followed her gaze. Seeing the snake, he ran to Angelika and scooped her in his arms and ran back toward the house. Maria was already loading the shotgun she had pulled down from the beams in the roof. She pulled back the hammer and moved slowly across the yard.

Her heart was racing, her hands shaking as her finger hovered over the trigger. Perspiration grew over her brow as adrenaline coursed through her body. She glanced over her shoulder once more to make sure the children were out of the way, and then fixed her eye, and her aim, on the intruder.

The iridescent scales of the large snake sparkled in the afternoon sun. Maria stopped a few yards away from the coop and steadied the shotgun against her shoulder. The chickens flapped their wings and clucked in a haphazardly manner, making it difficult for her to keep her eye on the snake.

When the cloud of plumage settled, Maria aimed the gun on the snake's body. With one swift pull of the trigger, the snake stopped slithering, and the hens went wild. Maria lowered the gun, her chest rising and falling prominently. Blood streamed out of the motionless reptile. She stepped over the low wire fence into the coop and lifted the dead snake by its tail. With the head trailing in the dirt behind her, she wandered into the brush behind the house and discarded it.

The children were ordered to continue their chores as soon as she got back to the house. She returned the shotgun to its place in the rafters and wondered if her oma ever had to shoot snakes in their yard in Ebenfeld. From all the stories she had heard about the place, she had the impression it was somewhat more civilized than Chaco life. Mind you, they did have money back then, which would have made life easier, in general.

Maria shook her head and smiled. This was her life. It wasn't the first time, or the last, that she would shoot a snake on their yard, among other random events. Like the times they kept strange animals at their house for a friend who sold animals to zoos. When he couldn't make it into town from Asuncion, he asked Jacob and Maria to take care of them until he could arrange to pick them up. One time, they had a tapir, another time it was an anteater, but the most memorable animal he ever asked them to take care of was a baby jaguar. It wasn't with them for long, much to Erwin's disappointment. The animal, though small, was still wild, with paws larger than Erwin's face. The young cat would chase him playfully, and stand on its hind legs, with its paws on Erwin's shoulders. It was quite the sight, but it was the sight of the cat viciously eating raw meat that changed Maria's mind about the whole arrangement.

With the chores behind them, Maria began preparing the meal for supper. Sylvia sat at the table with pen in hand, drawing elaborate details on the paper in front of her. Her tongue sat at the corner of her mouth, signalling her deep concentration. Erwin lay on his bed, reading. She couldn't see the title from where she stood, but knew it was likely another Karl May novel, as that was his current favourite author.

Maria looked at the clock – only five more minutes until the whistle would blow and mark the end of another day. With a wet cloth, she wiped the layer of dust off the table. The plates were placed upside down to keep them clean until it was time to eat. She put a few *tweeback* in a bowl and set it on the table. In the pantry, she grabbed a jar of guava jam – made from fresh guavas from Kaethe's tree – and some mustard. Finally, she placed a plate of cold, sliced meat, left over from lunch, on the table.

Maria looked at the spread before her, mentally checking her list to make sure she hadn't forgotten anything. Someone knocked on the door and Sylvia and Maria looked toward it simultaneously. Curious, Maria opened it and looked down at a young boy, cheeks flushed from running. Jacob walked up behind him and towered over the young boy.

"Erwin? Are you expecting a friend today?" Maria called over her shoulder. Erwin sat up on his bed and looked toward the door.

"Helmut? What are you doing here?" Erwin walked out of his room and stood beside Maria.

"I'm not here to play, *Tante* Maria" Helmut said through laboured breaths. Jacob looked down on the boy quizzically. "I was sent to tell you that there was an accident, with Hans Loewen. He was working on the electrical wires when one of the wires got loose and hit Hans. It electrocuted him. I'm so sorry."

Everything went silent, save for the sound of horse hooves on the street, and birds chirping in the trees. Slowly, the gravity of what they had just been told settled over the room. Sylvia screamed and slid off her chair and hid under the table. She hugged her knees and buried her face in her arms. Helmut's eyes brimmed with tears as the sound of grief filled the space, and he turned and ran out of the yard.

Erwin looked up at Maria, tears chasing each other down his cheeks. "Mutti, it's not true, is it?"

Maria put her arm around his shoulder and squeezed his arm. With more effort than she thought she possessed, she forced back her own tears and used every bit of strength she had to keep her legs upright. She looked at Jacob's pale face. Without saying anything, he turned and walked toward their bedroom.

"We'll find out what happened," she told Erwin.

Angelika started crying but Maria didn't notice. The sounds around her funneled into nothingness until she heard only the voice in her head. She leaned against the nearest wall and pressed her hand against it, feeling the firmness of it. She kept her eyes closed, willing it all to be a dream.

Hans is dead? she asked herself, not able to believe it.

As the sounds began to rise around her, she heard more crying coming from outside. Louder, deeper moans, intensifying as they approached the house. Maria stepped outside and saw Gerlinda shuffling up the yard with Roswitha, who was also wailing. The look on Gerlinda's face broke Maria, and her tears began to flow. She fought to breathe through her sobs and rushed to Gerlinda. The woman collapsed into Maria's arms, nearly dropping the child. Maria slowly ushered all three of them to the ground and wrapped her arms tightly around Gerlinda's shaking body.

"He can't be dead," Gerlinda howled. "He can't be dead. He can't be!"

There was nothing Maria could say to Gerlinda, so she held her dear friend and sister, and cried with her.

Jacob eventually emerged from his room with red, swollen eyes. He walked solemnly toward the women. When he reached them, he took Gerlinda's hand and lifted her off the ground and embraced her. She beat his chest with her fists, anger rushing through her as she grappled with reality. Tears fell silently from Jacob's eyes. Gerlinda relaxed into his strong body and he tightened his grip on her. For the next few minutes he held his brother's wife as she cried.

"I'm so sorry, Gerlinda," Jacob offered his sympathy, but his words felt empty. He wanted to turn back time, to bring Hans back to them. He cleared his throat, attempting to clear the emotion lodged inside. "Stay here as long as you need. I'll let you know as soon as I finish the coffin. I'll stop by Gerhard and Marieche's and ask Marieche to sort the details for the funeral and send out the notification. We'll plan everything for the burial tonight. You stay here with Maria."

Jacob lowered Gerlinda back to the ground, into the safety of Maria's arms. He turned to Maria and she placed a hand on his wet cheek. The pain in Jacob's eyes hurt her physically. He kissed her and made his way to the shop.

—

There were no stars in the sky that night as Jacob and Maria sat on the porch. The evening was simultaneously peaceful and eerie. Clouds rolled above them, hiding the stars. Jacob's fingers were intertwined with Maria's, and stayed that way for hours as they sat together.

"Gerlinda thinks she's pregnant." Maria looked into her lap. A fresh round of tears fell from her cheeks, camouflaged against her black dress.

"No." Jacob looked at her with disbelief, hoping it wasn't true. Maria nodded. He ran his fingers through his hair and shook his head.

"Yes," she squeezed his hand. "She told me this morning. It isn't for certain yet. Not for another week or so. But she has a strong notion that she is."

"Did Hans know?" he whispered into the night.

"No."

Jacob rubbed his temples with his fingers. He licked his teeth under his lips, rage seeping to the surface again. He had lost control at one point while he was building the coffin, and threw a box of nails against the wall. He couldn't understand why Hans had to die. What possible purpose did it serve?

He pictured Hans, lying in the coffin, his arms crossed over his chest and a shiver ran through his body. His anger slowly subsided as he reflected on everything that had happened that day.

"Do you think Hans was ready? To die, that is?"

"What do you mean, Jasch?"

Jacob rubbed his neck. "Do you think … Did he have Jesus … Was he spiritually ready to die?"

Maria saw the fear in Jacob's eyes. She knew what he was thinking, if there was such a thing as heaven or hell, would Hans be in the former? She wondered why he was so concerned about the spiritual well-being of Hans, yet had never showed any concern for himself.

"Do you have reason to believe he wasn't?" she asked him, curious to know his thoughts.

"I don't know. That's the problem. He was never baptized, and we didn't talk much about it when we were together. Did Gerlinda ever say anything to you?"

"Well, he went to church with her every Sunday, and sang in the choir, as well. She's mentioned in passing that he read his Bible in the evenings, after Roswitha was asleep. So, even though he was never baptized, I'm quite certain he chose to live his life reflecting Christ's."

Satisfied for the time being, Jacob squeezed her hand as more tears fell down his face.

25

March 1967

MARIA CARRIED A TRAY WITH FOUR ICED COFFEES OUTSIDE AND OFFERED one to Jacob, Ernst and Gredel before sitting down and taking a sip of her own. Gredel nudged Ernst subtly in the arm. The slight nod of her head was all it took for him to understand what she wanted from him. He cleared his throat and folded his hands in his lap.

"So, you know my sister, the one that lives in Canada?" Jacob and Maria nodded. "Well, she's offered to sponsor me to go there, as well."

"Oh, Ernst! That's wonderful!" Maria exclaimed. "We've been hearing so many great things about Canada lately, haven't we, Jasch? It's quite the popular place to move to these days. Seems there are more opportunities there, with work and whatnot. But without a sponsor, it's near impossible. What a blessing for you to have your sister to help you."

"Yes, I'm grateful for her offer. But she doesn't want to stay in Canada. She and her husband want to move back to Paraguay, as soon as possible. So, that means I would need to go soon, if I wanted to take advantage of her sponsorship."

Maria frowned. "When would you leave?"

Ernst looked at Gredel and then back to Maria. "The thing is, as much as I'd love to move to Canada, I won't go without Gredel." He reached over and held her hand in his. Gredel smiled at him and turned to face her parents.

"You want Gredel to move to Canada with you?" Jacob asked skeptically.

"Yes, I do. But that's not all. We'd like to get married first. We were hoping we would have your blessing."

Jacob looked at Maria and she smiled at him, giving him a slight nod.

"Of course you have our blessing, son." Jacob assured him. "So, I guess that means Gredel will be moving to Canada, too."

"Yes," Gredel spoke with fondness in her voice. "And we can't start the paperwork to immigrate until we're married. And I also need to be eighteen."

The thought of Gredel moving to Canada formed a pit in Maria's chest. "So, what does that mean?"

"Well, we'd like to get married this winter, after my birthday, and start the application process right after. His sister is eager to get back. They're only staying in Canada right now so that they can sponsor us."

"All right. Let's start planning your wedding then." Maria feigned a smile, but inside she ached. The thought of her baby getting married was a big enough change on its own, never mind moving to another continent. Memories of Gredel as a baby flooded her mind as she sat back in her chair. Her blonde curls bouncing as she ran; her explorative personality; the constant mess around the house. Seventeen years had passed by her in a flash. She had the sudden urge to pull Gredel onto her lap and rock her like she did when she was a babe, and never let go. Thankfully she restrained herself, but the urge continued.

"Thank you, both of you," Gredel said. "And Mutti, I already have a few ideas for my wedding dress! I'll show you the pictures in the magazines tonight."

With that, the newly engaged couple left. Jacob and Maria watched them walk away, hand in hand. They had never seen Gredel happier.

"I know it's a good thing, the right thing, for them, but I can't help but feel sad. Is that selfish?" Maria asked Jacob.

"It's called being a mother." Jacob patted her leg and lit a cigarette. They reflected on what the next few months would look like. They sat silently for some time before Jacob cleared his throat and changed the subject.

"Another man approached me today to settle debts that Hans had with him."

That week marked two years since Hans passed away. Since then, men from the colony, and nearby colonies, had started approaching Jacob looking to be compensated for the debt Hans owed them. Jacob offered to pay them back, he would do anything for Hans and Gerlinda, and couldn't bear the thought of Gerlinda being burdened with such matters, but he was also a smart man. He knew once word got around that he was paying back Hans's debt, that some men might take advantage of him. He ended up telling each man that if he could provide a signed document saying how much Hans owed, he would pay them.

"Did he bring you signed papers?"

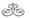

"No. So I told him I wouldn't pay him. He didn't like that very much. I'm hoping he'll be the last one, though. I just want to put this whole thing behind us. Move on."

"Have you seen Gerlinda recently?"

"No, have you?"

Maria shook her head. She hadn't talked to Gerlinda much since Hans passed away. Gerlinda stopped coming by the house, and didn't invite Sylvia over to play with Roswitha, or Birgitta, their youngest daughter, anymore, either.

Gerlinda had indeed been pregnant when Hans died, just as she suspected. She was a single mom of two very young daughters, and Jacob worried about her. He felt it was his duty to help her, even though she hardly visited anymore. She lived in a very small house with the two girls, so Jacob built them another house that they could grow into with room to spare, which had been Hans's original plan. When the house was done, Gerlinda and the girls moved in, though Jacob sensed they weren't as grateful for his gift as he expected they would be.

"At least we have a wedding to preoccupy our minds with now." Maria sipped the last of her cold coffee and put the four empty cups back on the tray and brought them inside.

—

Life went on as per usual, despite Gredel's absence that winter. Aside from Angelika moving into Sylvia's room, not much else changed physically after the wedding. Maria felt the void, though, even if no one else did. It was on quiet days, when the children and Jacob were out and about, doing their own thing, when she'd feel loneliness creeping in.

The children were on summer holidays, and Erwin had gone hunting for the day, as he did most Saturdays when he wasn't working at the mechanics shop. He didn't end up going hunting the weekend after Hans died, but Jacob had taken him a few weeks later. Erwin learned to shoot a gun on that trip, but he still hadn't yet shot a deer.

Maria buttoned the front of her blouse and tucked it into her skirt. She could already feel drops of sweat trickle between her breasts and down her spine. She grabbed her handkerchief and dabbed her face. Finding her lipstick in her night-stand drawer, she applied a thin layer to her lips and threw the stick in her purse.

Jacob sat on the porch, coughing. Maria gagged at the sound of his mucus-filled lungs. If she hadn't forced him to see a doctor to confirm he wasn't dying, she would swear he was. She sat beside him and looked at the street impatiently.

"He's coming," Jacob answered the question he knew she was thinking.

"I hope so. I don't want to be late."

"Is this the last night?"

"Yes, this is the last meeting. The team will be speaking at church Sunday morning too, if you'd like to come hear what we've been listening to all week."

"You've told me plenty, dear." His tone was light, but she sensed a hint of irritation. He brought the cigarette to his lips and inhaled.

Erwin appeared from behind the trees and Jacob sat straighter, craning his neck to see past the cloud of smoke he'd exhaled. A deer lay slung over Erwin's shoulder, and Jacob's face beamed at the sight. "That's my boy," he said quietly to himself. Maria heard him and smiled at the pride he exuded.

The pride on Erwin's face echoed his father's. They could see his smile from across the yard. Jacob stood as Erwin neared and lowered the carcass to the ground. Jacob put an arm around his shoulders and shook him in a manly way.

"How'd I do?" Erwin pointed to his victory.

"Not bad, my boy. Not bad at all." Jacob patted him firmly on the back before he lifted the deer and brought it to the back of the house and hung it from the rafters.

"Shower and change as quick as you can. We need to leave shortly if we're going to make it to the Crusades meeting on time. There's hot water ready for you on the stove." Erwin made a fist and pointed his thumb to the sky as he ran past her.

Maria and Erwin arrived just as the meeting began. Every meeting followed the same structure – the group sung hymns together, then listened to a sermon, followed by a few testimonies of faith. Every night ended with an invitation for anyone who wanted to give their lives to Christ to come to the front of the church, where a member of their team would pray with them.

That evening was different, though. It was the moment Maria had prayed for, for all her children. Amongst the crowd of attendees that knelt at the front of the church was Erwin. Her heart swelled at the sight, and a tear rolled down her cheek as she watched a member of the team place his hand on Erwin's shoulder. It looked like the man was asking him some questions, based on Erwin's nodding head.

They walked home in awkward silence. Maria longed to bombard Erwin with questions, but she knew he wouldn't appreciate it, so she held her tongue. Not able to contain herself for very long, she swung her arms around his shoulders, in the middle of the street. Erwin stood still, arms hanging straight at his sides. She didn't say anything – she didn't have to, he knew the reason for her actions. When she let go, she tucked in her blouse and struck up conversation about his day.

When they arrived home, Jacob was lying on the bed outside, with Angelika was fast asleep beside him. Erwin waved as he walked by and went straight to his room.

Jacob lifted his head, "Did he?" He searched Maria's face for the answer to his question.

Maria nodded, face beaming. She went to the side of the bed where Angelika slept and cradled her in her arms as she carried her to her room.

—

When Maria confirmed that Erwin had accepted Christ that night, Jacob had felt relieved and happy. Why did he suddenly care so much about everyone else's spiritual state, but not his own? It was a question that came up often, but as he did every time it came up, he brushed the thought away, telling himself he'd come back to ponder over it another time.

He walked into the kitchen and saw that Erwin's bedroom door was open. Erwin lay on his bed, propped up on one elbow. A Bible lay open beside him and his finger moved along the black text as he read. The candle flickered on the nightstand, illuminating the room just enough to read the words. Jacob felt emotion well up in his chest as he moved toward the door. He tapped on it with one finger to get Erwin's attention.

"Did you accept Christ into your life tonight?" Jacob asked sincerely.

"Yes," Erwin replied confidently.

Jacob took a deep breath. "Never go back, son. You took a step tonight, never go back."

"I won't," Erwin looked slightly stunned at his father's advice. It was the most Jacob had ever said about anything spiritual.

"Well, *schlop goot*, sleep well." Jacob quickly pulled the door closed behind him, not wanting his son to see how much his decision was affecting him.

—

Alone in her bedroom, Maria wrapped the last of the gifts on the bed. Cicadas sang outside her window, a soundtrack to her thoughts. The girls were busy cleaning the house, while Erwin was in the forest with Jacob, cutting cedar branches into varying sizes. When all the gifts were wrapped, she tucked them back into her wardrobe. She sighed with a smile – Christmas Eve had arrived.

The smell of paint lingered in the kitchen, and the room felt brighter from the fresh coat applied to the walls that morning. Sage-green florals were freshly stenciled overtop, as well, adding a personal touch to the otherwise plain walls. Maria placed five plates on the dusty table where they sat empty for the time being.

Jacob was now crouched beside the pit in the backyard, stoking a fire. When the wood was ablaze with flames, he sat on the porch and waited for the others. Sylvia appeared first, donning a new dress Maria had sewn for her. She twirled in front of Jacob. He nodded his approval and complimented her on the beautiful gown, and the matching bow pinned to her hair. She beamed, pleased at his approval, and climbed onto his lap, smoothing out her skirt with her hands.

One by one, the rest of the family gathered on the porch, dressed in their nicest clothes, and together they walked toward the church. They hadn't even reached the end of their block when Maria stopped and gasped.

"Oh, dear, I've forgotten my purse." Erwin rolled his eyes, he had figured out Maria's scheme years ago, but kept his mouth shut, not wanting to spoil it for the younger girls. "You go on ahead," she told them, "I'll run back to the house and fetch it and meet you at the church."

"Don't be late, Mutti," Sylvia urged, "I don't want you to miss my poem."

"I promise I won't miss it. I'll see you shortly." She turned and walked briskly back in the direction they had come from, while the others continued toward the church.

In the corner of the kitchen stood their Christmas tree – a wooden stand, made by Jacob, with cedar branches sticking out from holes drilled around it, in a quasi pyramid shape. The children had decorated the tree with the usual handmade decorations they'd accumulated over the years. Maria placed four gifts under the tree before pulling the hidden bag of treats out of a pot from the top shelf in the pantry. She filled each of the children's plates with chocolates, candies, and an apple – which was a delicacy for them, making it the children's favourite.

Maria scanned the room, checking off her mental list of things to do. Satisfied she hadn't forgotten anything, she grabbed her 'forgotten' purse and walked to the church, not wanting to miss Sylvia's first poetry recital.

Eager to begin the evening's festivities, the children ran ahead after the program. All the shutters on the house were open to allow any breeze that might come through the village to easily move through their home. It did little to relieve the humidity in the small room, though.

The children's excited banter reached Jacob and Maria as they walked through the gate, Jacob's arm resting just below the small of Maria's back as he ushered her into their yard. When they reached the house, Jacob kissed Maria, holding on to her long enough for her toes to warm with sensation. He looked longingly into her eyes when their lips parted. Maria's cheeks flushed as she looked back at him, his eyes divulging the thoughts on his mind. Jacob stroked her cheek with his thumb before he walked to the backyard to check on the fire. Maria took a deep breath to slow her heart and joined the rest of the family in the kitchen.

While the beef steaks cooked over the coals, Maria passed out the gifts to the children, who sat on the newly tiled floor. Erwin opened his box and pulled out a soccer uniform for his favourite local team, and immediately tried it on over his clothes. Sylvia opened her gift next and screamed with excitement to find a box of coloured pencils. She ran to her bedroom to grab her sketchbook and made a few marks with each colour onto a clean page. Angelika's gift contained her favourite doll, mended and clean. She was equally as thrilled as the others, and hugged the doll close to her body, grateful for the reunion.

With the children's attention fixated on their new gifts, Maria grabbed a small box wrapped in newspaper from behind a vase and placed it on the table in front of Jacob.

"What's this?" he asked.

"Just a little something for you."

"I thought we didn't get each other gifts?"

"I know, but I wanted to this year. I've been saving up for it."

Skeptical, Jacob raised an eyebrow at her as he ripped the paper on both sides. A small velvet box appeared and he opened it to reveal a watch, with a metal band chain. "Oh Mariechen, you shouldn't have."

"But I wanted to. Now, stop telling me I shouldn't have, and try it on." Maria took the watch out and placed the silver face on Jacob's wrist. He turned his hand over and fastened it. "There. It fits perfectly. Do you like it?"

Jacob adjusted the watch and held his wrist in front of his face. "I do. *Dankscheen*, Mariechen." He leaned across the table and kissed her. He turned the crown to set it to the proper time, and checked it often throughout the rest of the night.

26

February 1971

GONE WERE THE DAYS OF FINE FURNITURE CRAFTING. INSTEAD, JACOB SAT crouching on a roof, hammering a wood shingle into another. He longed to be back in the shop with Gerd, carving out impeccably detailed edges of wardrobes or bed frames, rather than being perched on top of a house like a bird, with the fiery rays of the sun scorching his skin.

The occupation change was not by choice. Having been evicted from the shop two years prior, Jacob was forced, once again, to find new work. It wasn't fair, he thought. He and Gerd had been faithful tenants, always paying the landlord on time, and never causing him any aggravation. They had established a reputable business, one that thrived and brought both brothers steady incomes for their families. Clients had lavished them with compliments about their work, and their ethics. They had never cheated anyone, or cut corners to make a few extra dollars. They had proved themselves to be honourable men, which left them even more dumbfounded when they received their eviction notice.

The whistle blew and Jacob climbed down the wooden ladder leaning against the side of the house. He eyed the roof from the ground, estimating another day's worth of work until he'd be finished. He wiped his forehead with a dusty arm, streaking his arm with brown lines.

He couldn't help but feel discouraged. Finding another new job, and at the age of forty-seven, would never have been his idea. The word 'failure' kept creeping into his mind. Losing his job twice had left him with a shattered ego. Emotions aside, he worried about the logistics of feeding his family. At his age, it would be difficult to find another job.

Jacob stifled his concerns and kept his worries to himself. He refused to burden Maria with his problems, but the silence only intensified his insecurities.

Soon he felt weighed down by his own negative thoughts, and overwhelmed with shame.

Maybe Maria was right, he thought, maybe he should've built a shed on their lot and worked from home, building the same furniture he had with Gerd. He saw now that it wasn't altogether a terrible idea, but at the time, he unhesitatingly rejected the notion, claiming it wasn't what he wanted. Which was true. He didn't want to work from a shed on his property, he wanted to work at his shop, with Gerd. There, the customers and the income were steady, and his work had been easy and enjoyable.

In the end, he decided on selling lumber that he bought from across the river, in East Paraguay. Not many men wanted to make the trek out that way, so Jacob seized the business opportunity and imported the wood to Filadelfia. He purchased a Volkswagen Kombi from a friend in Asuncion to transport the lumber, and stored the wood in a pile on their front yard.

The new business took off fairly well, in his opinion. He had a fairly steady and loyal clientele, and profited from the sales. Herr Wieler, a local businessman who owned a woodshop, came to Jacob for all of his lumber needs, which provided the majority of Jacob's income.

After a few months, Herr Wieler asked Jacob if he would do some roofing projects for him. Jacob looked into it, and estimated the cost of lumber, factoring in the amount of time it would take to finish a roof, and gave Herr Wieler a quote. Satisfied with the number, he hired Jacob. Jacob had been his sole roofer for a few months now, and with the experience and practice, Jacob was able to finish a roof in a fraction of the time it originally took him. But he still didn't enjoy it.

A black lab barked as Jacob walked through the gate. The dog ran to him, tail wagging fiercely behind him. "Hey, Ali," Jacob greeted him, scratching behind his ears.

Ali was essentially Ralph's replacement. Having eaten rat poison at the neighbour's house, Ralph became very ill and Jacob ended his suffering with a bullet between the eyes. He had been reluctant to pull the trigger, Ralph was part of their family, in a way. A few months later, friends of theirs moved to Canada and asked Jacob if he wanted their dog. A little more spritely than Ralph, Ali livened up the place again, and Jacob was grateful for the nonverbal company.

Jacob and Erwin were especially fond of the dog when it came time to go hunting. Ali would run through the woods and chase wild boar into the clearing so the men could shoot them. Then the dog would climb eagerly back into the bed of the Kombi, tongue flapping in the wind the entire way home. If it wasn't for the thrill of the car rides, they knew the dog would have wandered off long ago.

Jacob heard the familiar sound of Sylvia and Angelika bickering as he walked into the kitchen. Maria stood leaning over the table, spooning soup into all five bowls. Jacob grazed her back with his hand and kissed her cheek before sitting in his usual place.

"What's going on here?" he asked the girls.

Sylvia sat straighter, a smug smile plastered on her face. "*I'm* going to sleep at Oma's house tonight. All by myself. Geli doesn't get to come."

"It's not fair!" Angelika crossed her arms and raised her shoulders.

"Yes, it is. Oma likes me better." Sylvia jeered.

"That's not true!" Angelika began to cry.

"That's enough," Jacob stepped in, voice firm and authoritative. "Sylvia, you know that's not true. Oma loves you all the same."

The girls continued yelling. Jacob and Maria looked at each other and rolled their eyes.

"I met with Gerhard this afternoon, on my way to work," Jacob spoke loudly so Maria could hear him over the squabbling. "He said the men met at the Colony House yesterday and unanimously agreed that I should take on the role of the town's bylaw officer."

"Jasch, that's great! What a compliment!" Maria acknowledged. "When do you start?"

"Today. Or, tonight. I have to go to a town meeting at the church later. I'm not sure what the meeting will be about, exactly, but I'll meet Gerhard after so he can give me some more information."

"I'm happy for you," Maria said sincerely, "you needed something like this. It might help take your mind off things."

Yeah, maybe, Jacob thought, though he wasn't convinced. He smiled, not wanting her to sense his defeat, and sat in his chair at the head of the table.

—

Maria was reading on the porch that evening when she saw Jacob's tall silhouette appear on the street. Looking up from her book, she watched him as he moved toward her. She had memorized his body by now, and could make out every feature, even in the dark. Every curve of his muscles, every wrinkle creased on his skin, was etched in her mind. She smiled as he approached, until she saw the look in his eyes. He sat down in a vacant chair and rubbed his face with both hands.

"What happened?" Maria asked.

Jacob stayed quiet as he organized his thoughts. He leaned forward, his elbows resting on his knees, and placed his chin in the palms of his hands. "It's not so much what happened, but rather what was said that bothered me."

"What was said?" Maria urged him, intrigued.

"There was a speaker, someone from the Colony House, I think. Or was he from one of the other colonies? I can't remember. It doesn't matter, anyway. Whoever it was, he had the audacity to say that if someone who isn't a Christian donates money or goods to a church or charity, they're sinning."

Maria's eyes grew wide. "Pardon me? Who would say such a stupid thing?"

"I don't know, but it isn't sitting well with me."

"And no wonder! That's ridiculous! I should find out who it was and give him a piece of my mind."

"Calm down, Mariechen."

"I will not! Is he really saying that all of the furniture that you've made and donated to the Indians, and all the other mission organizations, is unsuitable for the Lord's work because you're not a Christian? And that you're sinning because of it? How dare he!"

"Mariechen," Jacob squeezed her thigh to get her attention, "calm down."

"As if God can't use the gifts from non-Christians to further his Kingdom! Ha! But to verbalize that heretical opinion, and to a group of men who aren't all Christians – how *dare* he."

Her anger turned to fear as she realized the man's ignorant comment might have pushed Jacob further away from any chance of ever having a relationship with God. "It's not true," her tone contrary to what it had been moments before. "Jasch, please don't take his comment as truth, or as what the church believes. From everything I have ever known, or read about in the Bible, it never mentions that acts of kindness are only acceptable, and useable, if done by Christians. You have sacrificed time and money and energy into those pieces you've given away, and they have brought so much good to the people who received them. Don't be discouraged."

Jacob didn't reply. He lit a cigarette and changed the subject. "Well, I'm officially the new bylaw officer for Filadelfia."

"Oh, is that so?" Maria eyed him knowingly. "And what, may I ask, does that entail? We won't be housing criminals in our home or anything, will we?"

"Only on weekends. And only the really bad ones," he winked at her. "No, I'm basically responsible for maintaining peace in the community, on a smaller scale. No criminals, yet," he winked again and Maria laughed. "I'll mostly be giving fines to those who disregard the bylaws."

"What kind of bylaws?"

Before Jacob could answer, they heard metal hitting against metal coming from the street. They couldn't see what it was, but saw something moving. The sound stopped right in front of their fence and they heard the gate open, followed by some more clanking metal, and then the gate closed.

Jacob sighed. "Like riding your bike in the dark without the front light on," he said to Maria with obvious disapproval in his voice.

"*Goodenowent*, good evening." They recognized Erwin's voice, though his face was still hidden in the dark. He had come home from working at Franz's son's store that night. The metal sound they'd heard was coming from his bicycle, which he was pushing beside him.

"Is the light broken?" Jacob asked sternly.

Caught off guard by Jacob's unwelcoming tone, Erwin looked at Maria for an explanation, but she didn't offer one. He looked over Jacob's head, through the kitchen window where the lightbulb hanging from the middle of the room shone brightly. He was more confused than ever. "Pardon me?"

"On your bicycle! Why isn't the light turned on on your bicycle?" Jacob's voice grew louder.

"Oh," Erwin bent to the side and looked where the light was attached to the front of the bike. "I guess I forgot. What's the big deal?"

"The big deal is that it's the law, Erwin. You have to have your light on when you're riding in the dark."

Clearly worked up by the situation, Maria touched Jacob's arm. "It was an accident. He forgot."

"What is going on?" Erwin asked.

"Papa was delegated to be the colony's bylaw officer tonight."

"Oh," he took a moment to process her words. "Maybe you can let this one go? Give me a warning or something?" There was hope in his voice, but the look in Jacob's eyes made it clear that his request was not likely to be granted.

"I'm going to bed," Jacob announced and went to his room. Erwin leaned the bicycle against the side of the house and sat down next to Maria. Not sure what to say, he changed the subject.

"Looks like the roof on Ernst and Gredel's house is almost finished." Erwin said, pointing in front of him. Across the street, hidden in darkness, was a near-finished house that Ernst and Gredel had been building since they'd arrived back in Paraguay earlier that year.

"Yes, Gredel said today that it's going faster than they anticipated. They've had so much help. Which is good, since she can't do much of the work herself, in her condition."

"Will they stay in Paraguay for long after the baby is born? She's due in the winter? July, is it?"

"Yes, beginning of July. I do hope they stay, but it doesn't sound like that's the plan. She said there's a good chance they'll move back to Canada next fall."

The thought of having to say goodbye to Gredel again, and so soon after they'd come back, was so hard for Maria. Add to that the fact that they would also be saying goodbye to their first and only grandchild was too much for her to bear.

The subject changed again, and the two of them stayed outside for a long time, talking until well after the light in the kitchen turned off.

—

Everyone, except Jacob, and Sylvia, who was still at Kaethe's house, was eating breakfast in the kitchen the next morning. No one knew where Jacob was, and Maria was growing slightly concerned by his absence. The door opened then and Jacob entered. He sat at his usual spot at the table and reached for the jam.

"Where were you?" Maria inquired.

"At the Colony House," Jacob responded nonchalantly, spreading some jam on his *tweeback*.

"What were you doing there this early?"

"I had a fine to pay." He kept his eyes on his bun, but saw Erwin's stunned face turn to look at him.

"You paid my fine?" He asked humbly.

"Yes. But don't let me catch you without your light on at night again."

"Don't worry, Papa, you won't." Erwin looked meekly into his bowl, stirring his cooked oats with his spoon.

Jacob laid the *Mennoblatt* on the table in front of him and took a bit of his breakfast. Maria could tell by the gleam in his eye that he knew she was looking at him, but he refused to look up and meet her gaze. Instead, he smiled coyly behind his *tweeback,* and she smiled.

27

May 1972

SHADOWS DANCED ACROSS THE ROOM AS A CANDLE FLICKERED IMPULSIVELY on the table. The only sound in the room came from the crackling wick and the whir of the sewing machine. Maria lifted her foot off the pedal, trimmed some threads, and repositioned the fabric under the presser foot. It was well past midnight, but that was irrelevant at the moment. The pile of torn and worn-through clothes would not mend themselves.

The door to the kitchen opened and Sylvia walked in, eyes bleary and hair knotted from rubbing against her pillow.

"Sylvia, what are you doing awake at this hour?"

Sylvia rubbed her eyes. "I couldn't sleep," she said through a yawn. She went to the counter and filled a glass with water from the bucket before sitting cross-legged on a chair. Maria continued sewing, humming to herself. Sylvia pulled her housecoat tighter around herself and yawned again.

"What are you doing?" Sylvia asked.

"Mending the clothes. Here," Maria reached for a stack of folded clothes on the floor and placed them in front of Sylvia. "These are done. Take them with you back to your room. You need to go back to bed now."

Sylvia sat in her chair with no intention of going back to bed just then. Maria could tell her mind was preoccupied. "Mutti? When is Lucy coming back?"

Maria sighed and put both feet on the tiled floor. It was a question she often asked herself but didn't have an answer for. Ernst and Gredel had moved back to Canada two months ago, with their eight-month-old daughter, Lucy.

"Lucy isn't coming back, remember? She lives in Canada now. But I'm sure we'll see them again soon," she reassured herself as much as Sylvia.

The thought of Lucy made her smile. Maria had paced the street outside the hospital, the day Gredel went into labour, waiting for Ernst to bring her any news. When the baby had finally arrived, visiting hours were already over, but Maria had been relentless, and the poor nurse behind the counter eventually ceded and let Jacob and Maria see their granddaughter.

Having birthed and held four babies of her own, Maria thought she would know what to expect. But nothing could have prepared her for the overwhelming love she felt toward the little baby cradled in her arms. Lucy was tiny, despite coming two weeks past her estimated due date. She had very little hair, but the hair she did have was dark as ebony. Jacob and Maria were instantly smitten with their granddaughter.

"When is Erwin going to sleep here again?" Sylvia's groggy voice startled Maria from her memory.

"Pardon me?"

"Erwin – when is he going to start sleeping here again?"

"Oh. Soon, I'm sure. Oma's moving into her new house next week, just a few lots down from us. Then he'll come home. We'll be able to see Oma more often, too." Maria's smile turned into a frown as she placed the hem of the skirt back under the presser foot and gently pushed down on the treadle.

"Is she still sad that David died?" Kaethe and Sylvia had always had a special bond, and she could see how Kaethe's grieving was affecting Sylvia.

Kaethe was the strongest woman Maria knew, so on one hand she was dealing with David's passing very well, at least on the outside. But she had confided in Maria that she was having flashbacks of Nikolai's death. The images haunted her, and she woke from nightmares nearly every night. She couldn't understand why she had to go through the pain of losing another husband. Maria worried about her mother, as did her children, especially Erwin. With all David's children married and out of the house, Erwin asked if he could live with Kaethe until she felt better. He, too, had a fondness for his grandmother, and genuinely wanted to be with her as she grieved.

Maria held her emotions in check as she finished the hem and trimmed the loose threads with large, metal scissors. "Yes, sweetheart, Oma is still sad."

"But David is in heaven now. That's not so sad."

Maria smiled, a ball of emotion building in her throat. She coughed lightly before she could speak again.

"That's very true, Sylvia, but it doesn't mean it's easy to say goodbye."

"God has our lives in His hands, doesn't He?"

"Yes, He sure does," Maria affirmed.

"Then everything happens exactly as it should, right? So we should trust God with his timing, even if we don't like what happens."

"Exactly," she wondered when her daughter had become so wise and sure about her faith.

Maria placed the skirt on the pile of mended garments and moved herself away from the sewing machine. She hugged Sylvia and kissed the top of her head.

"Come, it's time for bed," Maria held out her hand for Sylvia to hold. With their hands clasped together, Maria blew out the candle on the table and walked Sylvia back to her room.

—

Jacob carried the tin bucket for Maria as they walked down the yard to where the cow and her calf grazed mindlessly. Maria yawned, not yet fully awake. She could smell coffee brewing and couldn't wait to get back inside and add a bit of fresh milk to her cup. Sophie, their cow, as named by Angelika, stood patiently as Maria began massaging the teats between her fingers. Jacob leaned against the fence, watching her work with finesse.

"Herr Wieler doesn't have any work for me again this week," he began. "He also hasn't bought lumber from me for quite some time now." Jacob looked at the full stack of wood on the other side of the yard. "Gerd said Wieler's been driving across the river and buying lumber himself, and selling it, too."

"What does that mean for you, then?" Maria asked, trying not to let her worry seep into her tone.

"I'm not quite sure what it means, in the long term, but for the time being, it means I don't have enough work. Just as Herr Wieler was a loyal customer to me, so his friends are loyal to him, which means many of my customers are now buying their lumber from him." Jacob walked around Sophie and crouched beside Maria. "Mariechen, the truth is, I'm not making money right now. I can't compete with him in the same village, it just doesn't work. I've tried to get new customers, but in a small town like this, it's not that easy."

"Are you sure you've tried everything? What about advertising in the other colonies?"

"Even if I could get some customers from other colonies, it still wouldn't provide enough income for us. I've thought about it for a long time, working out all the options and adding numbers. Mariechen, there is no future for me with this business anymore. I'm sorry."

"It's not your fault, Jasch," she moved the bucket out from under the cow and stood, facing him. His eyes were the saddest she had ever seen them. He was beyond defeated, and she knew he felt he was letting her down. She reached for his cheek, stroking it with her thumb. "It's not your fault, Jasch," she repeated. "We'll figure something out."

He placed his hand over hers, moving it to his mouth and kissed her fingers. "Thank you," he whispered. "But that doesn't change the fact that there is no work for me here. I've been looking, and talking to some people..." he paused, shifting his weight to his other leg. "I've been thinking a lot lately, and I wonder if we should move to Canada."

"Canada!" Maria took a step back, scanning Jacob's face for any hint that he might be pulling her leg. His expression didn't waver. "You're kidding, right? Why would we leave our home to move to Canada? Our whole lives are here! Mama, the kids, the kids' friends and school. *Our* friends! What about your family?" Maria laughed nervously. "Surely you're joking."

Jacob reached for Maria's hands and held them firmly in his own. "I'm not joking, Mariechen. I can't work here, and we need to be able to provide for our family. Canada could offer us so much more. Besides, don't you want to be close to Ernst, Gredel and Lucy again? They're not going to move back to Paraguay."

"Of course I want to be near them! And don't for a second accuse me of not wanting to. You know how much I miss them. But our lives are here, in Filadelfia. Mama would be completely alone if we left. I couldn't do that to her. I won't. She's all I have left of my family."

"You have me, and the kids."

"Jasch, you know that's not what I mean. Besides, we can't just pack up our lives and move to a different continent. That's ridiculous!"

"Why? Why is it so ridiculous? So many others have done it already. You've heard my brothers – they love it over there, as do their wives and children. And wouldn't it be great to watch Lucy grow up? I miss her, too, you know." Jacob did have an undeniably close bond with Lucy, one Maria envied. But that wouldn't be enough to persuade her to move.

They stood holding hands for a long time. Maria looked past him, at nothing in particular. Her mind raced with all the reasons they should stay. Above everything, she just couldn't fathom life anywhere but in Paraguay.

"And what kind of work do you think is waiting for you in Canada? Don't you dare say construction. If we moved over there, and I'm not saying we are, but if we did, and you got a job in construction, I wouldn't live with you." She said seriously, no hint of teasing in her voice.

"What? Why not?"

"You know why. You hate construction! On the few days it rains here every year, if you're working on a roof, you come home grumbling and miserable. You do realize it rains far more often in Canada, right? You would be impossible to live with, and I won't even consider it if that's what you intend to do."

"So, you're saying you'll consider it?"

"Of course not!" she yelled and dropped her hands to her sides. She grabbed the bucket of milk and started walking back toward the house.

"You always do what I want you to do, when it comes to these kinds of decisions," Jacob called after her.

Maria stopped and turned to face him. "That might be so, but not this. I'm not uprooting our family and moving to Canada. It's preposterous!" Her posture softened. "Do you honestly want to move to Canada?" Her voice was now soft and sincere.

Jacob shifted his weight and looked away. He shrugged his shoulders and exhaled long and slow. "Not ideally," he confided. "What I want is to have a steady job, with a good income, so we can stay here, and keep living as we have been. But that hasn't been working out for me for some time now. And I can't put that burden on you or the kids. I need to find work so I can support you."

"But do we really need to move to Canada to fulfill that?" Maria walked right up to him and looked up into his face.

"What would you suggest?" He resigned and his shoulders dropped, along with his spirit.

Maria sighed, "I don't know. Let me pray about it." She offered him a compassionate smile and turned back toward the house, praying as she walked.

Lord, if this is Your will for our family, show me a clear sign.

—

Jacob snored beside Maria as she lay awake in bed. She couldn't stop thinking about Jacob's suggestion to move to Canada. She mentally listed all the reasons for and against the idea, but still didn't feel sure one way or the other. God would have to give her a very obvious sign that they should move, or she wouldn't even consider it. And if that sign did come, then He would need to change her heart to be excited about it, and to actually follow through with the move.

Maria wanted to be with Ernest, Gredel and Lucy, but could she reconcile her need to be with them by asking the other children to leave all of their friends, and everything they knew, behind. But was that really her reason for not wanting to move? Were her excuses more selfish than that? The gnawing in her gut made her wonder if it was more her own life that she didn't want to interfere with.

Paraguay was all she knew; it was her home. Her mother was here, as well as her friends and church. It was here that she grew up, and also met Jacob, fell in love, got married and started her own family. All of their children's memories were in Paraguay, as were hers. Her parents and grandparents came here with nothing, and worked themselves to exhaustion to build a life for Maria, and it was here that her grandparents and father were buried.

And then there was Canada – a country filled with potential and prospects. A country filled with modern conveniences to ease life's everyday tasks. Although she loved the idea of possibly owning a dryer, along with other appliances, it was the education and job opportunities their children would have in Canada that appealed to Maria the most, though not quite enough to convince her to move.

She fell asleep to the lull of her own thoughts, and woke an hour later. Jacob was already awake and she found him sitting on the porch. She eased herself into a chair, cringing from the stabbing pain shooting up her back. As she settled into her seat, the gate opened and their friend, Art Friesen, waved at them.

"Were you expecting him?" Maria asked Jacob, waving back.

"No," Jacob looked at his watch. "I knew he was coming to visit, but didn't realize he was already in town."

They stood to greet him. Art shook both their hands and greeted them warmly. Jacob motioned for Art to take a seat, which he gratefully accepted.

"What brings you here on such a fine Saturday?" Jacob asked. "Don't you have family to visit?"

"We arrived at my in-law's yesterday to spend a few nights with them, so I've had quite enough visiting for one day. Fancied a bit of a change of scenery," he winked at them and they laughed.

"How's Canada treating you?" Jacob asked. He listened intently as Art spent the next few minutes sharing about life in Canada, and what it was like over there.

"After we acclimatized to the weather, and settled into the culture and language a bit better, I could finally start my own business. It's a cabinet shop – we build kitchen cabinets, among other things. It's called Montalco Cabinets." Art paused, contemplating his next thought. "I don't know if I'm supposed to know this or not, but I hear you're not getting much work these days, Jacob."

Jacob's eyebrows rose, "That's right."

"Well, if you ever want to move to Canada, you've got a job waiting for you at Montalco. We could always use more finely skilled craftsmen like yourself."

Maria's heart raced. She looked at Jacob who turned to her with eyes as wide as her own. Art stayed for a while longer but Maria didn't hear most of what was said after that. A knot formed in her stomach, and she couldn't deny what just happened.

Jacob walked Art to the gate and came and sat beside Maria, lighting a cigarette. They stared out toward the street, motionless.

"Well, I guess we're moving to Canada," Maria stated matter-of-factly.

Jacob smiled, "I suppose we are."

Maria turned to him and offered a smile, but the reality of their decision made her feel slightly sick.

"I'll write a letter to David right away. He mentioned a while ago that he would sponsor us if we ever did decide to move to Canada."

"So soon? We haven't even told the children. I hardly believe it myself."

"There's no point delaying it. The process will take a long time to get underway as it is. The letter itself will take a few weeks to get to David, and then he'll need to acquire the paperwork and send it back to us."

"Right. You're right. That makes sense. Go write the letter. Send David and Aganethe my love."

Jacob leaned toward Maria and smoothed back the few strands of hair that unravelled from her pins. Her heart weighed heavy with uncertainty, but his smile reassured her. They would do this together, and that, in itself, would get them through it, she thought. He kissed her, the taste of tobacco still on his lips, and went to the bedroom to write the letter.

After David Thielmann passed away, Kaethe moved to a house on the same street as Jacob and Maria. She was grateful to have her mother nearby, except today. She wished she had more time to process her words as she walked toward her house.

They finally received word from Jacob's brother that their application had been accepted, their paperwork already underway. They didn't tell anyone about their plan until it was official, not even the children, in case the whole thing fell through. But also because the whole thing made Maria feel extremely vulnerable

Maria spotted Kaethe sitting under a large tree, drinking *maté* by herself. Kaethe looked up when Maria reached the house and knew instantly that something was amiss. Maria cried as soon as she stood in front of her mother, and Kaethe held her until her breathing calmed and steadied.

"I'll be fine, Michi. Don't worry about me."

"But, you don't even know what I'm going to say," Maria looked stunned.

"I know," Kaethe corrected her.

"But how?"

"I just know."

"Oh, Mama," Maria broke down again. "I thought I could do this, I was sure God was telling us to move, but I don't think I can. I can't leave you. I can't."

"Hush, now. Of course you can." Kaethe held her emotion inside. "When God makes a path, you follow it, even if you're afraid. His plans are perfect, and cannot be thwarted, regardless what you may think. I trust He has something wonderful in store for you all in Canada. I'll be fine here, don't worry about me."

Maria nodded as tears fell steadily off the end of her chin. "I love you, Mama."

"Oh, I love you, too, Michi."

Four generations, taken mid-1949. Kaethe (40) holding Gredel (2 or 3 months).
Maria (21) standing, Johann (79) sitting.

Maria (44) and Gredel (4), taken around 1953.

A photo of Gredel (6) and Erwin (1) taken in 1955.

Family photo taken in 1963 at Hans and Gerlinda's wedding.

Maria (35), Gredel (14), Jacob (40), Sylvia (5), Erwin (9).

Gredel (15) holding Angelika.

Ernst and Gredel (18) on their wedding day, July 15, 1967.

Jacob's parents, Abram and Helena Loewen taken around 1968.

Photo of Jacob (late 40's) taken in early 1970s.

Erwin (17) standing in front of their VW Kombi, holding a boa constrictor snake he shot.

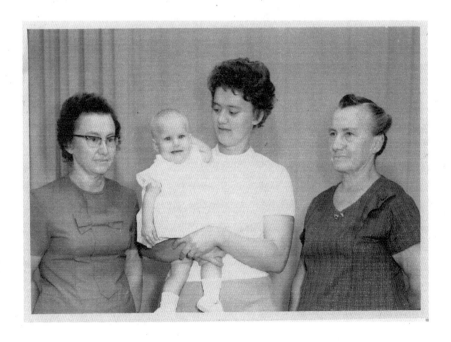

Four generations, taken late 1972. Maria (44), Lucy (6 months), Gredel (23), Kaethe (63).

PART
FIVE

28

March 1973

AS THE PLANE LEVELED OUT, MARIA LOOSENED HER GRIP ON THE ARMRESTS and the colour slowly returned to her knuckles. Angelika leaned over her to look out the small window, her mouth agape as she took in the view of the country beneath them. Everything looked so small as they soared higher into the sky, yet at the same time, the landscape grew larger and more vast than Maria had ever seen before.

The earth was brown for miles, with forests and rivers scattered throughout. From the seat behind her, she heard Sylvia asking Jacob what everything was, but he couldn't give her the answers she wanted. They had never seen the world from this vantage point before. The country they'd known for forty-three years looked foreign from above. The more Maria thought about it, the more overwhelmed she became. The whole move was overwhelming.

Maria pushed the button on her armrest and reclined her seat as far as it would go, which hardly changed her position. She closed her eyes, warding off the ebb and flow of nausea. The last few months had been such a whirlwind, she wanted nothing more than to relax and leave all their worries behind, but even moving halfway across the world wouldn't solve all their problems.

A week after Christmas, they received a letter informing them their papers had been cleared, and they were allowed to move to Canada. The children were excited, though Maria wondered if they understood the full impact it would have on them. Everyone did their part to prepare for the move. They sold all of their possessions, and gave or threw away any unnecessary items. Their furniture, household items, car and house were sold within weeks, leaving each member of the family with one suitcase filled with their own belongings.

Even after selling everything, they were still one thousand dollars short. They didn't have enough to cover the cost of airfare for the five of them. Jacob was forced to set his pride aside and borrowed the rest of the money from his brother. Maria had sold her most precious items – the nightstand Opa made her, the headboard Jacob gifted her, and all the children's drawings and schoolwork, items Maria considered priceless – and yet, it hadn't been sufficient enough.

As they neared Vancouver, snow-topped mountains rolled beneath the wings of the plane as they soared above them. In the distance, Maria saw a reflection glistening on what she assumed was the ocean. The warm hues of the sunrise, and the contours and shapes of the rigid mountains as they descended into the city, were a stark contrast to the dry, barren lands of Paraguay.

After many hours of travelling, the plane finally landed in Vancouver, British Columbia. They knew the seasons were opposite from what they were used to, but nothing could have prepared them for the chill they felt when they stepped off the plane. Spring had just begun in Canada, but the air was frigid. The family huddled together as they walked across the tarmac and into the airport.

The sheer size of the building took their breath away. They walked close together, not wanting to lose each other in the crowd. People moved all around them, rushing past with small suitcases trailing behind. Maria grew anxious as she looked at the signs above her. "*Welcome to Vancouver*"; "*Sunday, March 25*"; "*Baggage and Way Out*"; "*Customs.*" She pulled a paper from her purse, marked with notes that David had sent them. After landing, they were meant to go through customs, whatever that meant.

Maria pointed at the sign with the word 'Customs' typed in white font and the family moved as one entity toward a massive queue of passengers. Conversations buzzed around her, though she didn't understand any of it. If only she had learned English before they'd left, she thought. Her repertoire of English words consisted of five words – yes, no, little, boy and girl. Not very helpful in their current situation.

An officer behind a counter waved his hand at them and they shuffled toward him. Maria watched his lips move as he spoke, willing the language to be instantly translated in her mind. Somehow, despite the language barrier, their passports were stamped, and they followed the crowd once again, hoping they would guide them to where they needed to go next.

The carousel moved round and round, which fascinated Sylvia and Angelika. They watched with wonder as suitcases came down from the ceiling and fell onto the metal conveyor belt. Jacob and Erwin watched for their bags and when all five suitcases had been retrieved, they again followed the other passengers. A long hallway led to a sliding door that opened automatically, revealing glimpses of the crowds of friends and family awaiting the arrival of their loved ones.

As they neared the doors, Maria felt more anxious than she had the entire trip. Walking through those doors was the last step of their journey. On the other side, their future awaited them. Maria and Jacob turned and looked at each other and she knew the same thought had crossed his mind, too. He smiled half-heartedly at her and transferred his suitcase to his other hand and reached for Maria's. He squeezed it. Taking a deep breath, they walked through the doors together.

Sylvia and Angelika screamed when they saw Ernst, Gredel and Lucy. They ran to them, and Lucy bounced with excitement in Ernst's arms. When Jacob and Maria caught up to them, Lucy threw herself into Jacob's arms. Maria's throat caught with emotion as she looked around. Finally, they were all together again.

—

Jacob and Erwin started working at Montalco Cabinets the day after they arrived in Vancouver. Jacob refused to take time to settle in with a debt looming over his shoulders. All the money the two of them earned in the first year was used to repay David. With their debt behind them, they saved up and bought a house a few blocks away from Ernst and Gredel the following year.

Maria and the girls had no problem adjusting to the luxuries of Canadian living. Novelties like inside toilets, a freezer, running water, ovens that didn't require a fire, glass windows and central heating, greatly improved Maria's quality of life. Jacob was a bit more hesitant. He erred on the side of caution and claimed he would never in his life use a microwave. He preferred the *old way* of doing things, but Maria reminded him that he rarely had to use for the appliances himself.

Maria moved the wet clothes from the washing machine into the dryer. The clothes tumbled loudly as she walked down the hallway. She stopped to look at every photo hanging on the wall. There was much to be thankful for, she knew that. Her children were happy and healthy, and Jacob was working and doing what he loved. She looked at a picture of Angelika as a little girl, her blonde hair cut short, a kitten curled in her lap. Maria wondered how many memories of Paraguay Angelika would carry with her into adulthood. She didn't seem too rattled by the move and spoke English better than any of them. She was nearly fluent in the language after only a few months at school. Yet Maria couldn't help feeling guilty for uprooting her children and making them adjust to a whole new culture.

Maria heard someone plodding up the back steps. She went onto the porch and met Angelika at the top of the stairs. Maria hugged her daughter, not noticing the stunned look on the girl's face. Maria had never been one to show much physical affection to her children.

"I love you, Angelika," Maria told her.

"Uh, I love you, too, Mutti. Is everything all right?"

"Hm? Oh, yes." Maria loosened her grip on Angelika and pulled the sliding door open for her to walk through. "How was school today?"

"Ugh, I need to change my name."

"What? Why? I love your name! What's wrong with it?"

"No one can pronounce it. Everyone keeps calling me *An-jel-ee-ka*," she said with disgust.

"Why can't they say *Un-gay-lee-kah*? What's so hard about that?"

"I have no idea. I think I'll just tell them to call me Angie."

Angie, Maria thought, frowning. She loved the name Angelika. "If that's what you want, then Angie it is."

29

February 1983

THE KITCHEN SINK BRIMMED WITH SUDS, AND RAINBOWS SHIMMERED across the small bubbles. The room smelled of fragrant lemon. Maria rinsed another plate and set it in the rack on the counter. She looked over her shoulder, out the window, and saw a stream of smoke rising from Jacob's cigarette. It looked like it was dancing in the spotlight of the overhead light. She smiled at the image and scrubbed the next plate.

The phone rang as she set the plate in the rack with the others, water dripping onto the tray beneath it. She pulled on the fingers of the rubber gloves she wore, struggling to free her hand. On the fifth ring, she lifted the receiver from the wall and held it to her ear.

"Hello?"

"Hi, Mutti."

"Gredel. Hi, how are you?"

"I'm fine," though she sounded very much the opposite. "It's Oma. I'm worried about her."

"What happened now?"

"I was putting Cristina to bed when I smelled something burning. It was coming from the basement. I went downstairs and saw Oma talking on the phone in the living room and there was smoke coming from the kitchen. She left a pot on the stove – again. Mutti, this is the third time this week. It's not safe, for her or for us. I love her, but she just can't live with us anymore."

Maria lowered her head and rubbed her forehead with her gloved hand. Ernst and Gredel had been generous to let Kaethe live in their basement when she arrived in 1978, a few months before Erwin's wedding. In recent years, her mind had begun to wander, and Maria often received phone calls of concern from Gredel.

"I'll talk to Papa. We'll figure something out."

Maria finished washing and drying the dishes before changing into her nightgown. She grabbed the housecoat that hung from a hook on the back of the bedroom door and wrapped it around her body. Jacob was still on the porch, a glass of whiskey and water in hand. Maria grabbed a blanket from the couch and joined Jacob outside. Her presence seemed to have startled him. He lifted his wrist and looked at his watch – more so out of habit than an urge to know the time.

Maria settled into the white plastic chair and tucked the blanket under her thighs. Small patches of snow still lingered on the lawn below, glistening in the light of the street lamps.

"I just got off the phone with Gredel," Maria began, looking up into the dark, starless sky. She missed the skies in Paraguay, illuminated with stars as far as you could see. "Mama left a pot on the stove again. Third time this week." She turned to Jacob, "I think it's time we consider moving her into a different home. Gredel already has two little girls to take care of, she doesn't need the burden of taking care of my mother, too."

Jacob nodded, mumbling softly in agreement. Maria waited to see if he would add more in response, but he kept quiet. She sensed something was bothering him, he had been exceptionally quiet that day, more so than usual.

Ever since Jacob closed down his business with Gerd, he hadn't been the same bright-eyed, cheeky boy she had fallen in love with. She hardly ever saw his mischievous side anymore, and she missed it. Every now and again it came out. He'd walk past her in the kitchen, with that same cat-caught-the-bird grin she recognized so well, and she knew he was up to no good. Or the look of longing in his eyes as he subtly looked over her body while she laboured over a meal at the stove. She missed him, the real him, and, more than anything, she wished she could make him happy.

"I also talked to Erwin earlier," Maria continued, still searching Jacob's appearance for any signs of what might be bothering him. "He says Monica is doing well, or as well as she can be. They're just waiting impatiently for the baby to arrive. She's due in a few days, you know, at the end of the month." Jacob nodded again. "I wonder if we'll have another granddaughter, or if it'll be our first grandson." Again, Jacob nodded his head in silence.

Maria resigned and pulled the blanket tighter around her legs to ward off the cool draft. She placed her hands in her lap and turned her wedding rings around her finger. Her wedding band was now accompanied by another gold band with a modest sized diamond. Jacob had surprised Maria with the ring a few years after they moved to Canada.

"What's wrong, Jasch?" She couldn't handle the sadness looming over him any longer. "Something's bothering you."

Jacob looked at Maria with sombre eyes and placed a hand on her leg. She covered his hand with her own and squeezed it gently, encouraging him to confide in her.

"Art is letting me go."

"What do you mean he's letting you go? Go where?" She asked.

"There isn't enough work at the shop, so, in two weeks from now, I won't have a job."

Not this again, Maria thought. How many times could one man be told he didn't have a job anymore? Maria felt the heaviness of his shame. She rubbed his arm reassuringly.

"It's okay, Jasch. It's obviously meant to be this way, for whatever reason. God makes no mistakes, and He will provide another job for you, He always has." Maria unknowingly braced herself for his usual disagreeing response whenever she mentioned God.

"You say that like you really believe it," his tone was gentle, and curious, which caught her off guard.

"That's because I *do* believe it. Very much. God has yet to give me a reason to doubt that He will provide for us."

"But how do you *know*?" His eyes searched hers, desperate for answers, and hope.

"Because God loves us and the Bible is filled with His promises. His plans for us are greater than anything we could ever imagine."

Jacob leaned back in his chair and took another sip of his drink. "I walked away from God once before, you know."

"I know," Maria spoke softly and slowly. She didn't know where the conversation was headed, but she didn't want to risk disrupting Jacob's train of thought.

"How would it be any different if I tried again? What if I accepted Christ and then left – again?"

"You would have to *want* to leave."

"I don't want to, but I'm scared that I might."

Maria's hair stood on end and gooseflesh covered the skin on her arms and legs. This sort of conversation had never happened before, despite all Maria's hopes and prayers that it would. *Maybe I'm dreaming,* she thought. Jacob's eyes glossed over as he forced back tears. Maria's heart clenched and she held her own tears back. She wanted so badly to hold him, but pinned herself to her chair, afraid that any movement might end the conversation too early.

Lord, guide my words and fill me with Your wisdom. Speak Your truth through me to Jacob, she prayed. She excused herself and the blanket fell to the ground as she stood. A few moments later she returned with her Bible in hand and sat down again. *Okay, Lord, show me which verse You have prepared for Jacob. Give those words power to move through Him in a way that he can clearly understand.*

With shaky hands she opened the Bible to wherever it fell naturally. She looked at the top right-hand side of the page and saw the name 'Lukas', Luke, typed in bold, black serif font, all in capital letters. Without looking at the text on the page, she moved her index finger over the thin paper and stopped at random. She read aloud the verse her finger landed on, Luke 22:32, "But I have prayed for thee, that thy faith fail not: and when thou art converted, strengthen thy brethren."

Maria kept her gaze on the words in front of her, and prayed throughout the deafening silence that followed.

"How long have you been waiting to read that verse to me?" He asked quietly, his voice cracking from restrained emotion.

"I haven't. I prayed that God would give me a verse to read to you, and read the one my finger landed on."

He nodded his head slowly, rhythmically, and turned toward the street. Maria watched him with agony, longing to know the thoughts going through his mind. The minutes stretched themselves out and Maria grew restless as she considered what she should say, if anything.

When Jacob spoke again, he spoke with authority and confidence. "I'm ready."

—

Maria's smile was unbreakable the next morning as she ate breakfast, glancing at Jacob between spoonfuls of oatmeal. She glanced at the waste basket beside the counter where a pack of cigarettes, three quarters full, still lay at the top.

Jacob had thrown them away as soon as they went inside the night before. It was an important step for him to take, and she knew it meant he was serious about his decision.

There was a knock at the door and Maria answered it. Erwin stood on the other side, jacket buttoned up to the collar and a bright orange tuque on his head. Snow fell softly behind him and Maria thought of the lyrics from one of her favourite hymns, *Whiter than snow, whiter than snow, wash me and I will be whiter than snow.* She smiled and thought how perfectly timed the snow was, and the metaphor it represented.

Erwin brushed snowflakes off his shoulders and removed his tuque once he was inside. He embraced Maria, who hugged him tighter than usual. Maria didn't ask Erwin why he was there, or who he had come to see. The children were all called the night before, after Jacob had gone to bed. Maria couldn't sleep, though.

"Papa's upstairs," Maria told him as she took his coat and reached for a hanger in the closet. "I'll give you some time alone."

Jacob was reading the Vancouver Sun when Erwin appeared at the top of the stairs.

"Morje, Erwin."

"Morje, Papa."

Erwin sat down across from Jacob and cleared his throat. "Mutti called me last night and told me what happened."

Jacob smiled and folded the newspaper in front of him. "She did, did she? Well, I wouldn't expect anything less from her," he smiled lovingly and Erwin smiled back, grateful for the slight reprieve from the emotions he was feeling.

"Remember what you told me, the night I accepted Christ?" Erwin asked.

Jacob looked him in the eyes, "Yes."

Erwin's eyes glistened and his voice shook when he spoke. "Now I say it to you, never let it go."

"No, my boy, I won't."

—

At the beginning of April, a few weeks after Erwin and Monica's daughter, Victoria, was born, Jacob and Maria moved to Abbotsford to be closer to Jacob's new job at Columbia Kitchen Cabinets. Maria ordered all new furniture which felt both thrilling and wasteful at the same time. Having only ever owned used or handmade furniture up until that point, it felt odd to walk through the department store and select thousands of dollars' worth of brand new items.

Her guilt had quickly dissipated as the delivery truck arrived, when piece by piece, her home was filled with all their new furniture. When everything was in place, she sat on the long, soft brown velvet sofa and moved her finger along the wavy lines of the fabric. She looked around the room and imagined it filled with people. Many memories would be made in this home, she thought.

It didn't take long for their house to feel like home, either. With all of her picture frames strewn about the house, on every shelf, table and wall, she felt at peace knowing she was surrounded by loved ones.

In the weeks that followed, Maria took it upon herself to learn to drive. They bought a used, butter-yellow Chevrolet sedan and spent most Sunday afternoons driving around the city, exploring new roads and seeing new sights. Not wanting to learn to drive himself, Jacob gladly sat in the passenger seat, taking in the surroundings with awe.

Maria turned on the signal and merged into traffic on the freeway. They were on their way home from Jacob's father's house, who lived in Vancouver with his second wife, Lili. Jacob's mother passed away on his birthday in 1969, and his father had moved to Canada shortly after Jacob and Maria. Soon after he moved, he met and married Lili, who was also a widow. Jacob's siblings gladly called Lili *Mother*, mostly out of respect. She had lost all five of her own children in traumatic ways – either from starvation, freezing, or from a cat sleeping on one child's face.

Maria pressed down on the accelerator pedal until she was moving with the flow of traffic. Only then could her shoulders finally relax. Driving in Vancouver was stressful.

"If I didn't offer to clean your father and Lili's house, she would be doing it herself, despite having just had a mastectomy," Maria ranted. "Your father isn't much help, either. He would probably tell her to clean, even in her condition. The man hardly lifts a finger."

"Mariechen, don't start again."

Maria turned to him with fire in her eyes and adjusted her grip on the steering wheel. Not wanting to get into an argument, she took a deep breath and changed the subject. "I saw you on the deck with your dad when I was cleaning the kitchen. It looked like you were having a pretty serious discussion."

Maria looked at Jacob through the corner of her eye. He turned his face out the window and scratched his stubbled jaw.

"You know, that was the first time." Jacob said.

Maria looked at him, waiting for him to finish his thought. When he didn't, she furrowed her eyebrows. "What do you mean?"

"That was the first time I've ever had a conversation with my father."

Maria's face mirrored her shock. "Ever?"

"Yes, ever. I've never had an actual conversation with my dad before."

"Oh," Maria stared at the red lights on the car in front of her and gently applied pressure to the brakes.

"I told you, I've never been close to my parents. That's why I always envied your relationship with your mother, and grandparents, even. I think that's why I was so fond of your opa. He talked with me often, and gave me advice, like a father would."

They listened to the radio for the duration of the drive. Once home, Jacob poured himself a glass of whiskey and water and settled himself on the porch. Maria changed into her nightgown and tidied up the kitchen. When she lifted the newspaper from the table, a yellow paper fell to the floor. She noticed Jacob's handwriting and the title at the top of the page read, *Baptism Testimony*. She hadn't seen him write it, and wondered if he had prepared anything to say at his baptism the following day. Intrigued, she read the first line:

I'm standing here today, first, because of God, and second, because of my wife.

She stopped reading, not because she felt guilty, but because her vision was blurred from tears. Those were the words she needed to hear. Finally, everything made sense – Jacob's relentless pursuit of her; God filling her with a love for Jacob; the years of marriage filled with tension as she tried to live out her faith with a man who wanted nothing to do with religion.

Tomorrow, Jacob would be baptized, and everyone present would hear the story of how God had pursued *him* relentlessly throughout his entire life.

30

July 1989

"HE'S HERE SOMEWHERE," MARIA ASSURED HERSELF. JACOB WATCHED AS Maria stepped gently over the packed dirt behind the school in what remained of Friedensruh No. 6. Her eyes were fixed on the dry ground, trying to see through the earth at the hidden bodies buried beneath. "I know my father's here. Mama showed me once before, when I was younger. She knew exactly where he was, even without any markers over the graves. Why can't I find it?"

Panic washed over her and Jacob came to her side, slipping an arm around her shoulders. Unsuccessful, they walked back toward the street and down toward the house where Maria had spent the first many years of her life. She smiled as the familiar Flaschenbaum came into view. Her steps quickened, nostalgia bringing a wave of youthful excitement.

The yard was empty. The house she grew up in was nowhere to be seen. Maria's heart sank. She walked through the broken gate and lowered herself beside the Flaschenbaum, leaning her back against the round trunk, and closed her eyes. Memories of her childhood days played out in her mind. She saw herself as a young girl, hosting tea parties, or studying in the shade of the tree's overhanging boughs above her.

Jacob leaned against the fence and watched Maria from a distance, allowing her the space he knew she needed. She was excited to make the trip back to Paraguay with him, and he knew how much it meant to her to visit No. 6. It had been decades since she had been there, and her face showed her disappointment. Clearly the village no longer resembled the village she remembered.

When Maria was ready, she stood and wiped the dust off her skirt and they walked back to the car. Back at the house they were staying in, Maria brought the wet clothes from the washing machine outside to hang on the line. The sun shone bright, unobstructed by clouds, and warmed her skin enough to form little beads of sweat on her upper lip and between her eyebrows.

Maria wiped her forehead and noticed the wet streak of dirt it left on her arm – she had forgotten how dusty it was there. Reaching for a clean, wet towel among the stack of clothes, she wiped her face and arms. While she continued hanging the rest of the laundry, she thought of more memories from her childhood. Jacob sat along the wall of the house, his body darkened in the shade of the roof, with only his feet sticking out in the sun.

"Are you going to watch me all day?" Maria teased. "I'd much rather you helped, instead." She threw a wet shirt at him and he raised his arms reflexively and turned his face away from the flying object. The shirt fell in his lap and he instantly threw it back at Maria. It hit her back and fell to the ground. She looked at it, and shook her finger at Jacob. "You're going to wash that one yourself!"

Jacob laughed. Maria had forgotten what his laugh sounded like. She savoured the familiar melody. His lips were turned up in a smile, and it felt like she had reunited with an old friend.

Moving to Canada, and losing yet another job, led Jacob into a deeper depression. She fought to keep him afloat, to keep his mind on the positive, but nothing helped. After his decision to give his life to Christ, his spirit lifted slightly, but only temporarily.

"Would you want to move back?" His voice rang, lighthearted and full of hope. The unusual perk in his tone distracted her. She hung the last shirt and sat on a wooden chair next to Jacob, using the wet towel to wipe her face once more.

"What did you ask?" Maria asked, reclining into her chair.

"Would you want to move back here?" Jacob repeated.

"Back where?"

"Here. Paraguay."

"Move back to Paraguay? Are you daft?" Maria sat up straighter and looked at Jacob skeptically. "Why would I ever want to move back to Paraguay?"

As hard as it had been for her to leave Filadelfia, Canada was her home now. She had adapted to the culture and language, and established herself in their community, through church and friends. All of their children were married, and Jacob and Maria had seven grandchildren at that point, all living there, as well. Surely Jacob wasn't seriously considering the idea, or at least she hoped not.

"Jasch, I know being back here is bringing up many pleasant memories, for both of us, but you have to understand that we're reminiscent of the past. Life always looks more glamorous when you look back on it. Things would be so different if we moved back here now. We're older, for one thing, and wouldn't be able to keep up with all the chores and work that would need to get done around the house. Look at my back, I can hardly stand straight, and when I do, I suffer with the pain that follows. I couldn't go back to taking care of a house like I did when we lived in Filadelfia.

"Besides, our life is in Abbotsford now. And what about our grandchildren? Would you really want to leave them? Wasn't that how you got us to move to Canada in first place? Saying you wanted to live closer to Lucy."

"But life was good here, remember?" His eyes still glimmered with life.

Maria tilted her head slightly to one side, her eyes still fixed on him. She hadn't seen his eyes shine this blue or bright in so long. "Yes, it was good. But it was also really hard. We still have our memories from our years here, and they'll always be with us, wherever we go."

"It's warmer here – it would help your joints," he tried another angle, still hopeful.

"It does help them, but that's not reason enough for me to move back. Okay, Jasch, I still can't tell if you're pulling my leg or if you're actually being serious about this."

"I'm serious, Mariechen," she saw his desperation. As much as she wanted to keep this Jacob, the old Jacob, around, she knew moving back would not cure his unhappiness. Temporarily, perhaps, but inevitably it would fade.

"Then you're going to have to move here alone. I'm not leaving my home, or my children and grandchildren. I'll pack your bags for you, but that's about as much support as you'll get from me." She reached for his hand. "Trust me, once the nostalgia of being here wore off, you'd be crawling back home."

The hope left Jacob's eyes, and Maria saw the man she fell in love with slip away again. She called out to him with her soul, panic rising as his eyes darkened. He was gone. A frown replaced his smile.

—

Maria stood outside the church, staring at the large doors. She felt something akin to a homecoming as she walked into the building, but instinctively, her guard went up, and she wasn't quite sure why.

Women sat scattered around the room, laughing and sharing gossip they'd acquired throughout the week. Maria recognized most of them, aside from a few of the younger ones. The ladies greeted her with warm smiles and asked questions about life in Canada. Maria spoke in Plautdietsch, the words rolling effortlessly off her tongue. She missed this – the comfort, the familiarity, the ease. Though her English had improved greatly over the years, it didn't flow as melodiously as her Plautdietsch.

The leader of the women's group welcomed everyone and the meeting officially began. Maria was asked to share about their experience in Canada. She hesitated, sorting through all the years of struggles and successes, deciphering how much to share with these ladies that were now merely acquaintances. She didn't know if she should be honest, or give them the simple answers they were expecting. She decided on the former.

She shared details of the first years, about the challenges of learning a new language and adapting to a new culture, and all the ups and downs along the way. She spoke about her growing family with pride, naming each grandchild and their ages, and tidbits of information about each one.

"And, a few years ago, Jacob made a decision to follow Christ—" her sentence was cut off with clapping and gasps of relief. She heard the muted murmurs between the women with comments of, "Well, it's about time," and, "Finally their marriage means something," and, "It's such a shame it took so long. What a hard life she must have had, married to an *unbeliever* for so long."

The emphasis on *unbeliever* sent shivers through Maria's body and she felt her skin warm from her chest to her cheeks. The same feelings of rejection and judgement she'd felt when she had attended these meetings came creeping back, just as vividly as they used to be. She didn't even try to hold back her anger.

"You know," she said firmly, "ever since I started dating Jacob, I have been judged and shamed for my decision. The church wouldn't allow me to recite poems, a gift God has blessed me with, all because I was called to marry an '*unbeliever*.'" She said the word with the same intonation as the woman had earlier. "Not one of you in this room showed me love, grace, compassion, or any support. Not one." She held a finger in the air, slightly crooked from arthritis. "But in Canada, the ladies at my church *prayed* for me, and for Jacob, along with the other husbands who had yet to come to know Christ as their personal Lord and Saviour. And you know what? Five out of the six husbands are now believers."

Her cheeks burned. She took a few deep breaths and the room went eerily silent. With a shaky finger pointed at the group, and a quiver in her voice, she added, "It helps more to pray for those women than to cast them aside."

Maria slowly lowered herself into her chair, avoiding eye contact. She dabbed her cheeks with her handkerchief and sat quietly, anxiously waiting for the meeting to end. After the final "Amen," Maria grabbed her purse and made her way to the door without looking back.

She was a few steps from the street when she heard a young woman call her name. Maria turned around and waited as the woman ran toward her. Her cheeks looked glassy in the moonlight, and when she neared, Maria saw that she had been crying.

"Thank you," the woman said, "thank you so much for what you said earlier. My husband is not a Christian either, and I've been having such a hard time feeling accepted by the church." A tear clung desperately to the edge of her chin.

"What's your name?" Maria asked softly, seeing a version of her younger self in the woman before her.

"Elsie."

"I'll be praying for you, Elsie."

—

Kaethe's mind continued to deteriorate, little by little, until she was mostly unaware of her surroundings and behaviour. It was hard for Maria, and her children, to witness Kaethe, usually independent and capable, become weak and confused. She often forgot where she was, or who her grandchildren were, and in recent months, her actions in social settings mortified the family. It started with little oddities, like removing her false teeth during family meals and setting them beside her plate, which the children found amusing. Dentures on the table became the least of their worries after a few months, and then years.

Minor incidents occurred more frequently, much to the family's chagrin. Eventually, Jacob and Maria decided to move Kaethe from Menno Court apartments – a seniors' residence in Vancouver – to an assisted living facility in Abbotsford. There she received the proper care she needed.

When Jacob and Maria returned from their three month visit to Paraguay, Maria went to visit Kaethe. They sat beside each other by a window in the main hall. They faced the courtyard and watched the leaves of the large oak trees swing from side to side and they descended to the ground. The view before them was like a painting, with strokes of deep, warm hues brushed across the canvas. Mesmerized, Maria didn't hear a nurse approach them.

"There you go, Mrs. Thielmann," she said kindly as she placed a small plastic cup with pills, and a glass of water, on the table beside Kaethe. "I'll be back in a few hours for your next dose."

Kaethe smiled at the friendly nurse as she walked away, then leaned closer to Maria. Confusion swept across her face. She attempted to whisper, but her words were audible to those across the room. "Why did she call me Mrs. Thielmann? Doesn't she know I'm a Penner?"

Maria frowned at the sincere honesty in Kaethe's question. Larger pieces of her memory were fading away into the deep recesses of her mind. Maria answered the same questions, week after week – clarifying names of spouses and grandchildren – and it pained her to watch her mother drift away.

Maria tried to explain to Kaethe that she had remarried David Thielmann, but Kaethe didn't hear her. She spent the rest of the time talking about Nikolai, who was still very much alive in her mind. Maria loved hearing her mother's stories of her and her father from when they were dating. Even though she had no recollection of him from her own memory, she felt like she knew his character and personality simply from the stories her mother shared with her.

When it was time to leave, Maria kissed Kaethe on the top of her head and assured her she'd be back the next day. Kaethe told her to bring her children next time so they could sleepover and help her bake Trubochki.

Maria sighed. "I'm sure they'd like that very much, Mama."

—

Maria unlocked the front door, while balancing one bag of groceries on her knee. She hung the car keys on the hook and lugged the groceries upstairs. She winced as a sharp pain shot through her back. As she refilled the pantry, the pit in her stomach that had formed that morning grew as she reflected on her visit with Kaethe.

Maria shook her head and took a deep breath. She looked around the room, wondering what she could do to take her mind off her mother. She turned the coffee maker on – another Canadian novelty she was fond of – and sat at the table with her Elisabeth Dreisbach novel. The rich aroma of the coffee filled the room and Maria felt her nerves ease, ever so slightly. She read a few lines in her book, interrupted by the phone ringing.

"Hello?" She answered. "Pardon me? You're at the hospital? Why? Because of her flu?" Maria listened as Rudolf, Sylvia's husband, explained the situation. "Seizures?" Maria echoed him. Fear rose in her chest.

Sylvia had come down with a fever the previous weekend. The whole family had gone to Kelowna to celebrate Jacob's brother, Wilmar, and his wife Elsie's twenty-fifth wedding anniversary. While the others visited, Gredel and Angie nursed Sylvia, trying to lower the fever that gripped Sylvia's body.

The fever stayed for the rest of the following week. Sylvia wasn't able to care for the children in her daycare, or her own two boys, and spent her days shivering in bed. Maria knew she was ill, but couldn't understand why she would be hospitalized, and having seizures, from a case of influenza.

"Yes, sorry," Maria apologized. Rudolf had said her name a few times to get her attention and asked if she would watch Andy and Steven while he went to the hospital. "Of course. I'll be over as soon as possible. Which hospital is she at?"

—

In the days and weeks that followed Sylvia's admittance to the hospital, she endured every test imaginable, each one coming back negative. The doctors were baffled, which only filled the family with more worry. Not only was Sylvia's fever dangerously high, her white blood cell count was extremely elevated, as well. They tried everything to lower both, but to no avail. Specialists were called in to give their opinions, hoping to reveal what Sylvia's body was desperately fighting.

Five weeks later, Sylvia was moved to the Intensive Care Unit because her heart couldn't fight the infection any longer. Maria sat by her daughter's side as often as she could, her own heart falling apart as machines beeped around her. Sylvia's body lay motionless in a coma, a million tubes going in and out of her, keeping her alive.

Maria prayed ceaselessly during those weeks – for healing, for patience, for life, and for answers. Finally, after weeks of uncertainty, a multitude of tests, and nearly losing Sylvia on a few occasions, a young doctor suggested the diagnosis of Adult Onset Still's Disease – a rare type of inflammatory arthritis. There were no specific tests to confirm his suspicion, nor a cure.

The young doctor turned out to be right and Sylvia was diagnosed with Still's Disease. Treatment began immediately, which involved steroids and other medication. Her fever broke, and her symptoms eased, but not completely.

Shortly before Christmas, Sylvia was finally discharged from the hospital. The entire family, except for Kaethe, sat around the fully extended dining room table at Jacob and Maria's home. Maria looked around the table and felt immense pride and joy. Mothers lectured children to sit still and to keep their little fingers out of the food; wine was poured into glasses; and the aroma of the traditional Christmas barbecue feast filled the room. All was as it should be, Maria thought.

"Let's say grace," Jacob announced as he stood at the head of the table. He folded his hands and bowed his head. The others followed his lead. "Dear heavenly Father, we thank you for this day. Thank you for sending your Son to Earth as a baby to show us your love in the flesh. Thank you for Christ's death on the cross for the forgiveness of our sins. We especially thank you today for restoring Sylvia's health enough that she could be here today, and that we can celebrate Christmas as a family. We pray for your continued healing over her.

"Bless this food that we are about to eat. Amen."

"Amen." The others echoed in unison.

"Phew!" Three-year-old Steven said as he slumped in his chair. "That was a long one."

The room filled with laughter as food was piled on plates, and conversations hummed around the table.

31

June 1995

"REMEMBER THAT MARKET?" JACOB'S VOICE JARRED MARIA. THE PHOTO album sprawled open in her lap fell to the floor.

"You scared me."

"I can see that. I'm sorry."

Maria bent down and picked up the album, flipping through the pages until she found the image of the market Jacob was referring to. White canvas tents lined the Hawaiian streets on both sides, covering tables filled with bric-a-brac and overpriced souvenirs.

"You bought this candle from one of those vendors, didn't you?"

Maria turned to the mirror-topped side table where an elaborately carved candle stood, unlit. The intricately detailed cream wax, marbled with orange and brown, looked like a fountain, frozen mid-flow.

"Are we ever going to light it?" Jacob asked as he sat beside her on the couch.

Maria smiled at the animated decoration. "No. It's too pretty." Her voice was soft, lifeless.

"What's wrong?" Jacob put his arm around her shoulders and bent his head to look at her face.

"Oh, just a conversation I had with Steven today."

"What happened?"

"He asked me why God wasn't healing Sylvia. There are so many people praying for her, yet she's still sick"

"Ah," Jacob said, nodding his head. "And, what did you tell him?"

"The same thing I tell myself when I ask God the same question – that I don't know. And that I do know that God hears our prayers, and that He loves Sylvia very much. Sometimes it doesn't feel like God is listening to us, but He is. We have to trust that." She sighed.

They looked down at the album, filled with memories from their trip to Hawaii. They'd spent two weeks in Honolulu, just the two of them. It was a much needed break for Maria, though it was hard for her to relax. Sylvia's body hadn't fully recovered since her first episode of Still's. She had to close down her daycare, and needed help taking care of her boys.

Maria offered to help without hesitation. She slept at Sylvia's during the week, returning home to Jacob for the weekend, when Rudolf was home. For the last six years, Maria took care of both her home and Sylvia's, and helped with the boys. Her work doubled overnight, but there was no other option. Sylvia was sick and needed help, and there was no question of whether or not Maria would be the one to help.

She turned to the next page in the album and moved her fingers over a photo of the ocean, the same blue as Jacob's eyes. Beside it, tucked under the clear, cellophane protector, was a picture of Jacob sitting outside their hotel room. They had spent a lot of time on the small concrete slab outside their ground level suite. Every morning they drank coffee and ate breakfast at the round, glass table – plain bread and cold cuts for Jacob, and butter and jam spread on a slice of bread for Maria.

Maria closed the album and placed her hands on the cover brown cover, outlining the word 'Photos' written in gold foil. Jacob pulled her closer to him and kissed the top of her head.

"I've been thinking it might be time for us to go on another trip," he said.

"Oh, yeah?" Maria's spirit lifted at the thought of exploring new cities with Jacob. "Where to?"

"There's a guided tour bus that goes all over British Columbia. I thought it might be nice to see more of this beautiful province we live in. There's so much we haven't seen yet."

"Oh, Jasch! That would be wonderful!" She threw her arms around his neck.

"Then consider it done."

"When would we go?"

"Next week," he winked, thrilled to have been able to surprise her.

—

Jacob and Maria were mesmerized by the grand scenery rushing past them as the bus drove down long stretches of highway. They stopped in rural towns and fjords, where citizens dressed in period costumes, making it feel like they had gone back in time. It was in one of these fjords that Maria celebrated her sixty-seventh birthday, one of her most memorable birthdays to date.

One cloudless, Friday evening, Maria looked through her tinted window and stared at the stars dotting the sky. She hadn't seen that many stars since moving to Vancouver. They passed a large sign that read, "Welcome to Prince George, BC's Northern Capital". The moonlight silhouetted mountains towering over the city. The driver pulled up to their hotel and parked the bus in front of the entrance.

The passengers herded off the bus, anxious to stretch their legs. Jacob waited for the driver to unload the luggage while Maria checked them into their room. The numbers 3-2-5 were handwritten in black marker on the plastic, marquise shaped keychain. Following the clerk's instructions, they took the elevator to the third floor and settled into their room.

Jacob laid on the bed and turned on the TV. He browsed through channels until he'd settled on a news program. Maria listened to the monotonous male voice announce another horrid event while she unpacked their bags, placing clothes in the drawers, even though they would be moving on to another destination in two days. When the bags were empty, Maria changed into her nightgown and joined Jacob on the bed. She pulled the covers up to her shoulders and nestled in beside him.

They watched a woman in a cream pantsuit wave her hand over a map of British Columbia, pointing to an area where rain was expected to fall in the next few days. Maria wondered why all newscasters sounded the same. Surely they were allowed to have some personality in their tones, she mused. The screen zoomed in on the Lower Mainland, forecasting clear skies for the weekend. Then it moved further east, toward the Okanagan, where more sunshine was forecast.

"That's good," Maria said. "Wilmar and Elsie are having a barbecue get together this weekend. At least it won't rain."

"Are all the kids going to that?" Jacob asked, as the news program cut to a commercial.

"Just Erwin and Monica and Angie and Willy." They watched the next commercial, an ad for Pert Plus shampoo and conditioner, before Jacob grunted and hit the mute button. Commercials annoyed him.

"It's hard to believe we're actually here, isn't it?" Maria reflected in the silence. The colours of the screen lit the room sporadically.

"Here? Like, in Prince George?"

"No. Well, yes. The fact that we're in Canada, in general. It's hard to believe we've lived here for over twenty years already. Doesn't it feel like just yesterday we were standing in our empty house in Filadelfia, waiting for your brother to pick us up to bring us to the airport?"

"Mm-hmm," Jacob agreed.

"To think how much has happened in these last two decades. All of our children married, each with two children of their own, and lives of their own. They definitely adjusted much quicker to life here than we did. Remember when we first got off the plane, and couldn't read a single sign?"

"I still wouldn't be able to read many of the signs," Jacob admitted.

"Yes, but whose fault is that? You could have put more effort into learning the language, you know."

"I don't need to, you know enough for the both of us." He pinched her waist and she jumped. "And you're always with me, so you've been my personal translator." Maria punched him amicably in his side. A man and a woman sitting behind a desk appeared on the TV again. Jacob unmuted the volume and listened intently.

When the program was over, Jacob turned off the TV and the colours on the screen funneled into the centre before disappearing. He looked down at Maria, asleep on his arm. Jacob gently took her glasses off her face and placed them on the nightstand. He kissed the top of her head and moved his arm out from under her. She stirred and turned onto her side without waking. Jacob stroked her hair and smiled as he watched her chest rise and fall evenly, her eyes twitching as she dreamed.

"I love you, Mariechen," he whispered before turning off the lamp.

—

The next morning, Jacob and Maria joined a few of the other guests in the restaurant downstairs for their complimentary breakfast. They had all day to explore the city on their own, and Maria decided their first stop would be the Railway and Forestry Museum. She had seen advertisements for the museum in the hotel lobby when she was checking in the night before, and thought it looked interesting.

After breakfast, Jacob and Maria were invited for coffee and a game of Rook in another couple's room. Jacob and Maria grabbed the Rook cards from their room before going down the hall to meet John and Bev. Maria was glad she'd thought to grab the deck from the drawer, right before they left home.

The four friends sat at the small square table in John and Bev's hotel room. Bev turned on the coffee maker while Maria dealt the cards. Maria was instantly drawn to the couple on the first day of their tour. John and Bev's kind, outgoing personalities were magnetic, and the four of them enjoyed playing Rook in their hotel rooms between sightseeing.

The women were leading in points about half way through the game. There was laughter and excitement as they placed card after card on the pile in front of them, waiting for that sought after black bird to appear. Maria played a red fourteen on her turn and smiled smugly at Jacob.

Her smile faded instantly. Jacob stared in front of him. His face blanched and the cards he held fell through his fingers, onto the table. She could see the confusion in his eyes and she thought she saw his mouth twitch, trying to say something.

"Jasch? Jasch, are you all right?" Maria got out of her chair and put her arms around Jacob. His gaze never left the table. "Jasch, talk to me." Maria's voice grew more and more frightened as she tried to figure out what was happening to him.

"Help me get him up," she looked at John with desperation. She lifted one of Jacob's arms over her head, laying it across her shoulders, and held his wrist firmly. John went to Jacob's other side and did the same with his other arm. Together they lifted him out of the chair. Jacob stood, though most of his weight rested on John and Maria.

"I've got him, thank you," she said to John, and started walking to the door. All she could think of in that moment was that she needed to get him to their room. They were only a few doors down from John and Bev. She could do it, she assured herself. She moved slowly, burdened by the weight of Jacob's body.

"Let me help you," John offered, but Maria declined his offer.

Maria persevered, driven by adrenaline and fear. She struggled to grab the key from her pocket, but managed to unlock the door and usher Jacob inside. The moment the door closed behind them, Jacob's legs gave out beneath him. Maria, still holding his arm, fell to the floor with him. His body lay limp and heavy on top of her.

"JACOB!"

All rationale escaped her, replaced with sheer panic. She screamed his name over and over as she pushed herself out from under him and crawled to the nightstand. She lifted the receiver and dialed the room number of another guest on their tour, who happened to be a nurse. The woman answered and Maria told her what had happened, sobbing uncontrollably. The nurse stayed calm and apologetically explained that it sounded like Jacob had had a stroke.

At that point, there was a knock on the door. John's voice came barreling through, asking if everything was alright. She hung up the phone, and moved slowly toward the door. Her hands shook as she unlocked it. Medics rushed into the room and moved Maria aside while they assessed Jacob. John must have asked the front desk to call 9-1-1, she rationalized. The thought to call emergency hadn't even crossed her mind.

Maria felt like she was dreaming. She stood beside the bed, leaning against the wall. They turned Jacob onto his back and listened to his heart and checked his pulse. Her body didn't feel like her own, like she was floating outside of it. In her daze, she didn't hear the younger medic ask her to recall exactly what happened.

What did happen? She didn't even know, yet she was somehow expected to tell this man why Jacob went silent and lost control of his limbs. All she knew was that they were on a trip, enjoying their time together, playing a round of Rook, when all of a sudden Jacob fell to the floor, helpless and weak.

The room spun around her and she lowered herself onto the bed. The medic sat beside her and touched her upper arm, a look of sincere compassion in his eyes. Maria broke down once again.

"Ma'am, I know this is hard for you, and everything must have happened so quickly, but we're here to help your husband. In order to do that, though, we need to know exactly what happened. Please, can you tell me everything that happened this morning, leading up to his fall?"

Maria took a few deep breaths until her breathing was even and her cries were settled enough for her words to be understood. They strapped Jacob to a gurney and wheeled him down to the lobby. She watched in disbelief as they hoisted him into the ambulance. Maria climbed in after and sat beside Jacob, crying as she watched him lie there. His eyes darted back and forth, and he mumbled as he tried to speak. The lack of sound coming from his mouth brought him even more fear and he locked his eyes on Maria, his stare begging her to help him.

—

At the hospital, Maria filled out mounds of endless paperwork. Her English was good, but many of the words on the forms were words she had never seen before. Perspiration formed as she struggled to make sense of the questions and documents they needed her to provide.

Doctors and nurses were busily attaching Jacob to monitors and tubes, and Maria used the opportunity to look for a payphone. Her hands trembled as she scoured her purse for a quarter. She moved her hand up toward the coin slot, but the quarter fell out of her fingers. She picked it up and tried again, taking a deep breath to steady herself. The quarter made a clunk as it engaged into the phone and she dialed Erwin's phone number. The phone rang, and rang, and rang. No answer. She hung up and the quarter fell to the bottom of the phone. She scooped it out and inserted it into the slot again. This time she dialed Gredel's number.

"Hello?" Gredel answered.

Maria couldn't even speak. The tears flowed again, making it nearly impossible to catch her breath.

"Hello? Mutti? Is that you? What's wrong?"

"Papa," Maria sobbed, "he had a stroke."

It was the first time she had said the words out loud, and it knocked the wind out of her. She rested her forehead on the wall beside the phone as tears fell steadily onto her shoes. Gredel screamed on the other end of the line. For a few minutes, the two women cried together, until there was a 'click' and the dial tone droned in her ear.

—

Laughter filled Wilmar and Elsie's yard. Angie and her husband, Willy, along with Erwin and Monica, were in Kelowna for the weekend, without kids. The sun warmed their skin, the first glimpse of summer. The women congregated in their own circle of lawn chairs, while the men stood around the barbecue.

The phone rang and Elsie ran upstairs to answer it in the kitchen. She appeared again soon after and went to Erwin, quietly telling him Gredel was on the phone. Her voice and expression were sombre, and everyone quieted down, sensing something wasn't right. Angie watched with trepidation as Erwin ran up the steps, two at a time, and ducked into the kitchen where the phone lay waiting on the counter.

He slowly lifted the receiver to his ear, unsure of what to expect.

"Hello?"

"It's Papa," Gredel cried, "he had a stroke in Prince George. He's in the hospital there. Mutti is losing it."

She sobbed into the phone as Erwin tried to process her words. He wondered if he'd misunderstood, it was hard to understand her. Gredel repeated herself, thinking his silence was from a lack of hearing. Erwin was shocked.

As soon as he hung up, he lifted the phone again and dialed '0', asking the operator for the number for Prince George Regional Hospital. When he got through, he explained the situation to the kind nurse on the other end of the line, who connected him to the phone in Jacob's room. After two rings, he heard Maria's voice.

"Hi, Mutti. It's Erwin. How's Papa? What happened?" Maria fell apart on the other end. It took all Erwin's strength not to fall apart, too. "Hang in there, Mutti. I'll be there tomorrow."

"Don't drive at night, Erwin. It's not safe."

"I'll leave first thing in the morning. Hang in there." He hung up and took a deep breath before going back outside.

Angie sat restlessly in her chair, tapping her fingers on the armrest. There was silence as Erwin walked down the stairs. Monica waited at the bottom and wrapped her arm around his waist. Angie saw the redness in his eyes and stood, anxious to hear what Gredel had told him.

Erwin rubbed his mouth with his hand, forcing back the emotion that edged its way to the surface. He couldn't look at Angie, the worry in her eyes made his knees buckle, the gravity of the situation was too much. He cleared his throat, "My dad had a stroke."

Angie screamed, a deep, gut-wrenching wail that brought many others to tears, including Erwin. Monica held him, as Willy held Angie.

32

June 1995

JACOB LOOKED TO HIS RIGHT. MARIA SAT IN A CHAIR NEXT TO HIS BED, HER head downcast. He knew something bad had happened, though he didn't quite know what, exactly. He had seen the fear in her eyes, and even now, tears rolled down her cheeks, falling onto her blouse. He opened his mouth to say something, but only a sound resembling a grunt came out. It surprised him, and he tried again. Another mumbled grunt. Maria heard him and looked up.

Seeing the look on Jacob's face was too much. Maria folded her arms on the bed and hid her face in them. Her body shook as she cried. Jacob wanted to put his hand on her head to comfort her, but his arm didn't move. He looked at his right hand, lying limp on the bed beside him. He tried again, willing his arm to move, but nothing happened. He grew even more frightened, and tried to speak again, but it only resulted in more grunts.

What's happening to me? he thought, looking to Maria for answers. She lifted her head and looked into his eyes. Tears fell from his eyes and his lip quivered. He closed his eyes and leaned his head back into the pillow. He couldn't remember ever feeling as scared as he was in that moment.

A gentle touch caressed his cheek and he lifted his face.

"Stay calm, Jasch. Don't try to get up or move. You had a stroke. I'm waiting for the doctor to come back with some test results and more information. Stay calm. I'm right here."

A doctor came in and spoke to Maria. Jacob couldn't understand what he was saying. Maybe he should have put more effort into learning English, after all. It would have come in handy now.

"Mrs. Loewen, your husband suffered a serious stroke, which affected the left side of his brain. He won't be able to speak again, and the right side of his body will be paralyzed. Unfortunately, I can't give you a good prognosis. Jacob will either die tonight, or, if he lives, he will lie like this for the rest of his life, never to walk again."

He may not have understood the doctor, but he saw Maria's fingers curl and tighten into fists, and Jacob was glad he wasn't on the receiving end of what would ensue. She was getting ready to stand her ground.

"I understand that, Doctor, but we have a great God."

The doctor guffawed, a sly smirk across his smug face. "God has nothing to do with this." With that, he turned and walked out of the room, shaking his head at Maria's comment.

Maria sat beside Jacob again, his eyes inviting her to relay what the doctor had said. Maria explained it all to him, minus what the doctor said about Jacob possibly dying that night. Jacob looked at his left hand, resting beside him on the bed, and lifted it with ease. He grunted, waving it at Maria.

"I know, you're left handed, which is a blessing. We can thank God for that."

—

Maria didn't sleep that night. She heard Jacob breathing heavily beside her, but she couldn't quiet her thoughts. She spent the whole night reliving every horrid moment of the day, crying into her pillow to muffle her sobs so as not to wake Jacob, or the others in the room. She felt a heaviness inside her like she'd never experienced before. It was the weight of a loss, and in this case, she grieved the loss of the husband she knew. Life would never be as it was before, she dreaded.

Dear Lord, help, Maria prayed. It was all she could pray in that moment. She was completely overwhelmed.

She cried on and off all night long, until the room slowly illuminated with warm, orange tones from the rising sun. A nurse came in to check on Jacob shortly after six. Jacob was still sleeping and Maria sat on the edge of her bed, reading from a Bible she found in the nightstand drawer.

"Good morning," the nurse greeted her with a warm smile.

"Good morning," Maria replied, though there wasn't much good about it, in her opinion.

"How did you sleep?"

"Just fine, thanks," she didn't know why she felt the need to lie to the nurse. Surely it was common for wives not to sleep after their husbands had suffered strokes. She couldn't be the first.

"Your husband loves you very much." Maria looked at her with a raised eyebrow. How could she possibly make such a statement, having never met this woman before in her life? Seeing the confusion in Maria's expression, she elaborated. "Every time I looked in the room during the night to check on him, he was looking over to where you were lying to make sure you were still there."

Maria smiled. He had always told her he'd be lost without her. Maria turned to Jacob, her attention drawn to his now greying hair. She moved closer and ran her hand through it. His head, once full of dark brown hair, was now scattered with strands of grey and white throughout, aging him overnight. Her touch roused him, and he smiled when he saw her face, until he realized where he was.

"Good morning, Jasch. It's okay. Erwin will be here today. We'll get everything sorted out. Just stay calm."

You too, Maria, she thought. *Stay calm. Erwin will be here soon.*

<hr />

"Life will never be the same again," Maria told Sylvia over the phone that afternoon.

"Mutti, it's only the first day. It's still bad right now, but you don't know what's going to happen."

"Sylvia, you have no idea. You're not here, you haven't seen him."

After she hung up the phone, she felt so very alone. Their tour bus had left that morning, as scheduled, leaving them behind. The walls of the room felt tighter that morning, and she pulled on the collar of her blouse.

Maria lifted herself onto the bed beside Jacob, and held his hand in silence. Every now and then, he would squeeze her hand. She squeezed back every time, reassuring him that she wasn't going anywhere.

"Hi"

They both looked toward the door and saw Erwin standing there. He looked tired and weary from the ten-hour drive. Maria got off the bed and wrapped her arms around him. It felt so good to see a familiar face. When she finally pulled away from him, his shirt was wet where her tears had soaked through the fabric. She started wiping his shirt with her hand but he moved her aside and walked toward Jacob.

Erwin held out his right hand, offering a handshake. Jacob let down his guard, his tears falling freely and unabashedly. He lifted his left hand and placed it in Erwin's, squeezing it. Erwin wiped his own tears before turning back to Maria.

"Have you eaten today, Mutti?" He cleared his throat to dislodge the emotion welled up in his chest.

His question caught her off guard. Had she eaten? Of course not. She couldn't fathom eating at a time like this.

"No, I'm not hungry," she replied curtly. He didn't believe her, and sent her down to the cafeteria. He promised to stay with Jacob while she was away.

Maria reluctantly heeded her son's advice and walked through the sterile hallways, taking the elevator down to the empty cafeteria. She bought a sandwich and sat at a table by herself. She took a bite and realized just how hungry she really was, and devoured the rest of the sandwich, wiping her hand and mouth with a napkin when she'd finished.

She sat back in the chair and began to cry, again. This time she cried tears of relief. Relief that she wasn't alone anymore, that Erwin could help her discern the doctor's words and take some of the burden off her shoulders.

And he did. That night, Erwin booked two rooms at a hotel closer to the hospital, and by the next day, Jacob's name was on the waitlist to be transferred back to Abbotsford by helicopter. In the meantime, Erwin spent each day at the hospital with Maria, reassuring both his mother and father that everything would be all right.

—

On Monday, two days after his stroke, Jacob desperately wanted to get out of bed. He had grown restless and irritated from being so restricted. Maria didn't want to encourage him to try, she didn't think she could handle the disappointment that would inevitably wash over his face when he wasn't able to stand on his own. But Jacob was adamant. Erwin stood beside him, one arm wrapped around his waist, with Jacob's left arm around his shoulders for support. They all watched with bated breath as Erwin lifted his father off the bed.

Jacob stood. He actually stood. Maria's face beamed as she watched her husband standing, regardless how shaky his legs were, he was standing. At the same moment, the rude doctor that had given Maria the grave prognosis, walked in to witness the miracle. His face paled with disbelief and embarrassment.

"Mrs. Loewen, I owe you an apology," he said sincerely, clearly struggling to make sense of the phenomenon in front of him. "You were right, and I was wrong. I honestly didn't believe your husband would ever stand again."

"I forgive you. I believe in a God who can do the impossible."

On Wednesday, they cleared Jacob for transfer to Abbotsford. There wasn't enough room in the aircraft for Maria to fly with him, but the doctor advised her to arrange for someone to be at the hospital when Jacob arrived that afternoon.

After watching the helicopter take off from the pad, Erwin and Maria gathered their bags and started the long journey home.

—

Sylvia waited anxiously in the ambulance loading area of MSA General Hospital. Her heart was pounding inside her chest and she felt herself perspiring as anticipation grew. She watched ambulance after ambulance arrive, yet none of them carried her father. Another ambulance pulled in and she wondered again if that would finally be him.

The driver got out and walked to the back of the ambulance and unlocked the doors. He pulled the gurney out, revealing Jacob's body. Sylvia froze when she saw Jacob's face. His appearance had changed so much. Her dad had brown hair, yet this man had nearly a full head of grey. She looked closer at his face. Yes, it was definitely him.

Once the whole gurney was standing on its wheels in front of her, she went beside it and grabbed Jacob's hand. He looked at her and wept. She had seen her father cry before, but never like that. His emotion overwhelmed her and she sobbed as the paramedics wheeled him into the hospital. She tried to encourage him, tried to reassure him everything would be all right. He tried talking to her, but again, only grunting sounds came out of his mouth. He tossed his head to the side in frustration. She realized then just how severe his stroke had been.

Sylvia stayed with Jacob the whole day, talked to him, and asking him questions. He could never answer with words, which only frustrated him more. Most of his attempts to speak ended with him flailing his left hand in the air in defeat. There was no mutual conversation to be had, and it pained Sylvia to see her dad like that.

—

The drive from Prince George to Abbotsford was long. Erwin stayed calm, focusing his attention on the road, trying to compose his emotions every time Maria spontaneously burst into tears, which happened often.

Maria was grieving the loss of her husband, or at least the way she knew him. Their marriage and relationship would never be the same, she knew that much. Her chest tightened every time she thought about the future, the reality of what was in store for them. If Jacob did survive, he would never be the same.

"Mutti, it will all work out. With God's help, we'll get through this. Others have. It won't be easy but we'll get through it." Maria appreciated his optimism, but it wasn't much comfort.

The sun had just dipped behind the mountains when Erwin pulled into the parking lot of MSA General Hospital. Maria opened the door to Jacob's room and saw Sylvia sitting in a chair beside his bed. Jacob looked at Maria and his eyes filled with relief. He reached his left hand out toward her, begging her to come to him.

She sat on the bed next to him and kissed his cheek, savouring the familiar warmth of his skin against hers.

"Try to sleep, Jasch. I'll come back first thing in the morning."

He grunted, trying to speak. The look in his eyes told Maria he didn't want her to go, but she needed to unpack and have a shower, and sleep. She kissed him again and reiterated that she would be back first thing in the morning. The nurses would be there to help him if he needed anything, she assured him, and herself.

Erwin followed Maria down the dingy hallways and out into the warm, summer night air. They got back into the car and drove the short distance to Maria's house in silence.

—

The next few days, weeks and months were a blur. Each day bore the same monotonous routine as the day before. Maria couldn't stop dwelling on the fact that life would never be the same. That the hospital visits, and the constant support, would be her life, for the rest of Jacob's life. It was hard to watch her once strong and able husband lay in a bed, frail and weak, unable to speak or walk.

It was evident, after a few weeks in the hospital, that Jacob would never walk unsupported again. Maria reluctantly made the decision, with the help of her children, to sell their home and move into an apartment.

Maria stood in the kitchen of their beloved house one last time, and looked out the window to the porch, where Jacob had spent many hours. Suddenly it hit her – Jacob would never set foot in that house again. He left that home – *his* home – four months before, for a getaway with Maria, and would never return.

As she unpacked boxes in their new condo, she couldn't help but feel out of place. The apartment lacked the warmth and familiarity a home should have. For weeks she felt like a guest in her own house. The confined space was difficult to get used to, as well. She knew Jacob would hate it, and dreaded the day they would bring him home, only for that reason.

When Jacob was discharged from the hospital, Maria and Jacob's brother, Hein, helped him into their new minivan – another change needed to adapt Jacob's condition. The care aid Maria was promised didn't actually start visiting them for another few weeks, which left Maria to tend to Jacob, and the rest of the household chores, on her own. At least Jacob was able to move from one room to another, with the aid of his walker. His steps were small, and slow, but at least he could move, which saved Maria's back from the strain of carrying his weight.

Despite his best efforts, there were still moments when Jacob's legs couldn't support him and he would fall to the ground. Maria's breath caught every time she heard the familiar sound of his body hitting the carpet, followed by groans of pain and frustration. Sometimes he fell onto Maria while she helped him into bed, or out of his chair. In those moments, as she lay on her back on the floor, with Jacob's large body on top of her, she could only free herself if he shimmied his body down her stomach and onto his knees. With the majority of his weight off her, she could slide out from underneath him. Then she'd fetch a chair and set it right beside Jacob so he could pull himself up, with Maria aiding him from behind.

The following year, Jacob had another stroke, causing even more damage to his brain and nerves. His symptoms became even more severe. His left hand now lacked strength, making it hard for him to do anything on his own. His legs weren't able to hold his weight, so he couldn't move around, even with a walker. The children voiced their concerns for him, and urged Maria to move Jacob into an assisted living facility.

Maria dwelled on the decision for a long time, crying endlessly over what to do. She knew her children were right, she wasn't physically able to take care for him anymore, but the thought of sending him to a home made her feel sick, and incredibly guilty. Eventually, Maria knew what she needed to do. With both of their best interests at heart, she put Jacob's name on the waitlist for a room at Tabor Home. A few months later, they settled him into his new home.

Maria visited Jacob at Tabor Home faithfully every single day. He waited for her every morning, grateful when she walked through the door. She was the only light left in his life, it seemed. He grew more and more depressed with each passing day, with each failed conversation, and each embarrassing experience.

Jacob was done. He was done with living life in that way, needing to be cared for in every aspect of his life, even to go to the washroom. He hated living in a home with lots of people, another nightmare for him, and worst of all, Maria no longer slept beside him. The one thing he loved more than anything in the world was no longer at his side when he fell asleep, and when he woke. Instead, he fell asleep to the sounds of his neighbour choking on his own phlegm.

Jacob wanted to be free, not just physically, but spiritually. Nearly every day, on more than one occasion, he would point a finger to the ceiling and say, "*Hüss*, home." He wanted to be with Jesus, now more than ever before. Maria's response was always the same. While choking back tears at the thought of Jacob not being alive, she'd hold his hands and reassure him with the same words every time, "I don't know why you're still here, but God has a reason, and He doesn't make mistakes."

33

January 1999

MARIA SAT AT HER KITCHEN TABLE, STEAM RISING FROM THE MUG IN FRONT of her. A half-eaten slice of bread with butter and jam sat untouched on a little plate off to the side. The calendar on the wall had a blue circle around that day's date. It was January 26, Kaethe had been dead for two years. Maria took another sip of her coffee.

In her last days, Kaethe wasn't able to eat, and struggled to breathe. She was admitted to the hospital and Maria watched as her mother clung to what little life she had left in her, holding her hand the entire time. Kaethe drifted in and out of consciousness the whole day, never showing any signs that she knew Maria was even with her. Before Maria left that night, she laid down next to her mother and stroked Kaethe's soft, wrinkled cheeks. Maria knew it would be the last time she would see her mother alive.

"I love you, Mama. Thank you for everything you've done for me. Say hi to Papa when you see him," Maria had whispered through tears.

Kaethe died in her sleep that night. Maria still felt a surge of guilt every time she thought about the fact that she hadn't been by her mother's side when she took her last breath. But Maria was completely exhausted by then. Visiting Jacob and Kaethe every day for two years, while still maintaining her house and finding time to eat and sleep, and help Sylvia with the boys, had utterly depleted her. Emotionally, she was drained. And physically, her back pain was almost unbearable. But she kept that to herself, and prayed for the strength she needed every morning to get through one more day.

The phone rang suddenly and Maria jumped in her seat, interrupting her thoughts. She turned around and reached for the phone on the counter behind her.

"Hello?"

"Is this Mrs. Loewen?"

"Yes, this is she."

"Mrs. Loewen, this is Sandy calling from Tabor Home. Your husband was struggling to breathe so we called the ambulance. He's being transported to MSA General Hospital as we speak."

"Oh. Okay, thank you."

Maria hung up the phone, her heart racing. How bad was it this time? she wondered.

She called all of her children. The only one she didn't get in touch with was Erwin, who was out of town on business. She would figure out a way to contact him later. Grabbing her keys, she ran out of the apartment.

Maria's thoughts ran wild as she drove to Sylvia's house, who had wanted to accompany Maria to the hospital. Maria hadn't objected. She was afraid of what she might find when they arrived, and wanted the support.

Jacob was lying on a bed in a private area of the emergency ward. He was hooked up to all sorts of machines, which wasn't an uncommon sight. Angie arrived about an hour later, and soon after, Jacob was wheeled upstairs to a room with three other patients in as dire condition as himself.

The room felt eerily morbid. Even though all the patients in it were still alive, there was a smell that nauseated Maria. It was what she imagined death to smell like. It might have been the smell of over sterilized products lying around them, or chamber pots needing to be emptied, but regardless, the smell took some getting used to. There were four beds in the room, all of which were occupied by men, lying motionless, with eyes closed and loved ones surrounding them.

Angie and Sylvia sat on the bed on either side of Jacob while Maria talked to the doctor.

"What's going on, Doctor? What's happening?" Maria asked, desperate for answers. She hoped he would assure her it wasn't as bad as she thought it was.

"Mrs. Loewen, your husband is having congestive heart failure. I'm so sorry, but at this point, there really isn't much we can do to fix it. We can either prolong death by putting him on life support, or we can make him as comfortable as possible until he passes."

Maria turned her gaze to the white tiled floor beneath her feet, processing the doctor's words. "So, are you saying this is it? Either way, my husband is going to die?" Angie and Sylvia looked toward them, waiting for the doctor to correct her.

"I'm afraid so. I'm so sorry. Does Jacob have a living will?" The doctor asked, as if it were a normal, casual, everyday question.

"No, he doesn't. But we've talked about it many times." Jacob and Maria were both adamant that their bodies never be kept alive by machines. If they were old, and it was time for them to die, they wanted to be set free. Being kept alive through life support was no way to live, in their opinion.

Maria's mind spun. *What is happening?* she thought. These were questions she hadn't been prepared for, not because she didn't know the answers to them, but because she wasn't prepared to have to follow through on them. Maria felt her chest constrict. She took a few sharp breaths and moved her arms around to find something stable to lean on. She cried breathlessly as the room dimmed and her mind went blank, until all she saw was Jacob. She went to him and Angie moved further down the bed so Maria could sit closer to him.

Maria, Sylvia and Angie stayed by Jacob's side for the rest of the day. He went in and out of consciousness, but he was never coherent enough to interact with them. The light in the room slowly dimmed, filling the space with a golden glow as the sun set, until the only light in the room came from one small lamp in the corner.

Jacob's lips were dry and cracked. Sylvia asked the nurse if there was anything they could do for him. The nurse brought Sylvia some cotton swabs and a white paper cup filled with water to dip them in. Sylvia pressed the damp swabs against Jacob's dry lips, and along the inside of his mouth. She didn't know if it actually made a difference, but she needed to feel like she was helping him.

Maria had spent many nights at the hospital with Jacob in the first few weeks of January. One complication followed another, none of which had been all that serious, until the middle of January. He ended up needing to have surgery on his gall bladder right away, or the doctor guaranteed he'd be dead that night. She knew Jacob wouldn't have wanted the surgery – he was desperate to die and go to heaven – but Maria wasn't ready for him to leave her yet. She listened to her heart, and a few hours later, Jacob was wheeled into the operating room. She almost lost him that night, and she believed it was her prayers, pleading with God to keep him alive, that made him pull through.

Jacob survived that day, but this time was different, and Maria sensed that. The end was near, and there was no way to avoid it. Not even prayers could keep his body from shutting down now.

Having spent the majority of the past month sleeping on uncomfortable cots in the hospital, the girls urged Maria to go home to sleep. Sylvia volunteered to stay with Jacob throughout the night until Maria returned in the morning. Maria was reluctant to leave, but consented in the end.

When she finished buttoning up her jacket, she sat on the bed beside Jacob. Sylvia and Angie moved aside, giving them some privacy. Maria held Jacob's face in her hands as her tears fell onto his cheeks. To her surprise, his eyes opened and he looked clearly into her eyes. She smiled. They were the same eyes that could always tell her what he could not say with words; the same eyes she fell in love with all those years ago; and the same eyes that looked into her soul and knew exactly what she needed, at any given moment. Those eyes that once were filled with so much joy and zest for life, and then filled with sorrow and longing to die. And now, those same eyes pierced her to her very core as she understood what his eyes were telling her, "*Goodbye.*"

Through tears, Maria whispered, "*Ekj sie die goot, Jasch.*" She kissed his lips, and he kissed her back. She wished that moment could go on forever. She wanted to hold on to him, and never let go. She ran her fingers through his hair a few times, watching as his eyes slowly closed and he drifted off again. Maria kissed his forehead and forced herself off the bed.

When Maria and Angie walked out of the room, Sylvia moved up further on the bed to be closer to Jacob. Tears streaked her face as she looked at her dad. His eyes slowly opened again, and he met her gaze. She reached for his hand and placed it on her cheek. Tears moved over his fingers and she savoured the warmth of his fatherly touch on her skin.

With much effort, and a deep, raspy voice, Sylvia faintly heard Jacob say, "*Bliewe schmock,* stay true to yourself," and then he was out of consciousness once more.

—

Maria moved lethargically down the corridor toward her apartment. In front of her door, she searched her purse and retrieved her keys. Once inside, she dropped her purse on the floor and moved toward the living room. She sat on the brown velvet armchair, her hands folded in her lap. A large photo set in a gold frame hung on the opposite wall. It was a photo taken on their fiftieth wedding anniversary.

Jacob and Maria were centred in the photo. Jacob was sitting in his wheel-chair, wearing a fine navy suit – one of Maria's favourites – and a grey and blue striped tie hung from his neck. Maria stood beside him, her hand resting on his shoulder. She wore a pale yellow dress, knee length and fitted in the bodice, with a short sleeve jacket of the same material. A single black button closed the jacket at the front. The jacket, as well as the sleeves, were trimmed with black, satin fabric. Their whole family was standing around them – children and grandchil-dren, and even their unborn great-grandchild that Lucy was expecting.

Maria frowned at the sadness in Jacob's eyes. It was meant to be a joyous occasion, but there was nothing joyful about the look on Jacob's face. The room had been filled with all their dearest friends and family, yet Jacob couldn't help but feel discouraged and frustrated. He had never been fond of large gatherings to begin with, but the fact that he couldn't even join in any conversations only added to his grievance and disappointment.

Maria tried to sleep that night, but her attempts were futile. She couldn't fall asleep knowing her soulmate, her best friend, was slowly dying at the hospital. She tossed and turned in the darkness of her room. Every now and then, she reached her arm across the bed and moved it up and down the sheets where Jacob's body once lay beside hers. She recalled with pleasure the way he used to nestle her into himself, stroking her arm. Her small frame fit perfectly into his.

She cried on and off for the rest of the night, until the room brightened softly. Tired of lying restlessly in bed, she threw on her clothes and drove straight to the hospital.

Maria entered Jacob's room breathless from running from the parking lot. Sylvia sat in a chair beside the bed, resting her head in her hands, her eyes barely open. Angie was already there, sitting on the other side of Jacob.

"Mutti," Sylvia said, "you're supposed to be at home, sleeping."

"I couldn't sleep. I need to be here, with him."

Sylvia left soon after. Maria and Angie sat quietly, listening to Jacob breathe. It sounded like he was inhaling mouthfuls of water. Angie grew more and more concerned and disturbed with each breath.

"Is he going to drown?" Angie asked the nurse when she came in to check on Jacob.

"No, he won't drown. This is common with heart failure," the nurse tried to reassure her, but Angie wasn't convinced. With every gargled breath, Angie winced and prayed he wouldn't suffocate from the fluid in his lungs.

Ernst and Gredel arrived later that morning. Gredel sat in a wheelchair, uncomfortable and in pain as she was recovering from a kidney operation. She had only been discharged from the hospital the day before and got special permission to make the drive out to Abbotsford to visit Jacob.

The four of them sat around the small space designated to Jacob, and silently watched him. The room was quiet, save for the occasional sniffle and gasps of breaths from Jacob and the other patients in the room. They held hands with each other, and supported each other in turn, as each of the girls went through cycles of grieving.

Around two o'clock, Gredel couldn't endure her pain any longer, and she and Ernst decided to go home. Ernst moved her wheelchair closer to Jacob. She held his hand and kissed his fingers as she cried. She told him she loved him, but he showed no signs of hearing her.

The room fell quiet again after they left. No one was interested in conversation, or doing anything else.

After some time, Angie raised her head and sniffed the air around her. "What's that smell?"

Maria lifted her face and sniffed, catching a waft of the strange smell. It seemed to be coming from Jacob, but they didn't know what it was. The nurse walked in, and Angie asked her to identify the unpleasant odour.

"It's the smell of death," she told them sympathetically.

The nurse moved the sheets off Jacob and looked at his legs, squeezing his knees gently. There was a purplish colour on the skin. Seeing the frown spread across the nurse's face, they knew that was what she had been looking for, but hoping she wouldn't find. She pulled the sheets back over Jacob and made some notes on his chart before hanging it back on the hook at the end of the bed. She looked at the women with compassion.

"It won't be long now," she said softly, apologetically.

The doctor came in after the nurse had left and reiterated what the nurse had told them.

"It'll only be a few more hours, if that. You might want to phone your family."

A few more hours.

What did he mean by 'a few more hours'? Surely not only a few more hours until Jacob was gone, forever. Maria and Jacob had been together for over fifty years, and now the doctor was telling her that she only had a few more hours with him?

Maria's heart started pounded intensely. She brought her hand to her chest and felt the strength of her pulse against her skin. The doctor's words rang through her head, like the soundtrack to a horror movie. *A few more hours*. It wasn't enough time. She wasn't finished with Jacob yet. She knew this was going to happen eventually, but she never thought the day would *actually* arrive, let alone the *hour*.

Maria reached for the phone beside Jacob's bed, trying to drown out Angie's cries, which only spurred her own tears to flow even more. The phone rang three times before Sylvia answered, her voice groggy from sleep.

"Sylvia, you need to come back to the hospital right away."

She called Gredel right after but they hadn't arrived home yet. The phone kept ringing, and ringing. Erwin was still out of town, so she phoned Monica and asked her to get a hold of him. She hung up and sat on the bed beside Jacob, stroking his arm and his cheek. Sylvia arrived within minutes, and sat beside Angie on the bed, across from Maria. They talked to Jacob, despite his unconscious state. They shared their favourite memories of him, and what they would miss most about him. Their clothes, and the linen on Jacob's bed, were dotted from where their tears fell as they reminisced, clinging to their final moments with him.

The nurses unhooked Jacob from the machines at Maria's request. The only sound in the room came from Jacob's laboured breathing. Maria wondered if he was in pain, and asked the nurse if they could administer some morphine. The nurse assured her he couldn't feel anything, and that an IV would only liven his body up again, which would inadvertently cause pain.

"He will be so happy when this is all over," Angie spoke softly.

Maria and Sylvia nodded. They fixed their eyes on Jacob, not wanting to miss a second of his final moments. His breathing grew slower and slower, and he struggled to get air into his lungs, but his body lay so still. Not a finger twitched, nor an eyelid flinched.

The chaplain from Tabor Home entered the room and prayed over Jacob. The women bowed their heads, leaning over Jacob, and nodded in agreement with the words he prayed and the blessings he bestowed on Jacob. By this point, tears flowed endlessly and continuously among all three women. They didn't even bother drying their cheeks anymore. Each drop, filled with so much love for their father, streamed gracefully off the edge of their faces and onto the one they mourned.

When the prayer was over, Maria leaned her body onto Jacob's, resting her forehead against the side of his head so her mouth was beside his ear. With much effort, she controlled her tears and whispered, "I'm going to be all right, Jasch. You can go now."

His next breath would be his last. As he exhaled, they could faintly hear him whisper, "*Entlich*, finally." A smile brushed across his face, a look of utter peace resting over him. They knew in that very moment that he was in heaven.

Maria screamed, calling Jacob's name. She clung to him, lifting his body into her arms. Tears ran down her cheeks and onto his. It felt like something inside Maria had physically been ripped out of her. She felt sick, and hollow, and lost. She thought she might die from the immense pain she was feeling in her heart. Her lungs were taut with despair and she was struggling to breathe.

Sylvia and Angie hugged each other on the other side of Jacob. Their three lamenting voices carried through the room, and down the halls of the hospital.

A nurse spoke softly over their wails, "Time of death: 4:08 p.m."

34

November 2015

I SAT AT MY DINING ROOM TABLE, CURLING THE EDGE OF THE PLASTIC, LACE-printed tablecloth. I remembered that afternoon like it was yesterday. Every moment of that day played out in vivid pictures in my memory. Amidst the sea of picture frames standing on the table in front of me, I saw the black and white photo of Jacob and me on our wedding day. I reached for it with a shaky arm and wondered when I had gotten so old. The joints on my fingers were swollen with arthritis, and the skin on my arms hung loosely.

"What happened after that?"

My granddaughter's voice startled me. I forgot for a moment that she was there. I placed the picture frame back on the table and looked at Vanessa, sitting cross-legged on the wooden dining room chair beside me. Her eyes were glistening. I wondered how much she remembered about her opa.

"We stayed at the hospital for another hour, just sitting together, beside Jacob," I continued, my thoughts back on track. "Angie phoned Gredel a few minutes after he died – they had just arrived home by that time. She was so upset. If she had known it would have happened that soon, they wouldn't have left the hospital. Erwin, your dad, I mean, was in Las Vegas with your Uncle Art, so Hein called Art at the hotel and Art told your dad. He flew home the next day."

Even after nearly seventeen years, it was hard to relive those final moments. I could still smell the hospital room, and feel the stiffness of the sheets. I cleared my throat and began fidgeting with the tablecloth again. I rolled it up and then let it go, repeating the motion again and again. Recalling Jasch's final minutes made me feel extremely vulnerable. I could feel emotion working its way up my throat, but I forced back the tears. I knew Vanessa was crying beside me, even though I wasn't looking at her. Her hand moved to her cheek, wiping away her tears. I focused on the tablecloth. If I looked at her, it would surely make me cry, too.

"I stayed at Sylvia's for a few nights," I continued, "but eventually I needed to go home and start the grieving process by myself. Sometimes it was hard to be sad, because Jacob wanted so badly to die and be with Jesus. So, in some ways, I was happy, even relieved, that Jacob was gone, and not suffering anymore. But that didn't feel right either. I think it was about six months after he passed away that it really hit me, the reality that Jacob was never coming home. If I didn't know with certainty that Jacob was with the Lord, I don't know how I would have continued living after he died."

One tear managed to escape me and I quickly wiped it away. I looked behind me, toward the kitchen, and smiled as another memory came to mind.

"Even though Jacob was such a different man for those last few years after his stroke, he was still my husband, and I loved him very much. Sometimes I still think he's going to come around the corner, with that mischievous look on his face, like the cat-caught-the-canary. He was always up to something." My shoulders bounced softly as I laughed to myself. He always knew how to make me laugh. He was funny, my Jasch. I suddenly felt a chill in the air and my smile dissipated.

"I miss the way he would always graze my lower back when he walked behind me, or the way he stroked my arm when we were lying in bed together. He was so loving, so affectionate. I was his Mariechen, and he always made sure I knew how much I meant to him."

I stopped to take a deep breath and steady my emotions. Sometimes it still felt like he was there with me, and other times his absence paralyzed me. Vanessa reached into her purse for a tissue and wiped her eyes. Her mascara left dark marks under her eyes. She sat quietly, patiently waiting for me to continue.

"A few days after Jacob passed away, I was lying in my bed here, thinking about him, like I always do, when I had a vision. I saw heaven opening up and Jacob looking down at me, smiling. He looked so happy. I hadn't seen him smile like that in decades ..." *Keep yourself together, Maria*, I said to myself. I moved my fingers to the edge of the tablecloth and began rolling it again. "I felt like it was Jacob's way of saying goodbye."

"Another time I was watching TV in my little room there, while I was knitting, when a man came on the news wearing a suit, the same blue colour as the suit Jacob wore for our wedding. I lost it. The memory overwhelmed me, and I missed him so much in that moment." I sat quietly for a moment.

"Anyway, Jacob had a watch he always wore – I told you about it during one of our interviews, the one I gave him for Christmas that one year. Your dad had the idea of setting the watch to the time that Jacob died, and then stopping it. So we did. And he was buried with that watch on his wrist. He wore the navy suit he wore for our fiftieth wedding anniversary for the funeral. I always liked that suit on him." It wasn't as nice as the one he wore for our wedding, but it was still blue, and it made his eyes even brighter when he wore it.

It was silent for a minute again, and I sat in my chair, staring at the pictures in front of me. There were so many faces of loved ones. I turned to Vanessa and watched as she found her next question in her pink notebook. She looked up at me and I smiled when her blue eyes met mine.

"If you could go back to yourself as a young woman, what would you tell yourself?"

I looked over the table, into the living room, where more photographs of my family members were displayed on the mantle above the fireplace. There were wedding pictures, graduation pictures, elementary school photos of grandchildren, and even great-grandchildren. I was so blessed, there was no question about that. I thought about Vanessa's question, trying to visualize myself as a young woman. It wasn't easy, but I think I had a pretty good idea what I would say.

"I would tell myself," I began, "'Life is hard, and you won't always understand everything that happens, but know that it will all be worth it. Jacob becomes a Christian and everything happens for a reason.'"

"And what would you say is the biggest lesson you've learned in your lifetime, looking back on all eighty-seven years of your life?"

I smiled. That was an easy one, although thinking about it made me choke up.

"Give everything to God. Trust Him with all of your being, because God is almighty, all-knowing and always there. And He doesn't make mistakes. Not ever. Even if I don't understand why something is happening, I know and trust and believe that He makes no mistakes. Trust in the Lord.

"And then He says, 'Be still and know that I am God,' though that part is never easy," I laughed. Patience had never been my strong suit. Vanessa laughed, too. From the conversations we'd recently had, I knew patience wasn't her strong suit either. I told her to blame me for that, it must run in my family.

One final thought crossed my mind, and my demeanor sobered. She must have sensed the shift, as well, because her eyes brimmed with tears again. I sighed, grateful to have spent this time with her, and sad that our interviews were coming to an end.

"I know one day I will see Jacob again when I meet him in heaven, but until then, I will continue to pray for those I love. As long as God gives me clear thinking, I pray for everybody, by name. I have the time. Prayer is my only weapon. Nothing physical to fight with, I am too weak. I have only prayer. And that is my biggest strength."

EPILOGUE

AS I REFLECT BACK ON THE PROCESS OF WRITING MY BOOK, I AM OVERCOME with awe – not just for the overwhelming joy I've experienced from physically writing each word, but for the honour of being able to spend hours upon hours listening to Oma share her memories with me.

Through this process, I have gained a new appreciation for my family history; a plethora of knowledge on matters I otherwise would never have known; and so much wisdom and insight gleaned from an incredibly wise woman. Above all, though, I fell more in love with a woman whom I will always cherish. She has made a lasting impact on my life and heart.

This book also brought me closer to my dad and my aunts, who willingly sat down with me and answered the many questions I had for them regarding their parents. Those are some moments I will always cherish, considering the tragedy that befell our family soon after.

On August 22, 2016, at the age of fifty-seven, Sylvia passed away from complications from her Still's Disease. Oma shared with me one day that it was one thing to lose your spouse, but it was an entirely different matter to lose your own child. The pain of losing her daughter was more severe than she could have expected, but still her faith did not waver.

That was a heartbreaking experience for our whole family, but it was only the beginning. In November of that same year, Oma was diagnosed with leiomyosarcoma, cancer in her soft tissue. I drove to her house shortly after hearing the news and cried into her shoulder as she held me and rubbed my back. She comforted me with the words she'd said many times throughout our interviews, "*God makes no mistakes.*"

Oma underwent radiation in December, but the treatment only left her fragile and weak, and the cancer had spread to other organs. Soon after, she was admitted to Abbotsford Memorial Hospital, where she remained until she was transferred to the Mission Hospice Society in early January 2017. There, she was treated with the utmost care and respect from the lovely staff and volunteers, who were such a blessing to her and our family.

On Saturday, January 21, 2017, Maria Loewen went to be with her Heavenly Father, reunited with her Jasch, her mother and father, her grandparents, her daughter, and many other friends and family. She left behind a legacy of love and faith for her remaining family, which now consists of thirty members, including two more great-grandsons since this book was written.

On May 7, 2016, I finished writing the first draft of my book, and the following day, on Mother's Day, I delivered the printed pages of Oma's story to her in person. I cannot express what that moment meant to me, and likely to her. The fact that Oma was able to read my book, *her* book, before she passed away means everything to me. God's timing in all of this has truly been divine.

Thank you for reading *The Girl from No. 6.*
xoxo
Vanessa

Elizabeth Penner (Kornelius's wife, Maria's aunt), Jacob, Maria and Kaethe, taken in early 1980s.

Photo of Angie (19) and Maria (55) taken at Angie and Willy's engagement party, July 1983.

Family photo taken at Angie and Willy's wedding on June 23, 1984. Left to right: Victoria, Erwin, Monica, Andy, Rudolf, Sylvia, Maria, Angie, Willy, Jacob, Cristina, Gredel, Lucy and Ernst.

Jacob's baptism at King Road MB Church in May 1985.

Portrait of Jacob and Maria from the late 1980s.

Maria (69) and Jacob (73) at their 50th anniversary celebration.

The Loewen family at Jacob and Maria's 50th wedding anniversary.
Back row: Willy, Andy, Rudolf, Steven, Sylvia, Victoria, Monica, Erwin, Cristina, Ernst, Aldo.
Front row: James, Angie, Maria, Jacob, Gredel, Lucy. Sitting: Tami and Vanessa.

Five generations: Abram, Jacob, Gredel, Lucy and Talia. Late 1997.

Maria and her children taken in 2013.
Maria (85), Erwin (59), Sylvia (55), Gredel (64), and Angie (49).

May 8, 2016, Mother's Day – the day after I finished writing my book and delivered it to Oma to read.

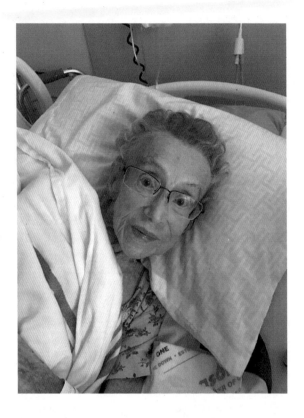

The last photo taken of Oma, while she was in hospice. It was the last time I ever had a conversation with her. In a way it was our final interview. I asked her any questions I could think of, that I didn't already know the answer to, and she answered each one. Those four hours with her are some of the most memorable and treasured moments I ever had with her. The lovely nurse had curled her hair in rollers that morning, and Oma felt so beautiful, even though she hadn't actually seen herself yet. So I snapped a photo of her with my phone so I could show her how radiant she was. This was the photo, and I will cherish it always.

Printed in Canada